Business BASICS

A study guide for degree students

INFORMATION TECHNOLOGY

PUBLISHING

First edition May 1995
Second edition May 1997

ISBN 0 7517 2119 0 (previous edition 0 7517 2073 9)

British Library Cataloguing-in Publication Data

A catalogue record for this book
is available from the British Library

Published by
BPP Publishing Limited
Aldine House, Aldine Place
London W12 8AW

Our thanks are due to *Cordelia Gerard-Sharp* for
assisting in developing the open learning aspects of
the text and to *Genesys Editorial* for additional
editorial and production work.

We are grateful to the Institute of Chartered
Secretaries and Administrators and the Association
of Chartered Certified Accountants for permission
to reproduce prior examination questions, the
answers to which have been prepared by BPP
Publishing Ltd.

CONTENTS

PREFACE

BUSINESS BASICS are targeted specifically at the needs of:

- students taking business studies degrees;
- students taking business-related modules of other degrees;
- students on courses at a comparable level;
- others requiring business information at this level.

This *Information Technology* text has been written with two key goals in mind.

- To present a substantial and useful body of knowledge on information technology at degree level. This is not just a set of revision notes – it explains the subject in detail and does not assume prior knowledge.
- To make learning and revision as easy as possible. Therefore, each chapter:
  - starts with an introduction and clear objectives;
  - contains numerous activities;
  - includes a chapter roundup summarising the points made; and
  - ends with a quick quiz

and at the back of the book you will find

  - multiple choice questions and solutions;
  - exam style questions and solutions.

The philosophy of the series is thus to combine techniques which actively promote learning with a no-nonsense, systematic approach to the necessary factual content of the course.

BPP Publishing have for many years been the leading providers of targeted texts for professional qualifications. We know that our customers need to study effectively in order to pass their exams, and that they cannot afford to waste time. They expect clear, concise and highly-focused study material. As university and college education becomes more market driven, students rightly demand the same high standards of efficiency in their learning material. The BUSINESS BASICS series meets those demands.

BPP Publishing
June 1997

Titles in this series

Accounting
Law
Information Technology
Economics
Marketing
Human Resource Management
Quantitative Methods
Organisational Behaviour

You may order other titles in the series using the form at the end of this text. If you would like to send in your comments on this book, please turn to the review form following the order form.

HOW TO USE THIS STUDY GUIDE

This book can simply be read straight through from beginning to end, but you will get far more out of it if you keep a pen and paper to hand. The most effective form of learning is *active learning*, and we have therefore filled the text with activities for you to try as you go along. We have also provided objectives, a chapter roundup and a quick quiz for each chapter. Here is a suggested approach to enable you to get the most out of this book.

(a) Select a chapter to study, and read the introduction and objectives at the start of the chapter.

(b) Next read the chapter roundup at the end of the chapter (before the quick quiz and the solutions to exercises). Do not expect this brief summary to mean too much at this stage, but see whether you can relate some of the points made in it to some of the objectives.

(c) Next read the chapter itself. Do attempt each activity as you come to it. You will derive the greatest benefit from the activities if you write down your solutions before checking them against the answers at the end of the chapter.

(d) As you read, make use of the 'notes' column to add your own comments, references to other material and so on. Do try to formulate your own views. In business, many things are matters of interpretation and there is often scope for alternative views. The more you engage in a dialogue with the book, the more you will get out of your study.

(e) When you reach the end of the chapter, read the chapter roundup again. Then go back to the objectives at the start of the chapter, and ask yourself whether you have achieved them.

(f) Finally, consolidate your knowledge by writing down your answers to the quick quiz. You can check your answers by going back to the text. The very act of going back and searching the text for relevant details will further improve your grasp of the subject.

(g) You can then try the multiple choice questions at the end of the book and the exam style questions, to which you are referred at the end of the chapter. Alternatively, you could wait to do these until you have started your revision – its up to you.

Further reading

While we are confident that the BUSINESS BASICS books offer excellent range and depth of subject coverage, we are aware that you will be encouraged to follow up particular points in books other than your main textbook, in order to get alternative points of view and more detail on key topics.

Information Technology is a fast-moving discipline in which books rapidly become outdated. For applications, the "... for Dummies" (IDG Books), the "... for Idiots" (QUE) and "In easy steps" (Computer Steps) series are extremely good. See the latest volumes relating to the applications in which you are interested.

We recommend that you regularly browse in a good book shop; look at the latest titles as they appear and buy those which you find most user-friendly and applicable to your needs and interests.

You should also use the Internet to keep yourself informed:

see Krol & Ferguson, *The Whole Internet for Windows 95*, 1995, O'Reilly Press (also available on the Internet at address www.ora.com.catalog/twiwin)

Chapter 1

COMPUTERS

Introduction

Computers were first used in business in the 1960s. The development of the integrated circuit, in the 1970s, incorporating a number of circuits in a single chip, has led to their use becoming widespread.

Compared with manual data processing, computers have the advantages of speed, accuracy and the ability to process large volumes of data to perform complex operations. Initially, their main commercial use was to process large volumes of transactions data, but over time they have been used increasingly to provide management information.

Computers have also penetrated the home. Originally intended as educational or games systems for children, they are now able to manage a wide range of mundane tasks such as household bills and communications.

The input-process-output cycle inherent in computer processing mirrors the operation of any system, whether this be sociological, biological, organisational or financial. Data for input can be recorded either manually, for example as a hand-written sales order, or in computer-sensible form.

Output can be either human-sensible, for example printed as text or graphics on paper, or computer-sensible, stored for later processing by another computer.

Computers can be classified as supercomputers, mainframes, minicomputers and PCs. Supercomputers are used in specialist applications only (for example, weather forecasting). There is now no real distinction between minicomputers and PCs (or microcomputers); the difference is becoming more a matter of size than type.

Today, many computers are described as workstations, file servers, desktop PCs or portables. These terms will be described in the following chapters.

In these first chapters, we will also introduce the basic building blocks of computing technology. This will include the distinction between hardware, that is the physical parts of a computer system such as printer or screen, and software, that is the programs which enable tasks or applications to be carried out.

We will also look at the types of computer memory, and the way in which memory, speed and power are measured.

Your objectives

After completing this chapter you should:

(a) know the components of a computer's hardware;

(b) be able to explain the distinction between hardware and software;

(c) know the main types of computer;

(d) understand the functions of a processor;

(e) know the different types of computer memory;

(f) know what factors determine the power of a computer.

1   WHAT IS A COMPUTER?

A computer is an electronic machine for handling information. Thus when talking about computers, people refer to *information technology* (ways of handling information) and to *data processing*. Data is the input to a computer, such as a list of employees to be paid. Information is the product or end result.

Definition

Data processing is the use of automation (ie computers) to process raw data (input) to create meaningful information (output)

We can make the following initial points about computers.

(a) The machines themselves, that is the physical components of a computer system, such as processor, screen, keyboard and printer, are referred to as the computer *hardware*.

(b) A computer *processes* data. The elements of data processing are input, processing, storage and output.

(c) A computer's operations are performed under the control of a program. Programs are needed to make the computer's hardware process data. A program is a set of instructions which tells the computer what to do. General terms used to describe programs are software or applications.

(d) Almost all business computers (and most scientific computers) are digital computers. This means that they operate by performing arithmetical operations on exact numbers, such as amounts of money, albeit in a coded (binary) form. They do not measure continuously variable quantities, such as electrical voltages. Analogue computers, used primarily in scientific and industrial applications, measure rather than count.

Definition

Software is the intangible part of the system, which comprises the instructions to perform given tasks, ie the programs

Hardware is the physical part of the system; the computer, peripheral devices, etc.

The basic components of a computer's hardware consist of the following.

(a) Input devices accept input data for processing, converting it, if necessary, into a form which the computer can understand and operate on. A keyboard is an example of an input device.

(b) Storage devices hold data and programs on file until they are needed for processing and also hold the results after processing. A hard disk is an example of a storage device.

(c) Output devices accept output from the data processing device and convert it into a usable form. A printer is an example of an output device.

(d) A processor performs the data processing by taking in data from input devices and storage devices, processing it, and then transferring the processed information to an output device or storage device. The processor has its own *memory* to hold instructions, data and results while it is working.

Activity 1

A small computer is used to process the payroll for a large organisation, but it cannot hold the data for all the employees in memory at once. Which hardware component would solve this problem?

Input devices, storage devices and output devices are often referred to collectively as peripherals. The term 'computer system' refers to the processor together with its associated peripheral equipment. The links between all the devices can be shown diagrammatically, as follows.

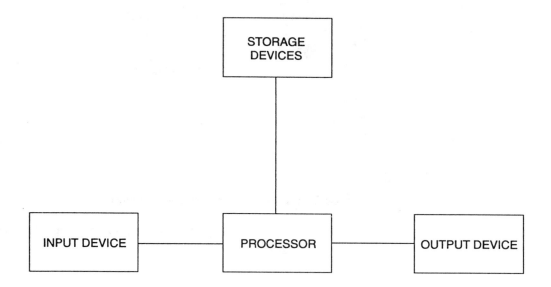

Figure 1.1 How a processor is linked to its peripherals

2   THE DIFFERENT TYPES OF COMPUTER

Computers are classified according to size, although the differences between these categories can be quite vague.

2.1   Supercomputers

Supercomputers are used to process very large amounts of data very quickly. They are particularly useful for occasions when many calculations need to be performed, for example in weather forecasting. Manufacturers of supercomputers include Cray and Fujitsu.

2.2   Mainframes

Mainframe computers are large computers in terms of price, power and speed. Typically, they cost over £1 million and support several hundred users. Well-known manufacturers include IBM and ICL.

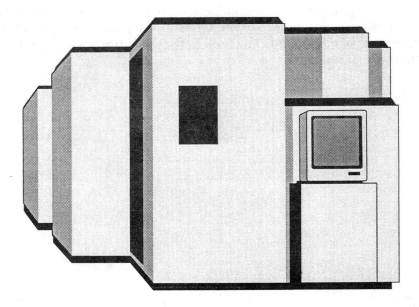

Figure 1.2 A mainframe computer

2.3   Minicomputers

Originally used to describe computers which were cheaper and less well equipped than mainframes, this term is becoming obsolete.

2.4   Microcomputers

The term microcomputer, originally used for a independent 'free-standing' computer, has become largely out-dated and replaced by the term personal computer (PC).

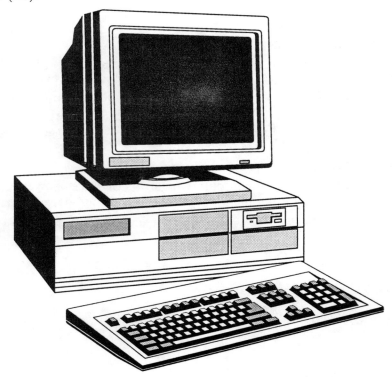

Figure 1.3 A stand-alone personal computer

Activity 2

A major bank processes all cheques written by its customers on one computer. What sort of computer is it likely to use?

2.5 Workstations

Originally, a workstation was a computer used by one person, particularly for graphics and design applications (such as computer aided design) and was used primarily in engineering. It had a fast and powerful central processor, a high resolution monitor, a large memory, and would, almost certainly, run on UNIX. This enabled complex designs to be easily manipulated. Such characteristics, however, are no longer unique to workstations as high performance personal computers can offer very similar services. The distinction, therefore, is a historical one based on the very noticeable difference between early 8-bit personal computers and powerful workstations. More powerful PCs mean that the distinction is eroding.

2.6 PCs

The personal computer market was first developed by companies like Apple Computers. Then, in August 1981, the IBM PC was launched. In the early years of the development of the PC, the Apple Macintosh (technically not a PC) became the standard for graphics-based applications and the IBM PC and a host of IBM-compatibles, or clones, were chosen for text-based (business) applications. However, as chips have become more powerful, the difference in emphasis has become less important.

The PC consists of three major components.

(a) The basic module contains the processing device, one or two floppy disk drives and an integrated hard disk unit. (These are storage devices, which store data and programs on magnetic disks. Details are given in the next chapter.) The processing device is on a chip (a piece of silicon containing complex electronic circuitry) and the type of chip (such as 386, 486 or Pentium) is often incorporated into the computer's name. The basic module can also act as a pedestal for the visual display unit.

(b) The keyboard is connected to the basic module by a cable. A mouse, a device used in conjunction with and sometimes as an alternative to the keyboard to input instructions, is usually plugged into the basic module via another socket.

(c) The visual display unit (VDU), or screen or monitor, displays input or output items, as letters and numbers or in graphical or picture form. It may display in colour or in black and white (monochrome), and, like a television set, has contrast and brightness controls. The screen is usually adjustable in all directions so that it can be placed where the user can see it without eye or neck strain.

2.7 File servers

A file server is a PC or minicomputer which provides additional services for users of networked PCs.

2.8 Portables

As the name implies, portables are small enough to be carried from place to place and can be powered from batteries or from the mains. Increased efficiency of design means that they can support as much memory as stand-alone PCs.

Portables are described as laptops, notebooks and handheld (or pocket) computers. These pocket computers may or may not be compatible with PCs, and range from machines that are little more than electronic organisers to relatively powerful processors with compatibility and full communications features.

It is estimated that portable computers now represent over 50% in volume of all types of personal computer sold. They offer considerable space saving.

Activity 3

Give three examples of businesses where it would be especially useful for staff to have portable computers.

3 THE PROCESSOR

The processor, or 'brain' of the computer, is a collection of electronic circuitry and registers. Sometimes referred to as the central processing unit (CPU), the processor is divided into three areas: the control unit; the arithmetic and logic unit; and the memory. The set of operations that the processor performs is known as the instruction set, or repertoire, and this determines in part the speed at which processing can be performed. Processors for PCs are located on single chips (very small pieces of silicon or some other substance, containing complex electronic circuits).

Definition

A *processor* is the part of the computer that coordinates its actions

3.1 The control unit

The control unit receives program instructions, one at a time, from the computer's memory. It supervises the execution of these instructions and sends out control signals to peripheral (input and output) devices, co-ordinated by a clock. The number of pulses (cycles) produced per second is an indication of processing speed, and is usually measured in megahertz (MHz). One MHz is one million pulses (cycles) per second. A typical PC might have a specification of 133 MHz to 200 MHz.

3.2 The arithmetic and logic unit (ALU)

This is the part of the processor where the arithmetical, logical and other operations are carried out. These include arithmetic (such as add, subtract, multiply and divide), comparison (such as 'does selling price exceed cost?'), branch operations (which change the order of program instructions) and the movement of data.

3.3 Memory

This is circuitry used to store data within the processor while the computer is operating.

A personal computer has two types of memory.

Storage memory (or ROM – read only memory)

It is useful to think of the hard disk of a computer as a compact disc on which, instead of tunes, applications (or software) are recorded (or stored). When an application is called up we can play it (or use it). In addition, we can record our work onto the hard disk as individual files, and call up these files again when we need them.

We can also over-record (over-write) files, for example when we have edited a previously created document and wish to keep only the latest version. Or we can over-write programs, for example when we are upgrading our software to a later version.

ROM is 'non-volatile' memory because its contents do not disappear when the computer's power source is switched off. A computer's start-up program is always held in a form of ROM, so that the computer can boot up (pull itself up by its bootstraps, ie start itself).

Working memory (or RAM – random access memory)

Working memory enables the computer to execute program instructions rapidly, by 'holding' the whole program in a work area rather than going back to the storage area to call up routines. This memory is 'volatile' in that its contents will disappear if the computer is switched off.

Data representation in memory

A computer's operations depend on simple circuits which can be switched on or off. These two states can be expressed as binary digits, ie, as the numbers 1 and 0 respectively. Any piece of data must be coded in these symbols before processing can commence. For example, in a commonly used code (ASCII), the capital letter A is coded as 1000001.

A single binary digit (1 or 0) is known as a bit. A group of 8 bits is a byte. Memory size is calculated in kilobytes, megabytes and gigabytes.

1 kB	= 1 kilobyte	= 1,024 bytes
1 MB	= 1 megabyte	= 1,024 kilobytes
1 GM	= 1 gigabyte	= 1,024 megabytes

So a computer described as having a 1.2 GB hard disk (storage memory) would have a memory of:

$$1.2 \times 1,024 \times 1,024 \times 1,024 = 1,288,490,189 \text{ bytes.}$$

And a computer described as having 32 MB RAM memory would have a memory of:

$$32 \times 1,024 \times 1,025 = 33,554,432 \text{ bytes.}$$

Activity 4

An electronic diary stores all its software on a chip. It includes a program to work out the days of the week for dates up to the year 2100. In what sort of memory should that program be stored?

Many PCs offer the user the option of increasing the size of RAM, so that larger programs can be run. Memory can be increased in the following ways.

(a) An *expansion slot* allows a chip providing extra RAM to be plugged into the PC, so as to become a part of the computer's main memory.

(b) An *extension card* or board fulfils the same function, but fits inside the PC box itself. A PC may have space inside it to accept extra printed circuit boards, to enhance its memory or its processing capabilities.

3.4   Buses

Data is transferred within the processor or between the processor and peripherals by means of buses. A bus carries a number of bits (depending on its size) along a number of tracks. A bus with eight tracks therefore carries one byte at a time.

4   THE POWER OF A COMPUTER

The factors that determine the power of a computer (how much it can do, and how fast) are as follows.

(a) The speed of handling program instructions, which for a mainframe is measured in millions of instructions per second (MIPS). Smaller mainframes only manage 11 MIPS, whereas the largest IBM mainframe can handle 80 MIPS. Alternatively, speed and power can be measured in megaflops (millions of floating point instructions per second).

(b) The MHz (Megahertz) rate of the internal clock (the rate at which timing pulses are emitted from the control unit). The higher the rate, the faster the computer can work.

(c) The efficiency of the instruction set. Some computers combine a fairly small set of instructions in clever ways to increase efficiency.

(d) The size of the processor's memory.

(e) The number of tracks on the computer's buses.

Activity 5

Computer A has a 33 MHz chip and 4 MB of RAM. Computer B has a 25 MHz chip and 8 MB of RAM. Which computer could handle larger quantities of data, and which could run smaller quantities of data faster?

Chapter roundup

- A computer operates under the command of stored programs. These programs are software, as distinct from the physical components which are hardware.
- Computers may be supercomputers, mainframe computers, minicomputers or PCs. Different sizes of computer are suitable for different applications.
- A PC's components are a basic module, a keyboard and a VDU. In some small computers, such as laptop and pocket computers, these components are combined in a single unit.
- The processor processes input to produce the desired output. It includes a control unit which is in overall charge, an arithmetic and logic unit to do the computations and a memory in which to hold data about to be worked on and put output ready to be worked on further or sent to an output device.
- The main types of memory are RAM and ROM. Memory is usually measured in megabytes.
- Several factors affect the power of a computer.

Quick quiz

1 Distinguish between memory and storage devices.
2 For what sorts of application are supercomputers suitable?
3 What is the smallest type of computer in common use?
4 What, in a computer, is measured in MHz?
5 When a computer is executing an instruction in a program, where will that instruction be held?
6 How is data represented in memory?
7 How may a computer's memory be enlarged?
8 What does MIPS stand for?

Answers to activities

1 Storage devices
2 A mainframe computer
3 Architects: computers could be taken to building sites.

   Accountants: computers could be taken to clients' offices.

   Insurance loss adjusters: computers could be taken to the sites of damage.
4 ROM
5 Computer B could handle larger quantities of data, but computer A could run small quantities of data faster.

Further question practice

Now try the following practice questions at the end of this text.

Multiple choice questions   **1 to 7**

Exam style question   **1**

Chapter 2

STORAGE

Introduction

In the last chapter, we saw the distinction between working memory and storage memory. Because RAM memory can only hold a limited amount of data and program instructions, and is in any case volatile, it is necessary to utilise other forms of storage medium. Magnetic disk is the most widely used commercial storage device, magnetic tape being suited primarily for backup applications. Once we have looked at the devices, we will look briefly at computer files and their purpose, before going on to discuss file design (relevant to storage selection).

Your objectives

After completing this chapter you should:

(a) understand the function of storage devices;

(b) know the different types of magnetic disk;

(c) know how data is stored on magnetic disks;

(d) know how data is stored on magnetic tape;

(e) know the capabilities of optical storage devices;

(f) understand the hierarchy of files, records, fields and characters;

(g) be able to distinguish between transaction files, master files and reference files;

(h) understand the different methods of file organisation and file access;

(i) know which methods of access can be used with disks, and which can be used with tape;

(j) know the steps in updating disk and tape master files.

1 STORAGE DEVICES

A processor has a certain amount of memory. However, as business computer files are required to hold far more data than any memory can handle, there has to be a method of holding data on file when it is not required inside the processor. The function of storage devices is to hold data until it is needed for further processing. Storage devices must therefore operate as input/output devices, capable of use for both the input and output of data.

1.1 Magnetic disks

The most commonly used storage medium with computers is magnetic disk. A magnetic disk consists of a flat circular disk covered on both sides with a magnetic material. Data is held on a number of circular, concentric tracks on the surfaces of the disk and is read or written by rotating the disk past read/write heads, which can either write data from memory on to disk, or read data from it for input to memory. To make it easier to locate data, each circular track is divided into several sectors. Data can then be found by its track number and its sector number. The mechanism that causes the disk to rotate is called a disk drive.

Hard disks

Most modern business PCs have internal magnetic hard disks. To increase storage capacity, external disks can also be used. An external disk sits alongside the computer in an extra 'box' with its own power supply and plug socket. An internal disk is incorporated inside the microcomputer box itself.

Definition

A *hard disk* is a direct storage device which uses a magnetic recording medium coated onto a rigid disk. The rigidity allows a greater spin speed, hence faster access/read times.

The standard size of the hard disk has increased dramatically in recent years as ever more space-hungry Windows-based software is released.

Large computers, such as mainframes, used to use exchangeable disk packs, in which several flat disks are mounted on a spindle and each surface has a read/write head. (Substantial storage capacity is also offered by the Winchester disk, which holds a number of flat disks sealed onto an airtight pack.)

It is common to back up important data by copying it onto floppy disk or magnetic tape.

Hard disk assemblies (HDA), typically using small computer systems interfaces (SCSI), are capable of holding vast amounts of data (3–9 Gb) and are relatively cheap due to the mass marketing of PCs.

This has led to the development of RAID (redundant array of inexpensive disks) devices which allow mainframe computer users to access the data stored in a group of these disks just as easily as their own proprietary storage devices, which are usually much more expensive. Furthermore, the data can be organised (striping) in such a manner that data can be recovered even if one of the units fail.

Activity 1

Why is it sensible to make an extra copy of the data on a hard disk?

Floppy disks

As well as a hard disk drive, a PC has one or two floppy disk drives, useful for storage, back-up and transportation between PCs.

A floppy disk is an exchangeable circular, flexible disk, typically 3.5 inches in diameter which is held permanently in a hard plastic sleeve. The sleeve cover on each disk will usually have an identification label for recognising the disk and its contents. A disk's sleeve usually incorporates a write protect facility, enabling the disk to be read but not altered or erased.

Definition

A *floppy disk* is a direct storage device which uses a magnetic recording medium coated onto a disk of mylar film.

The disk has a coating of magnetic material which is used to store data and may offer double density storage. Typically, floppy disks can store 1.44 MB of data. However, the time needed to read/write to a floppy disk is longer than that required for by a hard disk.

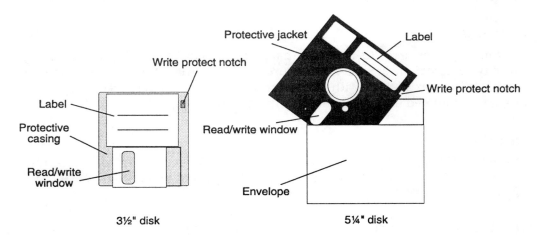

3½" disk   5¼" disk

Figure 2.1 Floppy disks

The disks must be compatible with the floppy disk drive being used, which might be for single-sided, double-sided or high density disks, and for $3\frac{1}{2}$ inch or $5\frac{1}{4}$ inch disks.

Floppy disks do not require special storage conditions and, indeed, they are often stored in open trays. However, data on them can easily be corrupted. In particular, they are subject to physical wear, because the read/write head actually comes into contact with the disk surface during operation. This is not the case with other types of disk. Because they can be left lying around an office, they are also prone to physical damage, such as having tea spilled over them.

Directories

As the files kept by PC users are usually quite small, it is common for the a disk, especially a hard disk, to hold a large number of files.

In order to organise these many files on the disk in such a way that they can be found easily and quickly when they are wanted, files are grouped into directories and sub-directories. There is a 'root' directory, from which sub-directories and files then branch out. For example, a computer user might organise his or her files so that the root directory includes a sub-directory for word processing (as well as a sub-directory for, say, a database).

The word processing sub-directory might include several files, such as a file for the word processing program itself and several data files, each for a particular document. The sub-directory might also include a sub-sub-directory for documents of a particular type, such as purchase orders. The purchase order sub-sub-directory might then include several data files, each for a different type of purchase order.

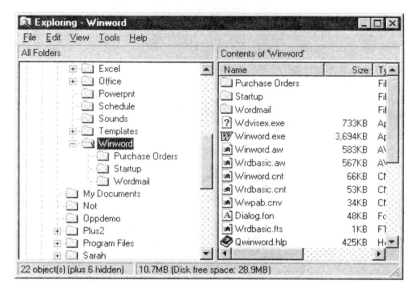

Figure 2.2 Ways of representing directories and sub-directories

Activity 2

A PC user wants to store about 5 MB of data, and to be able to pass the data to another user without setting up a direct physical link between their two computers. What storage medium would be appropriate, and why?

1.3   Magnetic tape

Magnetic tape consists of a strip of plastic tape coated with a magnetic material deposited in grains, each of which may be magnetised in one of two possible directions. To each of the directions, the significance 0 or 1 is attached so that data can be written on to, stored on and read from tape. As with domestic audio tape, a recording can be erased and the tape re-used. As data is read from a tape or written onto a tape, the tape moves past a read/write head, from one reel onto another, again like audio tape.

Data is held along the length of a tape in blocks. A block may consist of just one data record (for example, the data on one customer), but it might consist of several records. Blocks can be read from tape into memory, and written from memory on to tape, one at a time. After one block of data has been written, the tape stops (so as not to waste space) until the write instruction for the next block is given. This stop-start process involves slowing down the tape until it comes to rest, and then accelerating again to full speed. Data can only be read or recorded when the tape is moving at full speed and consequently there are blank stretches of tape between blocks. The existence of inter-block gaps means that the practical storage capacity of magnetic tape is usually less than two thirds of the maximum possible storage capacity.

Because the processor will only deal with one record at a time, the rest of the block will be held in a buffer area in memory. This is called buffering.

Business Basics: Information technology

In using magnetic tapes, it is not practical to read from and then write to a single piece of tape. Reading and writing are separate operations, using separate heads, and so two drives are necessary for the two operations.

Magnetic disk has replaced tape as the primary storage medium.

(a) It allows direct access, which is vital for real-time applications.

(b) It is more robust and reliable than tape.

(c) There is no risk of degradation from one generation of copy to the next.

Magnetic tape provides storage at a lower cost and is used primarily for back-up and archiving applications. Back-up can be defined as the process of taking machine readable copies of data or programs, normally onto a removable magnetic storage medium, to provide cover against a physical or processing disaster.

Magnetic tape cartridge and cassette

The development of minicomputer systems has led to the use of magnetic tape in cartridge form as a storage medium. A cartridge is similar to but larger in size than a normal audio cassette (being ½" wide). One of the most widely used, the IBM 3840 tape cartridge, is 2,400 feet long and has a capacity of up to 400 megabytes. Cartridges are being used increasingly in 'streaming mode' to provide back-up file copies for data held on hard disks. Fast tapes which can be used to create back-up files very quickly and can store up to 1 or 2 gigabytes of data are known as *tape streamers*. Cassette tapes are also used for back-up. Tapes based on 8mm videocassette technology can hold up to 2 gigabytes. These have the advantage of being small and easy to handle. A 4mm DAT (digital audio tape) with compression can hold 8 gigabytes.

Automated cartridge libraries (ACL) are a way of using legacy cartridge storage systems in an efficient manner. An industrial robot arm can replace human operators in servicing many cartridge drives at once. The robot can work 24 hours a day, removing the need for a full shift of operators performing mundane tasks.

Activity 3

The proportion of a reel of tape taken up by inter-block gaps could be reduced if more records were put into each block. Why might putting too many records into each block create a problem for the processor?

1.4 Optical disks

Optical disks are now being used for data storage. Optical technology is similar in principle to the compact disk (CD) used for audio recording. There are three basic types of optical disk: CD-ROM, WORM and magneto-optical.

Definition

A *CD-ROM* is a compact disk that records digital data, read by means of a laser

CD-ROM is a read-only technology. This means that all data is implanted at manufacture, in the same way as music is recorded on a CD. Users can only retrieve information; they cannot write their own data. CD-ROM is used primarily as a medium for publishing large amounts of data. Microsoft, for example, advertise the Microsoft Bookshelf (with such titles as Roget's II: Electronic Thesaurus, The US Zip Code Directory, Houghton Mifflin Spell Checker and Usage Alert, American Heritage Dictionary), and Microsoft Small Business Consultant containing tax, accountancy and legal information. In the UK data available on CD-ROM includes British Telecom's directory listings and company information published by Extel.

One application of CD-ROM is in multimedia. CD-ROM and multimedia are not the same thing, but CD-ROM is an integral element of multimedia. This involves the delivery of text, sound and pictures through a single terminal and is made possible by the comparatively high storage potential of optical disks.

Write once read many times (WORM) devices are more advanced than CD-ROM in that users can enter their own data. However, this data can never be erased. A WORM device is an alloy disk, covered on both sides with plastic. A laser burns holes in the plastic, and these burnt pits represent the data. To read the data, a low-powered laser is passed over the disk and the reflected light is detected. WORM devices have the following features.

(a) Most devices are written in sequence. Rather than arrange data in concentric tracks, data on many WORM devices is written into one long continuous spiral.

(b) It is not possible to erase data on a WORM device. Instead, if it is used to contain data which changes (such as records of goods in stock), new versions of the file are added to the disk. Some manufacturers make a virtue out of this necessity by advertising a history facility (the ability to look up old versions of a file on disk).

(c) The more a disk is used, the slower access speeds will be, as more old data is retained.

(d) WORM devices are ideal for archiving very large amounts of data (for example, where permanent records are required by legal or taxation authorities).

Definition

WORM, or write once read many, is a recordable form of CD-ROM

Recently, magneto-optical disks have been developed. These comprise a magnetised recording medium sandwiched between two plastic disks. The contents of the disk can be altered magnetically at high temperatures. The area to be altered is heated by a laser, and then its magnetic charge is reversed, a state in which it remains when cooled down. Bits are therefore represented by changed magnetic orientations in the disk. With these disks, old data need not build up but can be erased. Optical disks can also be arranged using a 'juke box' to automate the retrieval of large volumes of data.

The main advantage of optical disks over other storage media is that very large volumes of data can be stored on one disk. One writer has indicated that the cost per megabyte is only 1% of that of magnetic disk storage. However, before purchase, an organisation has to make sure that its data storage requirements are vast enough to warrant the use of optical disks.

Activity 4

Give three examples of businesses where a history facility might be particularly useful.

2 COMPUTER FILES

We will now look at how disks and tapes are actually used in the storage and processing of data.

In commercial data processing, a file is a collection of data records with similar characteristics. Every file has a name to distinguish it from other files. A file name is included as data on a file, as a 'header label'. Examples of files are:

(a) stock records;

(b) a price list;

(c) a report;

(d) data in a spreadsheet model (a spreadsheet file);

(e) a word processed letter (a document file);

(f) a sales ledger.

A record contains data relating to one logically definable unit of information, for example a customer record containing name, address and phone number. A collection of similar records makes up a file, for example a customer list.

Records consist of fields of information. For example, a record on a price list file might contain the following fields:

(a) catalogue number;

(b) description;

(c) colour;

(d) delivery times.

Fields are classified as types, for example alphanumeric, numeric and date, so that they can be manipulated more easily; for example, records can be sorted in date order.

Records on a file should contain at least one key field , that is an item of data which is unique to that record. In a price list file, the key field might be the catalogue number, as the colour and price might be duplicated in other records.

Activity 5

A company which is not organised into separate departments has a file of payroll data. What entity would each record represent? Give examples of the fields you would expect to find in each record.

2.1　Types of computer file

Transaction files, master files and reference files

In some systems files can be classified into transaction files, master files and reference files.

A *transaction file* is a file containing records relating to individual transactions that occur from day to day. The transaction records must all be processed. When a company sells its goods, the accounts staff might record the sales in a sales day book, which lists the sales made on a daily basis for which invoices have been issued. Eventually these transactions in the sales day book will be transferred ('posted') to the personal accounts of the individual customers in the sales ledger. The sales day book entries are examples of transaction records in a transaction file. Similarly, all receipts and payments of cash are recorded in the cash book; so the cash book acts as a transaction file

A *master file* in such a system is a file containing reference data, which is normally updated infrequently, and transaction data, which is built up over time. For example, in a purchase ledger system, the master file is the purchase ledger itself. This is a file consisting of 'standing' reference data for each supplier (supplier name and address, reference number, amount currently owed etc) and transaction data for each supplier, itemising purchases, purchase returns and payments to the supplier.

A *reference file* or index file is a file containing reference data, which is normally updated infrequently. It contains no transaction data. Examples of a reference file are a price list and manuals of company regulations and procedures. Reference files are often classified as a type of master file because they both contain 'standing' reference data.

Databases

A database contains a bank of data, which can be used in a more flexible way than the files above. For example, a database of sales data might contain details of each sale and might allow a user to find out about all sales of a particular product, all sales to a particular customer or all sales worth over £500.

Databases allow information to be input in any order, and to output in a variety of formats. Databases can be relational, allowing different files to be accessed simultaneously. For example, by querying both a salesperson's individual file and the client sales list, the database could allow you to calculate current commission due.

Large databases have made centralisation increasingly workable. For example, by telephoning your bank's central phone number, a computer operator is immediately able to read from the screen your current details, perhaps accessing this information by typing in a key field such as your account number or your post code.

Temporary files and permanent files

Files might be temporary or permanent . Master files and reference files are usually permanent, which means that they are never thrown away. As they will be updated from time to time, the information on the file might change, but the file itself will continue to exist.

A temporary file is one that is eventually scrapped. Many transaction files are held for a very short time, until the transaction records have been processed, and are then thrown away. The magnetic medium holding the file can be re-used.

Activity 6

A university keeps a file (A) of students' names and addresses, a file (B) of courses completed up to the end of the last academic year by each student and a file (C) of data on courses completed since the start of the current academic year waiting to be recorded in file B. Classify each of these three files as a master file, a transaction file or a reference file.

2.2   File organisation

File organisation refers to the way in which records are held on a file, with a view to the retrieval of data. File organisation may be sequential or non-sequential.

Sequential file organisation

A file's organisation is sequential if the records on the file are in a logical sequence according to their key field, for example in alphabetical order or in numerical order. On a price list, for example, the key field could be the product number.

Sequential files must be maintained in sequence. New records must be placed in their correct position in the file, and records which follow 'pushed back' to make room for the new records. In computer systems this could lead to a large number of 'accesses', moving each record in turn one position back in the file. To get round this problem, it is usual to leave spaces on a sequential file, to allow room for new records. This is done by grouping records together in 'buckets' with each bucket starting part-filled with records and part-empty for new additions. After a while, when the empty spaces start to fill up, records will be regrouped into new buckets with spaces. This process of tidying up the file is called housekeeping.

Non-sequential file organisation

Where records are not in a logical sequence according to a key field, the file is organised non-sequentially. This does not, however, make it impossible to find records, as we shall see in a minute.

2.3   File access

File access means locating individual records on the file. The way in which a file can be accessed depends on how the file is organised; access can be serial, sequential or random.

Serial access

Serial access is simply reading through the records on a file in whatever order they happen to be in.

(a) With transaction files, serial access will often be suitable, because every record on the file has to be processed.

(b) With master files, serial access to locate records would be very time consuming and so very inefficient.

Sequential access

With *sequential access*, the records on the file must be organised sequentially. Sequential access is the access of records on a sequentially organised file, without using an index. Sequential access is faster than serial access for two reasons.

(a) Since records on a sequentially organised file are in key field order, once the particular record has been located, there is no need to check serially through the rest of the file in case there is another record on file with the same key field number.

(b) There is a method of locating records on a sequential file, known as binary search, which means that individual records can be located more quickly than with serial access.

Random access

There are two methods of *random access:* indexed sequential access and direct access. They are methods of locating an individual record without having to look through any other records first.

The term *indexed sequential access* is used to describe random access to records that are held in a key field order in file, that is filed sequentially, using an index to locate individual records. Both the records on file and the index must be held in sequence, and new records must be placed in their correct positions on the file and their correct places on the index.

Indexed sequential access is often faster than sequential access, because any record can be located by reference to the index, which gives its address on file.

Direct access refers to the retrieval of data from a file which is not sequentially organised. The method of random access will depend on the method used to put records on to the file in the first place. This may be done by calculating a key value from data about the record, or by reference to an index.

Activity 7

The records in a telephone directory (names, addresses and telephone numbers) are organised sequentially by name. If you only had a directory in book form (and not in computer readable form), what method of access would you use:

(a) to find someone's telephone number when you know their name;

(b) to find someone's name when you know their telephone number?

2.4   File access with magnetic disk

The method of access on a disk may be one of the following.

(a) Serial access is only used for temporary files, for example, transaction files.

(b) Sequential access may be suitable for master files in a normal batch processing system (one which processes a large batch of data at once), but depending on the hit rate (the proportion of records on the file which need to be accessed), random access may be preferable. If the hit rate is low (that is, only a few records need to be accessed for each batch), it may be useful to be able to access those records without working through other records.

(c) Random access is useful where:

   (i) the hit rate is low;

   (ii) data cannot be conveniently batched or sorted;

   (iii) a fast response is required.

Updating disk files by overlay

A disk file could be updated by *file copying* with each record being written to a physically different file. The old records are thus preserved. However, updating by *file overlay* is more common. The updated record is written back to its original address location after update, ie the old record is overwritten by the new record.

The procedure for *batch processing* (dealing with a whole batch of transactions at once) with update by overlay is as follows.

(a) The transaction record is read into memory.

(b) The relevant master record is located on the disk and read into memory.

(c) The master record is updated in memory.

(d) The next transaction record is read into memory.

(e) The two record keys are compared. If they agree, the transaction data is used to update the master record (which is already in memory, updated with the first transaction). If the keys are different, the updated master is written back onto the disk.

(f) The relevant master record (for the transaction record now in memory) is now read into memory and updated.

(g) The whole process is repeated until all the transaction records have been processed.

The procedure for direct keyboard entry to update a master file for a single transaction is as follows.

(a) The transaction record is keyed in.

(b) The master file record is located by random access.

(c) The master file record is updated and written back onto the same master file.

(d) Any user output required is shown on a VDU screen or printed out.

There is a tendency for commercial files to expand and so in a sequentially organised file new records have to be placed in overflow areas. Also, when a variable length record has expanded to such an extent that it can no longer be accommodated in its own area, an overflow location must be used. The address of the overflow location is recorded in the original area and thus the records can still be accessed sequentially even though they are no longer physically held in sequence. This process of referencing is known as chaining. After a certain time, the structure of the file will become rather complex and it will have to be reorganised. File reorganisation (sometimes referred to as file maintenance) involves transferring the data on the disk onto a new disk, placing records back into sequence, deleting old records, rewriting the index and creating new (empty) overflow areas.

Databases do not have this problem. However, they require large storage capacity for their data.

Activity 8

A master file on disk of goods in stock is being updated by overlay. The master file contains records for products A, B, C, D, E and F. The transaction file contains four records, giving details of stock movements for products A, C, C (again) and F. Set out the sequence of readings of records from the master file, updatings of master file records and writings of records back to the master file, assuming that the transaction file records are processed sequentially but that random access to the master file is used.

2.5 File access with magnetic tape

With magnetic tapes, file access must be serial or sequential. It is impossible to have random access with magnetic tape, because the computer must work through the tape in order until it reaches the right place, rather than jumping straight to the middle of the tape.

It follows that magnetic tape is only usable in certain circumstances.

(a) It can be used for a transaction file, when every record on the file will be processed in turn. Since transaction data might not be pre-sorted when it is input to the computer, it must be sorted before the master file update. Sorting of transaction data would be done in a separate sort program, and the sorted data would be written to a new tape;

(b) It can be used for a master file, when the hit rate is high enough to make sequential access quicker than random access. The tape master file must be organised sequentially.

Another important feature of magnetic tapes is that it is usual to produce a new master file on a different physical tape from that used for the old master file.

The steps in master file updating with magnetic tape

The steps involved in updating a master file on magnetic tape are as follows.

(a) Read a transaction record into memory.

(b) Read a master record into memory.

(c) Compare the two key fields.

(i) If the fields agree, the master record is updated with the appropriate transaction record data and held in memory. Then read the next transaction record into the memory.

(ii) If the records do not agree, write the master record to the new tape and read the next master record into memory.

(d) Compare the key fields of the two records now in memory (transaction record and master file record).

(e) If they agree, update the master record; if not, write the master record (which obviously does not need updating) to the new tape. The process continues repetitively until all the records on the transaction file have been processed.

Tapes are organised in blocks of records. As blocks are read into memory from both transactions and master files, a number of buffer areas (areas to hold data waiting to be dealt with or waiting to be written to the new tape) are allocated for all the records in each block. The updating procedure is as outlined above, each record being processed in turn until the whole block can be written to the new tape.

File maintenance (amending standing data, removing records or adding records) is carried out in a similar manner. As a completely new tape reel is produced each time, there is no problem in inserting records in the correct sequence, or in having variable length records, so there is no need for 'buckets' and file housekeeping.

Activity 9

A master file on magnetic tape is being updated from a transaction file. The current master file record to be processed has a key field value of 75 (its serial number on the tape). The current transaction file record to be processed has a key field value of 183. What procedure should have been carried out to ensure that it is not now necessary to check through the transaction file for a record with a key field value of 75?

Chapter roundup

- Storage devices are used to hold data when it is not being processed.
- Magnetic disks may be exchangeable disk packs, smaller hard disks or floppy disks.
- PCs generally have an integral hard disk drive and one or two floppy disk drives.
- Magnetic tape can also be used to store large quantities of data.
- Optical storage devices have a very large capacity, but in most cases data cannot be erased.
- A file comprises many records, each of which has several fields.
- Master files are updated from transaction files.
- Data which is needed for processing but which rarely changes is stored in a reference file.
- Files can be organised sequentially or non-sequentially.
- Files can be accessed serially, sequentially or randomly.
- All methods of access are possible with magnetic disk files, and such files are usually updated by overlay.
- Only serial and sequential access are possible with magnetic tape files, and such files must be updated by producing a new tape.

Quick quiz

1 How is data laid out on a magnetic disk?

2 How may data on a small hard disk be dumped?

3 What are the two sizes of floppy disk, and how do they differ?

4 What is the capacity of a modern floppy disk?

5   Why are files grouped into directories and sub-directories?

6   Why must a magnetic tape include inter-block gaps?

7   What does WORM stand for?

8   A file includes a record for each supplier to a company. What might the fields be?

9   When can a transaction file be discarded?

10   How can records be found in a file with random organisation?

11   Which method of file access should not be used for master files?

12   When is random access useful?

13   What are the steps in update by overlay?

14   How does chaining arise?

15   What are the steps in updating a magnetic tape file?

Answers to activities

1   A hard disk might be damaged or a PC containing a hard disk might be stolen.

2   Floppy disks should be used, because only about four disks would be needed and they can be taken out of one PC and inserted in another.

3   There might not be enough space in memory for the contents of a whole block.

4   Banks: it may be useful to be able to see how an account has been conducted over several years.

     Retailers: it may be useful to see how sales and stock levels fluctuate over time.

     Solicitors: it may be important to keep all drafts of a contract drawn up for a client, in case it is later alleged that the firm was negligent.

5   Each record would represent an employee. Fields would include the following.

     (a)   Employee name

     (b)   Employee number

     (c)   National insurance number

     (d)   Tax code

     (e)   Weekly wage

     (f)   Gross pay for the year to date

     (g)   Tax for the year to date

     There would probably be other fields, depending on how the payroll system worked and on whether overtime was paid.

6   A: reference file

     B: master file

     C: transaction file

7   (a)   Indexed sequential access

     (b)   Serial access

8   Read in A, update A, write back A

     Read in C, update C, update C (again), write back C

     Read in F, update F, write back F

9   The transaction records should have been sorted into sequence, so that if a record with a value of 183 has been reached, any record with a value of 75 must already have been dealt with.

Further question practice

Now try the following practice questions at the end of this text.

Multiple choice questions   **8 to17**

Exam style question   **2**

Chapter 3

INPUT AND OUTPUT

Introduction

Input devices come in a wide variety of forms. They are used, quite simply, to 'get data into a computer'. Their function is to convert data in any form (figures, text, speech, images, etc.) into the binary signals recognised by the computer. The range of output device is smaller, the two most widely used being the printer and the visual display unit (VDU), also referred to as a screen or a monitor.

Your objectives

After completing this chapter you should:

(a) know the stages of input;

(b) understand how a computer keyboard is laid out;

(c) understand what a VDU is used for;

(d) understand how and when to use a mouse;

(e) know how to use menus;

(f) understand the WIMP user interface;

(g) know the advantages and disadvantages of direct keyboard input;

(h) know the stages in encoding to disk or to tape;

(i) know the main automatic document reading methods available;

(j) know the main types of card reading device;

(k) know the main types of printer available;

(l) know the methods of computer output on microform;

(m) be able to select a method of output appropriate to a given task.

1 INPUT

The stages of data input are as follows.

(a) *Origination of data* (the business transaction that gives rise to data which needs to be recorded and processed).

(b) *Transcription of data* into a machine-readable form (which the computer can take in), if this is necessary.

(c) *Data input.*

Data origination and collection where transcription is not necessary is known as data capture.

1.1 Keyboard, VDU and mouse

The usual way to get data into a computer directly (without any intermediate stages) is to use a keyboard with a VDU displaying the input data so that you can see what you are typing. Increasingly, a mouse may be used in conjunction with the keyboard; this allows quicker 'navigation' around the screen. VDUs and keyboards can be used for direct data entry as:

(a) *terminals* connected to a mainframe or minicomputer;

(b) an integral part of a personal computer.

Keyboard

You may be familiar with the basic QWERTY keyboard.

Definition

A *QWERTY keyboard* is a keyboard laid out in the standard typewriter pattern. It includes the alphabet, numbers 0-9 and some basic punctuation, plus other keys (eg space bar and a shift key, which allows the upper case alphabet keys and a second set of key features to be used)

A typical computer keyboard is a development of the QWERTY design. The standard keyboard now has 102 keys and includes the following.

(a) *Ordinary typing keys* used to enter data or text as with a manual or electronic typewriter. These may also be used to input *instructions or commands* if used with special keys called CTRL or ALT.

(b) *A numeric key pad* to use like a calculator or to enter lots of numbers. This key pad is usually sited to the right of the main keyboard and resembles a simple calculator. These keys may also double as cursor control keys.

(c) *Cursor control keys*, which in compact keyboards may be incorporated into the numeric section, but which in the 102-key keyboard are also grouped separately. These are up/down/left/right keys to move the cursor or writing point on the screen. There are also keys for more rapid movement through documents, for example 'Home', 'End', 'Page Up' and 'Page Down'.

(d) A number of *function keys* for use with software. These keys are numbered (F1, F2, etc) and preset to perform certain functions. The preset functions will vary depending on the particular software being used. F1 is often a 'help' key which can be used to call up a 'help screen'.

The actual positioning of these areas and what characters share certain keys may differ between keyboards.

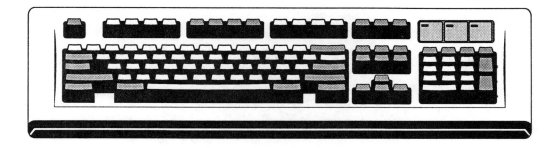

Figure 3.1 A typical keyboard

Activity 1

Find an actual keyboard, and locate on it:

(a) the function keys;

(b) the cursor control keys;

(c) the CTRL and ALT keys.

In addition to the function keys, there are special keys that must be used to let the computer know that you wish to enter or have finished entering a command, to correct a command and so on.

(a) *Return key* or *Enter key*. All commands direct to the system must be 'entered' with this key, to let the machine know that you have finished typing your command and wish it to be executed.

(b) *Escape (ESC) key*. This key can be used when, for example, you wish to stop using a procedure.

(c) *Control (CTRL) key*. This alters the meanings of some keys. Thus in word processing, pressing the key 'P' would type the letter P, but pressing the control key at the same time as the key 'P' might make the word processor start a new page.

(d) There may be another special key or combination which can be used to change the meanings of keys: there is no room on the QWERTY keyboard for characters such as accents, foreign alphabets, mathematical signs and so on. Such a key might change some letters to mean for example, $\alpha\,\beta\,\gamma\,\delta\,\Sigma\,\varsigma\,@$ etc

VDU

VDUs display text and graphics. They can be cathode ray tubes, liquid crystal displays or gas plasma displays, and can support colour and detailed display.

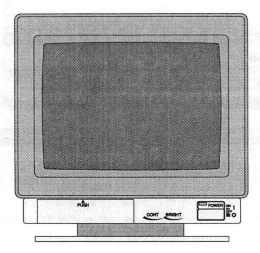

Figure 3.2 A VDU

The screen's resolution is the number of pixels that are lit up. A pixel is a pictorial element, a 'dot' on the screen, as it were. The fewer the pixels on screen, the larger they will be: the resolution of any picture with large pixels will be low. More and smaller pixels enable detailed high-resolution display. Currently, many PCs have a resolution of 640 × 480, the resolution offered by IBM's VGA standard. Higher resolution requires more processing power, but enables graphs and diagrams to be displayed. *High resolution monitors* currently available include 1024 (horizontal) × 768 (vertical). Super VGA, or SVGA, is becoming the standard specification for new PCs.

To view a different piece of text, the operators 'pans' up, down or sideways. Alternatively two or more bits of text which are in different places in the overall layout can be viewed on screen at the same time by making use of windows: a bit of text on screen is surrounded by a box, and two or more such boxes can be displayed at once.

A wrap-around facility enables the computer to display a line of text that is too long to be displayed on the screen in its entirety. The line appears on the VDU as two successive lines. Scrolling occurs when the screen is full of text: the computer moves each line of text up one line, thus removing the first line from view, so that text input can continue on the bottom line.

The screen is used to display text, to allow the operator to see what has been keyed in, to help the input of data by providing 'forms' on the screen for filling in (the screen's format can be specified by the program) and to display output, such as answers to enquiries. In addition, the screen can be used to give messages to the operator, and the operator can respond to messages by keying in new instructions.

Mouse

A mouse is often used in conjunction with a keyboard, particularly in Windows-based systems. A mouse is a handheld device with a rubber or metal ball protruding from a small hole in its base. The mouse is moved over a flat surface, usually a special mouse mat which is designed to possess enough friction to prevent the ball slipping and, as it moves, internal sensors pick up the motion and convert it into electronic signals which instruct the cursor on screen to move in the same direction.

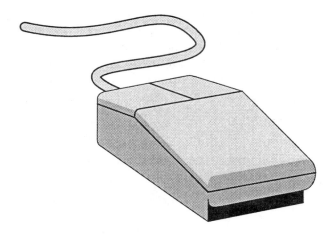

Figure 3.3 A mouse

The mouse has (usually) two or three buttons which can be pressed (clicked) to send specific signals. For example, a 'click' on the left hand button can be used to send the cursor to a new cell in a spreadsheet and a 'double click' can select a particular application from a Windows menu. A mouse largely removes the barrier of requiring keyboard skills for computer use. The term 'mouse' is loosely derived from the physical appearance of the object, particularly the long 'tail' which connects to the computer.

The advantage of the mouse is that it is much easier to use than the keyboard for navigating around the screen. With the keyboard, the user is often confined to using the directional arrow keys, but with the mouse, any movement in two dimensions is possible. This means that the mouse is particularly useful for:

(a) moving from one point to another in a file, for example, to a different location in a word processed report or a table of data;

(b) selecting an option from a menu-bar or a pulldown menu;

(c) graphics applications, as the mouse can be used to 'draw'.

Similar to the mouse is the *trackball*. This is prevalent on notebook computers, where there is not always space to place a mouse mat on a flat surface next to the computer. It operates in a similar way, except that the casing is fixed to the computer and a ball, which protrudes upwards, is manipulated by hand.

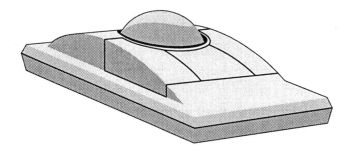

Figure 3.4 A trackball

The advantages of direct keyboard input

By far the most significant advantage of direct input via a keyboard (with or without a mouse) is that a computer user can have interactive processing. Interactive processing is when data can be input to a computer, output information can be received quickly, further input can be keyed in and output received. The computer user gets the information needed instantly.

Interactive processing is essential to some forms of data processing, and managers increasingly need to obtain information rapidly from a computer that would take far too long to prepare manually. The use of financial models and spreadsheets are examples of how managers rely on computers for planning and budgeting. The modern trend is towards putting a PC on every manager's desk.

This major advantage of keyboard input is only an advantage, of course, when the computer user wants interactive processing. For some data processing applications, routine batch processing in particular, interactive processing is not needed.

The other advantages of keyboard input are as follows.

(a) The person keying in the data can be in a location far away from the computer itself, with the keyboard and VDU linked to the computer by telephone. In such a case, the keyboard and VDU are used as a terminal for the remote computer, which may be a PC or a larger computer. The terminal may be just a terminal, or it may itself be a PC able to carry out some computing itself.

(b) The person keying in the data can check it on the VDU screen before pressing the 'Enter' key to input it to the computer. Any keying errors, or even errors in the data itself, might be identified and corrected on the spot.

The disadvantages of direct keyboard input

Direct keyboard input is unsuitable for large volumes of transaction data. Keying in takes a long time, and a computer waiting for data to be keyed in is idle for much of the time. The speed of keyboard input depends on the typing speed of the operator. A typical speed might be 200–250 characters (bytes) per minute. This is slow in computer terms.

Keyboard input is error-prone because the only data verification that can be done before input is a visual check of the data on the VDU screen.

There might also be security problems. Keyboard terminals are less secure than a computer centre: unauthorised users could gain access to a keyboard terminal in an office.

Activity 2

A company inputs data from all of its 2,500 employees' weekly timesheets into its computer for payroll purposes, and the production director occasionally inspects this data to check on the amount of overtime being worked in each department. Why would direct keyboard input be valuable for the production director's enquiries, but not for the weekly input of data?

1.2   The user interface

'User-friendly' is a term which has been used by many people to signify many different attributes of a computer system. Such a system is best described by reference to examples. Ways that help to make a system user-friendly include the following.

(a) A listing of valid commands can be provided on screen on request.

(b) Menu-driven routines are used.

(c) Errors entered by the user can be identified and diagnosed.

(d) A help system, whereby information pertaining to the current screen or location within the application can be provided at the touch of a key, is always available.

Definition

A *user-friendly system* is one which is designed to make the users task as easy as possible by providing feedback.

The introduction of PCs into business organisations marked a significant change in user profiles. Computers and terminals became available to many staff who had none or very little previous computing experience. This made it important that only the simplest interactions should be necessary for them to start making practical use of the system in question. For example, if a computer running a program encounters an error situation, it might simply stop running the program and display an error code, which the user could then look up in a handbook in order to discover how to proceed. A user-friendly computer would display on screen the nature of the error and offer the user alternatives for continuing processing from which the user could simply select by 'clicking' on the relevant option box using a mouse.

The mouse is at the heart of a particular widely-used approach to increasing user-friendliness of systems: WIMP. WIMP was designed to make computers more 'user-friendly' to people without experience of using them, and who might have difficulty in using a keyboard, or who might be resistant to the idea of becoming a computer user. WIMP involves the use of two design ideas and two operating methods. WIMP stands for windows icons mouse pull-down menu (or alternatively menu pointer) and is an environment which offers a method of accessing the computer without using the keyboard.

(a) *Windows*. The screen can be divided into sections, 'windows' of flexible size which can be opened and closed. This enables two or more documents to be viewed and edited together, and sections of one to be inserted into another. This is particularly useful for word processed documents and spreadsheets which are too large for the VDU screen. There are two main sorts of windows: 'directory' windows, which display the contents of a 'folder' on a dish; and 'application' windows, in which a part of the program actually being run is displayed.

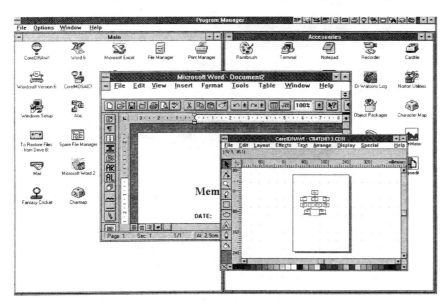

Figure 3.5 A windows screen

(b) *Icons*. An icon is an image of an object used to represent an abstract idea or process. In software design, icons may be used instead of numbers, letters or words to identify and describe the various functions available for selection, or files to access. A common icon is a waste paper bin to indicate the deletion of a document.

CLIPBOARD VIEWER

Clipboard provides temporary or permanent storage for information you want to move, save or share.

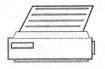

PRINT MANAGER

Print manager can be used to manage documents sent to a printer. It can also be used to install and configure printers.

CONTROL PANEL

Control panel is used to customise windows. It can be used to change your desktop colours, adding and removing fonts and setting up a screen saver etc

FILE MANAGER

File manager can help you organise files and directories on your disk drive.

Figure 3.6 Examples of icons

(c) *Mouse.* As the mouse moves around on the desktop, a pointer (cursor) on the VDU screen mimics its movements. A mouse can be used to pick out an appropriate icon (or other option), to mark out the area of a new window, to mark the beginning and end of a block for deletion or insertion and so on. It has a button to execute the appropriate command when the pointer is in the right place.

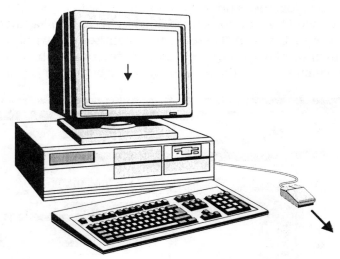

Figure 3.7 Mouse/pointer interaction

(d) *Pull-down menu.* An initial menu (or menu-bar) will be shown across the top of the VDU screen. Using the mouse to move the pointer to the required item in the menu, the pointer 'pulls down' a subsidiary menu, similar to pulling down a window blind in the room of a house. The pointer and mouse can then be used to select the required item on the menu pulled down.

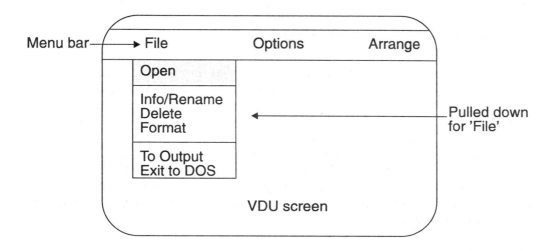

Menu bar

File   Options   Arrange

Open

Info/Rename
Delete
Format

To Output
Exit to DOS

Pulled down
for 'File'

VDU screen

Figure 3.8 A pull-down menu

Activity 3

A word processor offers an initial menu which includes the following options.

1 Text feature; 2 Search; 3 Tabs; 4 Delete.

Which of the above would you expect to give you a subsidiary menu including the following options?

1 Subscript; 2 Bold; 3 Italic; 4 Underline.

Graphical user interfaces (GUIs)

WIMP is an example of a trend towards *user-friendliness* and ease of use for computer operators, many of whom are not computer professionals. WIMP is a 'graphical user interface' in that dialogue is conducted through images rather than just typed text. The WIMP strategy is a feature of Apple Macintosh computers, and all software written for Apple Macintosh machines can be operated using a mouse. There are leading WIMP systems for IBM-compatible PCs, notably Windows (manufactured by Microsoft) and Presentation Manager, which is a part of IBM's OS/2.

WIMP is not used on all PCs: all the same operations can be performed by other means, using cursor control keys instead of the mouse, entering commands via codes or alphanumeric menu selection and so on. The WIMP strategy has several advantages, however.

(a) Icon selection is very easy to use, and less taxing for the user's memory than codes.

(b) The mouse/pointer/icon system means that the keyboard is not used for controls. This avoids confusion over keys which have different meanings in different modes and means that typing speed is no longer a constraint. (It may, however, be more convenient during the typing of documents to have the necessary controls also at the typist's fingertips.)

(c) The windows system is really the only way of viewing the contents of two files simultaneously. It also provides a convenient alternative to panning around documents covering large areas, for example, spreadsheets.

Manufacturers are now offering *pen-based systems*. In these systems, a 'pen' is used instead of a mouse; a sensor collects information about the strokes being formed and analyses the movements to identify the characters written. This is a development from mouse technology; however it has been criticised as being a backward step from the computer keyboard. Nevertheless, it is proving popular with people who cannot type.

The design of the *keyboard* reflects the way in which the user communicates with the computer to direct its operating processes and to provide and manipulate the contents of its memory. The *screen* is the means by which the computer communicates with the user. The way the keyboard is used, and what you would expect to see on the screen, will therefore depend on the particular strategy for *screen dialogue* that the software adopts. This dialogue between computer operator and computer might be a central feature of the running of a program, and the term *conversational mode* describes a method of operation in which the operator appears to be carrying on a continual dialogue with the computer, receiving immediate replies to input messages.

WYSIWYG (what you see is what you get)

Once you are using a GUI, the image of the text on screen can be made to appear exactly as it will look when printed. This means that what you see (on the screen) is what you get (on the printer), taking a lot of the guesswork out of text formatting.

The cursor

You know exactly where your next character will be if you enter data on a page by hand or typewriter, and in the same way the cursor (an arrow, line or box) shows you on screen the point in your text that will be affected by your keyboard entries.

Definition

A *cursor* is a marker of where the computer's attention is at any given moment. It can be moved about the screen by direction keys on the keyboard or by a mouse.

Activity 4

A computer screen displays a form, with boxes to be filled in. When the operator has finished filling in a box, he or she can move to the next box simply by pressing the Return key. Why would it still be useful to have a cursor displayed on the screen?

Broadly speaking, there are three ways of using a keyboard with VDU to input data. Many systems use a combination of the three.

(a) By selecting options from a *menu*. A menu is a display of a series of options, and the operator selects an option by keying in an appropriate letter or number, or perhaps by moving the cursor to the required option and then selecting the option.

(b) *Form filling*. The screen is laid out to match the design of the source document. When a field has been filled, the cursor moves on to the next field. This process resembles filling in a form.

(c) A *graphical user interface*, as described above.

Menu selection

A menu is a list of items to choose from. A VDU screen might list a number of different options, from which the computer user must choose what he or she wants to do next. For example, a main menu for word processing functions might include:

1 – Create new document

2 – Load saved document

3 – Edit document

4 – Print document

5 – Delete document

6 – Save document

By selecting 4, the operator chooses to do some printing. When 4 has been keyed in, another menu may be displayed, calling for the operator to narrow down the choice still further (for example, print the whole document or only part of it and specify the number of copies to be printed.). A menu system is thus a hierarchical list of options. In graphical user interfaces, many sub-menus are displayed as 'dialogue boxes'.

Form filling

The main part of the screen area, of course, will be the 'page' on which you will be entering data or text. In a standard word processing system, there is a 'blank page' available for document creation and manipulation. However, it is possible to have the screen laid out for specific user requirements. For spreadsheets, accounting applications and data files, there are suitable pre-formatted structures, into which items of data can simply be inserted. Formatting includes several features, such as:

(a) different colours for different screen areas;

(b) reverse video (where colours in a selected area are the reverse of the rest of the screen);

(c) flashing items;

(d) whole forms laid out on screen, with boxes marked out for data to be entered;

(e) larger characters for titles;

(f) paging or scrolling, depending on the volume of information.

1.3   Encoding to disk or tape

Data can be copied from source documents and written on to a magnetic disk or a magnetic tape from a keyboard or terminal. This process is called encoding. In short the data is transcribed into a machine-readable form.

Encoding can be done in one of two ways; either *off-line* using special key-to-disk encoding equipment, or *on-line* to a computer, so that the keyboard input is encoded on to a disk (or possibly a tape) via the computer. A device is on line when it is connected to a computer, which can receive signals from it or send signals to it before input to the main processing program(s). In both cases, the data (probably transaction data) that is encoded on to the disk will be sorted.

Generally, key-to-disk encoding systems are multi-station systems comprising a number of keyboard/VDU terminals on-line to a small computer. The system is controlled by the system's computer using a small library of programs. These are able to carry out some checks on the data as it is keyed in, and also control the encoding and verification processes. Checks may identify inconsistencies or logical errors.

The procedure is as follows.

(a) Data is keyed in, checked and shown on the VDU screen (detected errors are indicated on the screen) and, when accepted, written onto the magnetic disk or tape.

(b) Verification is carried out by another operator. Verification is the process of checking that data input is identical to source data. The data is keyed in again by the second operator, and the system checks that both versions are identical.

(c) Completed batches are grouped together to create the complete transaction file which is written from the working disks to another disk (or a magnetic tape).

(d) This disk (or tape) is then used as the input for the main computer.

Key-to-disk encoding is suitable in systems where large volumes of data are input for processing.

Data may also be keyed in to a floppy disk, rather than to a big tape reel or disk pack. This may be used when a small amount of data is collected by each recording device. Examples include the recording of sales on cash registers, keying in stock level details (for example, in a supermarket) and keying in household gas or electricity meter readings to a hand-held recording device.

Activity 5

Give two examples of situations where preliminary encoding to disk or tape would be preferable to direct keyboard input.

1.4 Document reading methods

Transcribing manually-prepared data into a computer-readable form such as disk or tape is costly and jeopardises accuracy. Document reading methods of data collection involve the use of a source document that both humans *and* computers can read. The data on the source document might be pre-printed, or added later by manual processing, but in either case the source document itself is fed in to the computer. Data transcription and verification are reduced or eliminated. Although the on-line input speed of document reading devices is slower than that of magnetic tape or disk devices, the saving in data collection time is considerable.

Magnetic ink character recognition (MICR)

MICR is recognition of characters by a machine that reads characters printed in magnetic ink. Using ink which contains a metallic powder, highly stylised characters are printed onto documents. The documents must be passed through a magnetic field before the characters can be detected by a suitable reading device.

The largest application of MICR is in banking. Cheques are pre-encoded with the customer account number, branch code and cheque number and, after use, post-encoded with the amount of the cheque. The cheques are then passed through the reading device and details are stored on magnetic disk or tape . The cheque data is now on magnetic storage for processing, while the cheques (sorted by the reading device into branch code order) are returned to the appropriate branches. MICR is particularly well suited for cheques, since although they may become dirty, overwritten or crumpled, they are still legible to the reading device.

The main advantage of MICR is its accuracy. However, as MICR documents are expensive to produce, it has only limited application in practice. A large MICR reader in the banking system can scan up to 2,000 documents per minute.

1 8 7

ENLARGED

1 2 3 4 5 6 7 8 9 0 :"#

ACTUAL SIZE

E 13 B FOUNT

Figure 3.9 Examples of characters printed in magnetic ink

Optical character recognition (OCR)

OCR involves a machine that is able to read characters by looking at their shapes. Optical scanners can read documents at up to 300 pages per hour. They recognise the characters, convert them into machine code (readable by the computer) and record them on to the magnetic medium being used. In practice, the difficulty of distinguishing between O and 0, and between I and 1, means that OCR applications are limited. Most machines still require special typefaces, although some can cope with any printed letters and even with handwriting.

Mark sensing and optical mark reading (OMR)

Mark sensing is generally used for numeric characters, their values being denoted by pencilled lines in boxes on the preprinted source document. The document is then read by a device which senses the graphite marks in the boxes.

OMR is similar, except that the reading device uses an artificial light source and the marks can be made with ball point pen or ink as well as with pencil.

The data recorded must be of a fairly limited nature, for example, yes/no responses on a questionnaire or answers to a multiple choice examination.

Bar coding

A bar code reader is a device which reads bar codes, which are groups of vertical lines whose spacing and thickness indicate specific codes or values. There is an example of a bar code on the back cover of this book. Bar codes are now commonly used in shops. When a customer buys some bar coded items and takes them to the check-out to pay, the shop assistant uses a bar code reader which transmits the bar coded data to a central computer in the store. The computer then provides the price of the item being purchased and this is output to the cashier's check-out point. The total cost of all the purchases is similarly calculated, displayed on a small screen for the customer to see and a receipt printed. At the same time, the data about the purchases that has been read into the computer from the bar codes can be used to update the stock file (so that goods which have sold well can be re-ordered) and to record the sales data for management information purposes.

Figure 3.10 A bar code

Turnround documents

OCR and OMR methods can make use of *turnround documents*.

Definition

A *turnround document* is a document that is initially produced by computer. It is then used to collect more data and then re-input to the computer for processing.

Examples of turnround documents are as follows.

(a) Credit card companies, for example, Visa and Mastercard, include payment counterfoils with their computer-produced statements, which will then be used for inputting payment data to a computer, using OCR.

(b) An examining body that stores multiple choice questions on a computer file can produce examination papers by computer. Candidates are then asked to make marks to indicate their answers, and the positions of the answer marks are detected by OMR readers. The examination papers can thus be marked by computer.

Activity 6

(a) Why would a warehouse prefer bar codes to MICR as a system for marking goods?

(b) Why is OMR, rather than OCR used to take the meter reading entered by a gas consumer on a form provided by the supplier?

Scanners

Scanners could be seen as a form of advanced OCR in that they are a means of inputting documents to a computer system. A document is fed into the scanner which passes a light band along the page. The pattern is transferred to the computer. Some scanners are used for document image processing (DIP). Alternatively they might be used in desk top publishing (DTP) to input an image to the desk-top published document. A computer with a fast hard disk is essential for scanning work. Scanning text and images uses up a great deal of processor capacity.

The camera used in a scanner consists of tiny cells which may be charged or uncharged, depending on whether the part of the image being scanned is light or dark. The resolution of a typical scanner is 300 dots per inch (dpi). This means that a matrix of 300 by 300 cells is created for each square inch of the document. The software in the scanner receives as input the electrical charges generated in the camera and stores them or prints them out in digital form.

1.5 Card reading devices

Magnetic stripe cards

Magnetic stripe cards have been widely distributed over the past decade, so that almost every person with a bank or building society account can use one. The standard magnetic stripe card is rectangular in shape, about 8.5 cm by 5.4 cm in area, and about 1mm thick. One face of the card shows the name of the issuer, the payments system the card applies to (such as Visa), and often a hologram image (a bird on Visa cards) for security purposes. The customer's name, the card number and the card expiry date also appear (in embossed form, so that the details can be printed on to credit card payment slips).

Figure 3.11 Magnetic stripe cards

However, none of this surface information is strictly necessary for data input to a computer system. All the machine-readable data is contained on the back, on a magnetic stripe. The card is passed through a reading device which converts this information into directly computer-readable form. The widest application of magnetic stripe cards is as bank credit or service cards, for use in automated teller machines (ATMs) and bank payment systems.

Smart cards

Smart cards are similar to magnetic stripe cards in that information is held on a plastic card for the customer to use at will. However, the technology by which this is achieved is quite different. Smart cards are much more versatile than magnetic stripe cards. They are currently most widely used in France. A smart card is a plastic card in which is embedded a microprocessor chip. The microprocessor includes a memory which retains its contents even when there is no power supply to the card. The smart card contains a great deal more information than a magnetic stripe card. Not only does it contain basic account details, but also a memory and a processing capability. The smart card is used in a similar way to a magnetic stripe card for money transmission.

One of the advantages of smart cards over magnetic stripe cards is that they are much harder to duplicate and, therefore, more secure. On the other hand, they are more expensive to produce.

Electronic point of sale (EPOS) devices

More and more large retail stores are introducing electronic point of sale (EPOS) devices which act both as cash registers and as terminals connected to a main computer. This enables the computer to produce useful management information such as sales details and analysis and stock control information very quickly. Many devices use bar coding, as described earlier, or direct keyboard entry.

A fully itemised and descriptive receipt can be produced for the customer, who will also feel the benefit of faster moving queues at the checkout. Management can obtain more information more quickly than was possible before, in particular immediate updating of stock levels, identification of fast-moving items for reordering and sales information.

The provision of immediate sales information, perhaps analysed on a branch basis, permits great speed and flexibility in decision-making (certainly of a short-term nature), as consumer wishes can be responded to quickly.

Activity 7

Suggest some applications for smart cards, where it is useful to be able to record data on the card as well as to read it.

EFTPOS

EFTPOS (electronic funds transfer at point of sale) aims to handle, electronically, the high volume of low value transactions which banks would otherwise have to process in paper form. EFTPOS systems integrate the retailer's POS system with an electronic payment system. By this means, stock control, retailing and receipt of funds can be fully automated.

The plastic cards used in EFTPOS transactions are known as debit cards. This is because the payment is debited to the purchaser's bank account, usually within two or three days of the transaction's taking place. It is important that the distinction between credit cards and debit cards is understood. A debit card functions as an electronic cheque book, providing access to the holder's current account, and allowing instant electronic authorisation of the transaction by the paying bank. A credit card provides a means of charging purchases to the cardholder's credit card account, on which credit is provided by the card issuer.

The Switch consortium was set up by Midland, National Westminster and Royal Bank of Scotland in 1988 and has gained widespread acceptance in the UK; it is accepted as a means of payment at many large retailer groups.

A typical EFTPOS transaction

The steps in a typical payment by debit card at the retailer's terminal are as follows.

(a) The cardholder's card is swiped through the terminal.

(b) Data is captured: the sort code, the account number, the card's expiry date and the card number;

(c) The amount of the purchase is keyed in (unless already captured by a barcode reader).

(d) The data, together with the retailer's identification, is coded and transmitted to a central electronic funds transfer switch.

(e) The central switch forwards an electronic message to the cardholder's bank's computer system for authorisation.

(f) The bank's computer decodes the message, checks the account balance and returns a coded approval (or refusal), logging the item against the cardholder's account.

(g) The central switch forwards a message to the retailer's terminal.

(h) The cardholder and cashier are advised of the approval and an advice slip is printed for signature.

(i) The customer signs the advice slip and the transaction is completed.

Settlement occurs two or three days later when the relevant bank accounts are debited and credited. There is no technical reason for the delay, but it is included because people are used to a short delay when they write cheques.

2   PRINTED OUTPUT

2.1   Large-scale printers

Line printers are printers that produce one line of print at a time, but at very high speeds, usually between 600 and 1,000 lines per minutes. Most large computer systems use line printers for the majority of printed output that the machine produces. The paper is in a continuous sheet, with perforations between 'pages', which is fed through the printer and can be separated into individual pages after printing. Such paper may be described as 'sprocket-fed' (moved by toothed wheels fitting into holes down the side of the paper) or as 'fan-folded' (because it is folded at the perforations). Chain line printers have characters embossed on the outside of a continuously revolving chain which moves past the print position. They are impact printers, suitable for printing multiple copies.

Large-scale laser printers, like line printers, are used in large computer systems. However, they print whole pages at a time using an electrostatic process and have a greater range of print characters and styles. They are a type of non-impact printer. Although speeds of 30,000 lines per minute have been achieved, quality is reduced and lower speeds (say 15,000–20,000 lines per minute) are a more practical proposition. Like line printers, large-scale laser printers use continuous stationery, but, unlike them, make little noise.

2.2   Desk-top printers

Most minicomputers and PCs generally have no need of such fast print capabilities. Small desk-top printers, using continuous (or sometimes single sheet) stationery, are used in such systems. Desk-top printers can also be used in mainframe computer systems where high quality (letter quality) output is required.

Printers for PCs can be divided into two broad categories, impact printers and non-impact printers.

(a) Impact printers work by means of the impact of a print hammer or pinheads on to a print ribbon and the paper, and they are therefore quite noisy.

(b) Non-impact printers work with different technologies. They do not rely on the impact of a hammer or other device and so they are much quieter to use.

The choice between different types of printer involves balancing cost, speed and print quality, although noise can be an important factor too.

2.3   Impact printers

Daisy wheel printers

In a daisy wheel printer, fully formed print characters are positioned at the end of long stems, which protrude from a central wheel. This gives the impression of a daisy-like flower, with a solid round centre and petals sticking out all around it, hence the name of the printer. The daisy wheel is inserted in the printer, and rotates until the desired character is in the right position. A hammer then strikes the end of the stem and the character appears on the paper.

Daisy wheels can be changed, if a different font is required (such as italics) but only one daisy wheel can be used at a time. Daisy wheel printers print one character at a time, rather than one line at a time. Print speeds can range from 10 to 80 characters per second, depending on the make and quality of printer. They are slow and noisy, but do produce a high quality print. Companies are increasingly unlikely to buy new daisy wheel printers today.

Dot matrix printers

A dot matrix printer has a head containing an array of steel pins or 'needles'. Characters are constructed by pressing a combination of these pins against the print ribbon, and so on paper each character appears as a matrix of small dots. It depends on which combination of pins is fired as to which character appears. The dots can be placed anywhere on paper, and so it is possible to produce graphics (of fairly low resolution) as well as characters.

Most dot matrix printers have print heads with a matrix of 9×9 pins or 9×7 pins, and so there are noticeable gaps between the dots. This lack of resolution is the main drawback of dot matrix printers. Like daisy wheel printers, dot matrix printers print one character at a time, rather than one line at a time. Dot matrix printers are faster than daisy wheel printers, printing typically 120 to 200 characters per second. They are also cheaper.

Most dot matrix printers can also be used to print better quality print (known as NLQ: near letter quality). This is still not up to daisy wheel standard but it is acceptable for many users. In NLQ mode, the pin head prints each line twice with the second pass slightly offset from the first. This has the effect of partially filling the gaps between the dots left by the previous run.

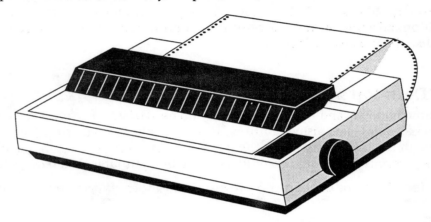

Figure 3.12 A dot matrix printer

Activity 8

A PC user needs to be able to print out about 25 pages of data a day, and has decided to buy an impact printer. Some of the pages are reports to the board of directors, and in order to make these reports easy to read they incorporate frequent changes of font for headings and sub-totals. None of the output goes to users outside the company. Recommend a suitable type of printer, explaining your choice.

2.4 Non-impact printers

Laser printers

Laser printers print whole page at a time, rather than printing line by line. They print onto individual sheets of paper (just as photocopiers do) and so they do not use continuous computer stationery (as daisywheel and dot matrix printers can).

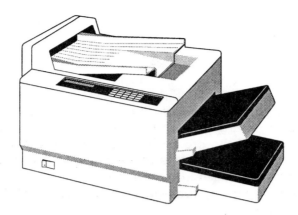

Figure 3.13 A laser printer

A laser printer works by means of a laser beam suppressing the charge on charged photoconductive material, typically selenium. The residual image then attracts toner which is fixed onto the paper by heat and pressure, to produce the printed page. The resolution of printed characters and diagrams with laser printers is very high, up to 600 dots per inch. A desk-top laser printer will print between 8 and 10 A4 pages a minute. Most laser printers have their own random access memory for storing data prior to printing, and also to store fonts. They can be used to combine different fonts, such as italics and bold characters and a wide range of other characters, including mathematical symbols and Greek letters.

Laser printers are quiet, because unlike daisy wheel and dot matrix printers, they are not impact printers which rely on the striking of hammers or pins. Their cost is higher than that of daisy wheel and dot matrix printers.

Page description languages

Some laser printers produce characters using selected patterns of dots, called *bitmaps* (each bit relating to the setting of an individual dot), while others use mathematical descriptions, called *outlines*. Printers which use the latter method feature a page description language. A page description language describes the output sent to a printer, describing individual character shapes, drawing lines and polygons, and scaling. The language deals with technical details, constructing a program describing the page and sending it to the printer. This enables more precise control over the way each page is printed. A widely used page description language is Adobe's PostScript, which provides faster text printing and faster and more accurate graphic images than most other protocols can offer. It can support complex fonts such as Arabic with its precise encoding and positioning requirements, and is becoming accepted as the standard for laser printers. Another example is Microsoft Windows' True Type.

Thermal printers

There are two types of thermal printer. Some work by heating thermally-sensitive paper with a printhead to form characters. An alternative form of thermal printer, a thermal transfer printer, uses a special printing ribbon with heat-sensitive ink, which melts on to the paper when either the hot printhead touches it, or an electric current is run through the ribbon.

Canon has manufactured a type of thermal printer for portable computers called a bubblejet printer. The print head heats up the ink and deposits it on paper. The inkhead and cartridge are removed when the ink runs out. Bubblejets are small and comparatively inexpensive. They are also quiet and fast, but they need special paper that can soak up the ink as quickly as it is squirted on to it, to avoid smudging and produce good quality copy. A more recent development is a solid inkjet printer, which uses a solid block of ink that melts on to a page to form characters, and is less messy than printers using liquid ink.

2.5 Buffering

Buffering is a method of storing output data in a printer, magnetic tape reader or other output device until the device becomes free and ready to accept it. By storing data in an output device, the processor is released for other work. The term 'buffering' can also be applied to cases where an input device feeds data to the processor, and the processor takes in more data than it needs immediately. Thus a block of records might be read in from a tape, and all the records but one would be put in a buffer area of memory.

This means that output devices, such as printers, need to have buffer storage areas for holding output data which they have not handled (for example, have not printed) yet. In a microcomputer system, the size of a printer's RAM buffer area should be at least 8 kB.

2.6 Plotters

Finally, in this category of output devices, some mention must be made of *plotters*. Graphics plotters are output devices which actually draw on paper or transparencies, using pens held in a mechanical arm. Unlike dot matrix printers, they can draw unbroken straight lines, and so are particularly useful for computer aided design work. Because they work by moving pens over the paper, they can be very slow output devices, which often makes graph plotters unsuitable for normal office applications (for example, producing a graphical presentation for a management report would be better done using a laser printer).

Activity 9

Why is a significant amount of buffering often needed when a processor is sending output to a printer, but very unlikely to be needed when a processor is receiving input from a keyboard?

---

3 COMPUTER OUTPUT ON MICROFORM (COM)

COM is a form of computer output whereby instead of printing the output on to paper, it is projected on to a cathode ray tube and then photographed into a very much reduced form, a microform. (Alternative methods of producing COM involve laser beam, electron beam or optical fibre technology.)

The microform is readable, but not by the naked eye, and a magnifying reading device (with a viewing screen) is needed by users. To assist the user in finding the records on the microform, 'eyeball' characters (letters or numbers visible to the eye without magnification) are shown on the microform.

(a) *Microfilm* is a continuous strip of film, with images in frames along the film. It is not simple to view or update, as a whole roll in a cartridge resembling a 35 mm roll of film needs to be changed at once.

(b) *Microfiche* on the other hand, consists of separate sheets of film (about the size of a postcard), each sheet containing over 100 frames. It is commonly used in lending libraries and in the book trade to store information on books in the system and titles in print respectively. A microfiche is about 6 inches by 4 inches in size and contains perhaps 200 pages of information, reduced at a ratio of 42:1, 48:1 or 72:1.

Large volumes of information can be condensed into a very small physical space so that savings in storage space can be considerable where printed matter would otherwise have to be kept for fairly long periods of time. Microform therefore provides a suitable storage medium for archive information or reference information. Microform frames or pages can be reproduced on paper in an enlarged, readable form, if required.

Microform has the disadvantage of needing special reading devices, so that if the output is in regular use by various staff in a department, there might be 'bottleneck' problems for them in getting access to the information they need, as they queue up to use the reading device.

In comparing microfilm with microfiche, the advantages of microfilm are that:

(a) microfilm readers can scan microfilm images quickly, to locate the information required. In contrast, information on microfiche takes longer to locate;

(b) where the information held is updated regularly, it is probably more convenient to produce a new microfilm at regular intervals, rather than to produce new sheets of microfiche with the updated information, for inserting manually into the appropriate place in the file of microfiche sheets. The regular change in information would probably justify the cost of producing new reels of microfilm.

The advantages of microfiche over microfilm are that:

(a) where information changes slowly, it would probably be more economical to produce a new microfiche occasionally than to produce a new microfilm every time a change occurs;

(b) where information is held for archive purposes, sheets of microfiche can be produced with updating information and added to the back of the file manually. With microfilm, however, it would be uneconomic to produce new information until enough is available to fill up a reel of film. This means that there would probably be a longer delay with microfilm in updating the archive records.

Microfilm and microfiche output are not common, and because of the expense of COM output devices, this form of output is generally reserved for organisations with a relatively large expenditure budget or for libraries which would otherwise have to hold large quantities of bulky books and articles in paper form.

Activity 10

Give three examples of data which might reasonably be stored on microfiche.

---

4 THE CHOICE OF OUTPUT MEDIUM

Choosing a suitable output medium depends on a number of factors, such as:

Is a *hard copy* of the output required? If so, what quality must the output be? If the output includes documents that are going to be used as, for example, OCR turnround documents, the quality of printing must be high. If the information will be used as a working document with a short life or limited use (such as a copy of text for checking) then low quality output on a dot matrix printer might be sufficient.

It should be remembered that a *screen* is an output medium. It is particularly suited for use where the volume of output is low (for example, the result of a single file enquiry) or where permanent output is not required (for example, the current balance on an account).

The *volume* of information produced may effect the decision. For example, a VDU screen can hold a certain amount of data, but it becomes more difficult to read when the information would more than fill a screen and can only be read a bit at a time.

The *speed* at which output is required may be critical. For example, to print a large volume of data, a high speed printer might be suitable to finish the work more quickly (and release the processor for other jobs).

The *suitability* of the output medium to the application should be considered. A VDU is well suited to interactive processing with a computer, while output onto a magnetic disk or tape is appropriate if the data is to be used in further processing. Large volumes of reference data for human users to hold in a library might be held on microfilm or microfiche, and so output in these forms would be appropriate.

Some output devices would not be worth having because their advantages would not justify their *cost*.

Activity 11

Suggest suitable input and output devices for a lending library which needs to:

(a) record the issue and return of books

(b) identify books already out on loan in response to readers' enquiries

(c) issue letters to recall books which are overdue or which have been requested by other readers.

Chapter roundup

- Data must be originated and in most cases transcribed before it can be input.
- A computer keyboard includes the normal typewriter keys and some additional keys.
- A VDU screen displays both data as it is input and the output from processing.
- A mouse may be used in conjunction with, or as an alternative to, a keyboard.
- The WIMP interface uses windows to display information, icons and menus to set out options and a mouse to allow the user to make choices.
- Direct keyboard input is particularly useful when the user wants interactive processing, but it is wasteful of processor time when large amounts of data are to be input for routine processing.
- Data can be encoded to disk or to tape off line, and then processed in batches.
- MICR, OCR, OMR and bar coding can all be used to reduce the amount of keying in required.

Chapter roundup (*continued*)

- Card reading devices enable information about cardholders to be input directly to a computer.
- Large-scale printers are much faster than desk-top printers.
- Desk-top printers may be impact printers (daisy wheel or dot matrix) or non-impact printers (laser, thermal, bubblejet or inkjet).
- Buffering enables better use to be made of the processor.
- Computers can output data to microfilm or microfiche.
- The choice of an output medium depends in part on whether hard copy is required, on the volume of output and on the speed and quality required.

Quick quiz

1 What are cursor control keys?

2 What is the resolution of a VDU screen?

3 How is a mouse used?

4 What is a GUI?

5 What items might be found on a menu for amending a personnel file?

6 What is a key-to-disk system and how is one used?

7 What is the largest application of MICR?

8 What are turnround documents?

9 What are EPOS devices?

10 What are the main types of large-scale printers?

11 How does a laser printer work?

12 How does buffering enable better use to be made of the processor?

13 What are the advantages of microfiche over microfilm?

14 What form of output is appropriate for data to be used in further processing?

Answers to activities

1 (a) The function keys, labelled F1 to F10 (or F12), are likely to be along the top or down the left hand side.

   (b) The cursor control keys will have arrows on them and may double up as number keys. The CTRL and ALT keys may well be near one end of the space bar.

2 The production director makes occasional brief enquiries, and is likely to want response immediately. Instant processing of each item of routine weekly input is not needed.

3 Option 1: text feature

4 The operator needs to be reminded where he or she has got to on the form. Having a cursor also makes it easy to pick out a character to be changed (for example, a mistyped letter in the middle of a name).

5 Recording responses to several thousand market research questionnaires; keying in data from credit card vouchers.

6 (a) Bar codes can be scanned quickly from a few inches away using a hand-held reader. MICR characters must first be magnetised and then read (requiring contact with the paper). This needs bulky equipment which it would be difficult to carry around a warehouse.

(b) People would write digits in many different styles, making it much harder to read hand-written digits than simple marks.

7 An individual's medical details (including required regular medication, and any allergies) could be kept on a smart card. Smart cards could be used as clock cards, to record hours worked in a factory.

8 A dot matrix printer should be used. The quality will be adequate for internal use, and it can handle changes of font easily.

9 A processor works much faster than either a printer or a keyboard operator, so it quickly generates enough output to keep a printer busy for a while, but can deal with data from a keyboard as soon as it is input.

10 Telephone directories; library catalogues; records of previous years' transactions which need to be kept for several years for tax purposes.

11 (a) Bar code readers (with each book and each membership card owning a bar code each membership card showing a bar code)

(b) A keyboard and a VDU

(c) A laser printer or a dot matrix printer

Further question practice

Now try the following practice questions at the end of this text.

Multiple choice questions   **18 to 24**

Chapter 4

DATA COMMUNICATIONS, NETWORKS AND PROCESSING METHODS

Introduction

As you will probably have realised from the earlier descriptions of computer types, larger computers support more than one user at a time and PCs are essentially single-user machines. This does not means that PCs are always used as stand-alone computers. PCs, and other types of processor, can be linked to one another for a number of reasons, for example, to share data files, to use a common printer or to increase available processing power.

In this chapter we start by describing some of the technical matters involved in computer communications. We say a little more about how signals are actually transmitted. We then move on to examine some of the ways in which computers are linked: the use of PCs in local and wide area networks is increasing and is likely to continue to do so.

Your objectives

After completing this chapter you should:

(a) understand the need for data communication;

(b) know the main data communication media;

(c) understand the concept of data switching;

(d) understand the difference between synchronous and asynchronous transmission;

(e) know the main items of data communication equipment;

(f) know the difficulties of direct links between computers;

(g) appreciate how a multi-user system is arranged;

(h) be able to distinguish between centralised and distributed processing;

(i) be able to distinguish between local area networks and wide area networks;

(j) be able to draw diagrams of some network topologies;

(k) know the advantages of distributed processing and networks;

(l) know the difference between batch processing and demand processing;

(m) appreciate when on-line, interactive and real-time processing should be used.

1   WHAT IS DATA COMMUNICATION?

Data communication means sending data between computers or other data processing devices.

When all data processing is done in the same office, no serious problem should arise with the transmission of data between input and output devices and the processor. The equipment will be joined together by internal cables.

When the input or output device is located away from the computer, so that data has to be sent along a communications link (such as a telephone line), additional items of equipment have to be used.

A communications link might typically connect any of the following.

(a) A computer and a remote terminal (consisting of keyboard and VDU). A computer may have a number of remote terminals linked to it.

(b) Two computers located some distance from each other (for example, a mainframe and a PC, which would use the link to exchange data).

(c) Several processors in a network, with each computer in the network able to send data to any other.

1.1   Who provides the communications link?

In the UK, British Telecom and Mercury and, gradually, other telecoms operators provide services to send data and can supply public or private lines for direct data links.

(a) Public lines use the ordinary telephone network and the cost depends upon the service used and the time for which the telephone link is maintained (as for any ordinary telephone call).

(b) Private lines also use the telephone network but a special line is provided at a fixed annual charge. Private lines are sometimes referred to as leased lines. Many organisations will lease a number of lines to construct their own private networks. Sometimes, they will be happy to allow other users to access them.

1.2   Data transmission media

These are a variety of physical media through which links are established.

(a) Copper wire, as used in current telephone systems.

(b) Coaxial cable, also copper, but more sophisticated than copper wire.

(c) Fibre optic cable, made out of thin glass strands, through which pulses of light (as opposed to electricity) are passed in digital form.

(d) Microwave radio links (for example, mobile telephones).

(e) Radio links via satellite, from one country to another.

Bandwidth

The amount of data that can be sent over a line is in part determined by the bandwidth. The bandwidth is the range of frequencies that the channel can carry. Frequencies are measured in Hertz (cycles per second). There are three ranges.

(a) Narrow band (up to 300 Hertz).

(b) Voice band (300–3,000 Hertz).

(c) Broad band (over 3,000 Hertz).

The greater the bandwidth, the greater the rate at which data can be sent, as a wider bandwidth enables messages to be transmitted simultaneously. (You might like to think of a motorway carrying three lanes of traffic at once.)

Bit serial and bit parallel transmission

Data transmission can be either bit serial transmission or bit parallel transmission. In bit serial transmission, the bits making up a character are sent one after the other down the line. In bit parallel transmission, eight lines are required as each bit in a byte is transmitted at the same time over its own channel. Bit serial transmission is the most common method. The number of bits transmitted per second is referred to as the baud rate.

Activity 1

Computer user A has large quantities of data to transmit every day. Computer user B has far less data to transmit. Which of these users is more likely to use:

(a) a leased line?

(b) bit serial transmission?

2 DATA SWITCHING

When the computer user has a number of computers (and terminals) which will transmit data to each other in an irregular and unpredictable way, it would be too expensive to rent dedicated private lines for direct data links. Instead, a data switching arrangement is used. A telecommunications link is a circuit like any other: when you are speaking to someone over the telephone a circuit exists between the two devices. In the telephone network, switches connect one set of lines to another.

Definition

A *switch* is a device for opening, closing or directing an electric circuit.

2.1 Circuit switching

Circuit switching occurs when the connection is maintained until broken at one end. If data is sent simply by circuit switching, the line between the sender and the recipient must be open for the duration of the message. Because much data transmission is irregular, this would be a wasteful use of the telephone line. Gaps in transmission of your message, when the line is idle, could be used by somebody else. Similarly, you may wish to transmit your data at a time when there is nobody on the other end of the line to receive it.

2.2 Packet switching

Packet switching seeks to overcome these problems, and operates as follows.

(a) A data message is divided up into packets of data of a fixed length, usually 128 bytes, and transmitted through the network (many processors all over the country, or even the world, linked together by cables or radio) in these separate packets. Each packet contains control data, which identifies the sender of the message and the address of the recipient. The first packet opens a route (or *virtual circuit*) from source to destination, which the others will follow.

(b) Each processor in the network receives packets of data from another processor, and redirects them to the next processor along the chain to the eventual recipient.

(c) At the local end of the link (the end near the recipient of the message) the packets of data are reassembled into the full message, which is transmitted to the recipient. If terminals are asynchronous (see below), they will be connected to the packet switching network by a packet assembler/disassembler (PAD).

The packet switching system in the UK is called PDN (Public Data Network).

Packet switching systems transmit data in digital form, that is as a series of pulses representing bits. When circuit switching is used to transmit data over ordinary telephone lines, the digital data is first converted into analogue (wave) form using a modem (see below).

2.3   Simplex, half duplex and full duplex transmission

There are three modes of transmission each of which requires different types of equipment (at increasing cost). These are:

(a) *Simplex* allows transmission in one direction only. A computer can be used to send messages to a peripheral device (for example, a remote printer or screen) but the peripheral cannot send data back.

(b) *Half duplex* allows transmission in both directions but not simultaneously;

(c) *Full duplex* allows transmission in both directions simultaneously.

2.4   Synchronous and asynchronous data transmission

Data transmission can be asynchronous or synchronous.

(a) With *asynchronous transmission*, one character at a time is sent. Each character is preceded by a start bit and followed by a stop bit with the bits of the character coming in between. The receiving device at the end of the line recognises a start signal which activates a clock and then reads the bits that follow until it comes to the stop signal which turns the clock off. PCs normally use asynchronous transmission. Asynchronous transmission is efficient and economical provided that very large quantities of data are not being transmitted.

(b) With *synchronous transmission*, data is transmitted between the sending and receiving machines at a constant rate, and so there is no need for start signals and stop signals between the characters. The rate of transmission is controlled by a clock, which is usually the computer's internal clock. Synchronous transmission is less error-prone than asynchronous transmission. Many mainframes normally use synchronous transmission, and can only communicate in the asynchronous mode by adding special items of equipment.

(c) One type of synchronous data transmission is BSC (binary synchronous communication) developed by IBM for communication between a mainframe and terminals. Special control characters are used to control the message. Synchronisation *characters* begin a message, followed by header, text and end of text characters.

Activity 2

In a commonly used binary code for characters (ASCII), the code for '5' is 1010110 and the code for 'j' is 0101011. Use this example to explain why start and stop bits are needed in asynchronous transmission but not in synchronous transmission.

3   DATA COMMUNICATION EQUIPMENT

3.1 Modems and multiplexors

Equipment used to connect terminals to a computer some distance away includes modems and multiplexors.

Computer equipment stores and uses data in discrete digital (or 'bit') form. Much of the telephone network, however, still handles data in analogue or wave form. For data transmission in analogue form through the telephone network to be possible, there has to be a device at each end of the telephone line that can convert (modulate) the data from digital form to analogue form, and demodulate from analogue form to digital form. This conversion of data is done by devices called *modems*. There must be a modem at each end of the telephone line.

Figure 4.1 A modem

In some computer systems, several terminals or local PCs share the same data link. A *multiplexor* is used where it is necessary to send data from several sources down a single line at the same time. It codes the data in a special way so that it can be sorted out at its destination. Where a number of terminals are linked to the central computer, the multiplexor is an essential piece of hardware handling the input/output and reducing line charges (as only one line, rather than several, is necessary).

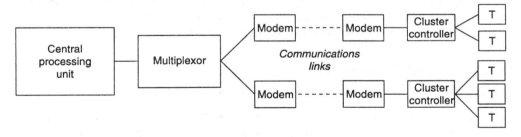

Figure 4.2 How a multiplexor works

One of the functions of a multiplexor is to stop the data from one source being mixed up with the data from another. In *time division multiplexing*, a device is allocated specific time slots in which to use the signal path. In *frequency division multiplexing*, the transmission medium is divided into a number of channels of smaller bandwidth.

3.2 Stand-alone computers and multi-user systems

A computer system might consist of a stand-alone computer (one not linked to other computers) with its peripheral equipment and one user, a computer whose peripheral equipment includes several terminals for several different users, or networks of inter-communicating computers with shared files.

Stand-alone computers

Stand-alone computers are used in the following situations.

(a) When the data processing requirements can be handled by one user with one computer. Office PCs are often stand-alone machines for use by individuals, for example, for developing a personal spreadsheet model.

(b) When the data processing is centralised, for example with very large volumes of transaction data being handled by a mainframe, or with a centralised minicomputer being used for the processing requirements of a department.

(c) When security could be compromised by the use of a multi-user system.

Multi-user systems

With mainframe computers, minicomputers and larger PCs, several users, each with their own terminal (VDU and keyboard), might be connected to the same computer, with all the users able to carry out processing work simultaneously. Computer systems of this type are called multi-user systems. The terminals are dumb terminals.

Definition

A *dumb terminal* is a terminal which does not have a processor and relies on the central computer for its data processing power.

The terminals in a multi-user system might be in the same room or building as the central computer, connected to the computer by internal cable or geographically distant from the central computer, in which case the terminals are connected to the central computer by an external data link, usually provided in the UK by British Telecom. Terminals can be used:

(a) for interactive computing with the central computer; or

(b) to input data into the computer from a remote location. Remote access describes access to a central computer installation from a terminal which is physically distant. The term *remote job entry* is used to describe a method of processing in which the computer user inputs data from a remote terminal.

Benefits of multi-user systems

The benefits of multi-user systems are as follows.

(a) More departments or sections can have access to the computer, its data files and its programs. This improves the data processing capabilities of local offices.

(b) By giving departments more computing power and access to centralised information files, multi-access systems also make it easier for an organisation to decentralise authority from head office to local managers.

(c) The speed of processing, for both local offices and head office, is very fast.

(d) Local offices retain their input documents, and do not have to send them to a remote computer centre for processing.

Activity 3

In what circumstances might a multi-user system encounter difficulties because the processor could not cope with the demands being made on it? How might such situations be prevented from arising?

4   COMPUTER-TO-COMPUTER LINKS

4.1   Purpose

We have already suggested that one computer can be connected to another computer, or to several other computers (depending on the size of computer). These computer-to-computer links might be via cable, or via a data communication link so that geographically distant computers can be made to communicate directly with each other. Why should computers need to communicate directly with each other?

(a) Two or more computers can share the data processing work.

(b) One computer can obtain data or programs from another computer's files.

(c) Database systems can be made more versatile and useful when several computers have access to the same database.

Large computers such as mainframes can be linked directly to each other, but more common types of computer-to-computer links involve PCs, in some form of *network* configuration.

4.2   The reasons for wanting mainframe to PC links

There are three main reasons for wanting to link a PC to a mainframe computer.

(a) Opening a communications link between a PC and a mainframe allows the PC user to run programs on the mainframe, using the PC as a terminal.

(b) When the computer user writes software for the mainframe computer, a PC can be used to create and correct programs on the PC using its 'text editor' software, before it is actually put into use on the mainframe.

(c) With the right software to link the PC and the mainframe, data can be exchanged between them, giving the PC user access to the mainframe's database files and integrating the organisation's data processing system.

4.3   Technical aspects of mainframe to PC links

Although many PCs used by large organisations are linked to a mainframe, there are problems with creating such a link which have to be overcome.

(a) PCs *normally use asynchronous transmission* whereas mainframes normally use synchronous transmission to transmit data.

(b) PCs *may use a different data alphabet to the mainframe*. A data alphabet is the combination of 0s and 1s used to represent each character. PCs use a data alphabet called ASCII whereas IBM and some other mainframe manufacturers use an alphabet called EBCDIC in their mainframes. To allow the PC and the mainframe to communicate, there must either be a special translation device (called a protocol converter) or special hardware and software added to the PC.

(c) *PCs have to be made to act like (emulate) mainframe terminals.* For example, an IBM PC might be linked to a mainframe and expected to act like an IBM 3270 terminal. This can be done by inserting an emulation board into the PC, and using this with an emulation program on a disk that comes with the emulation board. Even then, the computer user may have some problems because the keyboard on the PC will differ from the keyboard of a mainframe terminal, and so some keys may have to double up, with keys being used for two different purposes. This can make it difficult for the terminal user to learn which keys to use.

Activity 4

A company has a data input office in London, linked to a mainframe computer in Glasgow. The input office is equipped with 25 PCs, all of which use ASCII, whereas the mainframe uses EBCDIC. All of the PCs are in use for data input to the mainframe at the same time, and only one line is available to transmit the data. List the various additional items of hardware and software that might be required.

4   PROCESSING

4.1   Centralised data processing

Centralised data processing is carried out in a central location, such as a head office. The data for processing might be gathered from a wide area, for example from local offices or regional centres. The output will probably be distributed over a correspondingly wide area. But the actual processing of data is centralised.

Data might be fed in to the central processing system either:

(a) by physically transporting data records from their source to the central location; or

(b) electronically, for example from remote terminals linked to the central computer.

Similarly, output might be sent to local offices either:

(a) physically, by post or courier (for example, in printed form or on floppy disks); or

(b) electronically, to a remote terminal in the local office linked to the central computer.

4.2   Distributed processing

In *distributed processing*, there are several autonomous but interacting processors and/or data stores at different locations linked by a communications network. The key features of distributed processing are as follows.

(a) A computer can access the information files of other computers in the system.

(b) Computers within the system can process data jointly.

(c) Processing is carried out either centrally, or at dispersed locations.

(d) Files are held either centrally or at local sites.

(e) Authority is decentralised as processing can be performed autonomously by local computers.

Activity 5

What advantage does linking PCs to a mainframe in a distributed processing system have over linking dumb terminals to a mainframe in a multi-user system?

The key feature of a distributed system is that end users of computing facilities are given responsibility for, and control over, their own data.

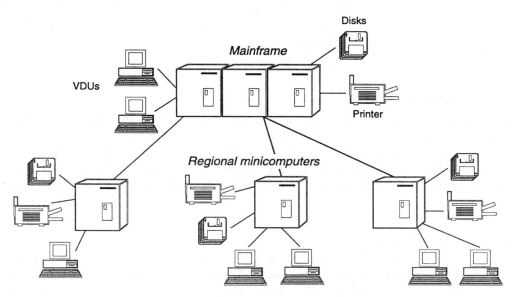

Figure 4.3 An example of a distributed processing system

The advantages and disadvantages of distributed processing

The advantages of using a distributed processing system compared with having a stand-alone centralised mainframe computer are as follows.

(a) There is greater flexibility in system design. The system can cater for both the specific needs of each local user of an individual computer and also for the needs of the organisation as a whole, by providing communications between different computers in the system.

(b) Since data files can be held locally, data transmission is reduced because each computer maintains its own files which provide most of the data it will need. This reduces the costs and security risks in data transmission.

(c) There is faster processing for both local offices and the central (head) office.

(d) There is scope for a distributed database. Data is held in a number of locations, but any user can access all of it for a global view.

(e) The effect of breakdowns is minimised, because a fault in one computer will not affect other computers in the system. With a centralised processing system, a fault in the mainframe computer would put the entire system out of service.

(f) The fact that it is possible to acquire powerful PCs cheaply enables an organisation to dedicate them to particular applications. This in turn means that the computer system can be more readily tailored to the organisation's systems, rather than forcing the organisation to change its systems to satisfy the requirements for a mainframe computer.

(g) Decentralisation allows for better local control over the physical and procedural aspects of the system.

(h) Decentralised processing may facilitate greater user involvement and increase familiarity with the use of computer technology. The end user must accept responsibility for the accuracy of locally held files and local data processing.

Distributed processing has the following disadvantages, some of which might be overcome by future technological developments.

(a) PCs have not had a large storage capacity in the past, and the programs needed for distributed processing have used up much of the storage capacity available. This disadvantage is now being eliminated by the development of more powerful PCs.

(b) There may be duplication of data on the files of different computers. If this is the case, there may be some unnecessary storage costs.

(c) A distributed network can be more difficult to administer and to maintain.

(d) The items of equipment used in the system must be compatible with each other.

4.3 Networks

Distributed processing systems are usually referred to as *networks*. However, not all distributed processing systems are networks. In a network, each user is aware that there are other users with their own computers, which he can communicate with. It is possible to have a distributed processing system in which a user is unaware of the existence of other users, and the system automatically shares work between computers.

Local area networks

A local area network (LAN) is a system of interconnected PCs and other devices over a small area, typically within a few hundred metres, linked directly by cables. This use of cables distinguishes LANs from wide area networks, which may use telephone lines or radio links.

Most LANs include a server computer. This may be a powerful PC or a minicomputer, but is increasingly likely to be machine which has actually been designed as a server. As its name implies, it serves the rest of the network:

(a) offering a shared hard disk file for all the other PCs (a *file server*);

(b) sometimes offering other resources, such as a shared printer for the network (a *printer server*);

(c) offering connections to long-distance communications links (a *communications server*);

(d) offering access to a collection of software (a *library server*).

Network topologies

There are several types of LAN configuration including bus systems, rings, stars and trees.

Definition

A *network topology* is the physical arrangement of nodes in a network. A node can be a computer or a peripheral device such as a printer.

In a bus network, messages are sent out from one point along a single bus, and the messages are received by other connected computers. Messages identify the intended recipient, and a computer only accepts messages which contain its unique identifying code. Nodes can be added or unplugged very easily.

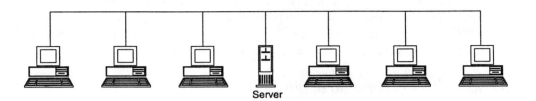

Figure 4.4 A bus system

In a ring network, the cable in the system, and the computers in it, are joined in a ring. There may or may not be a server.

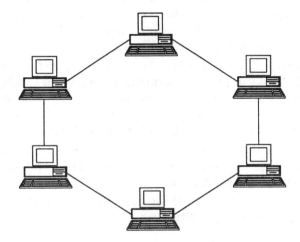

Figure 4.5 A ring system

In a star network, there is:

(a) a central disk file and program store, controlled by a server computer;

(b) a cable linking the central computer to the other computers. The terminals cannot communicate directly with each other, but must send messages to the central node.

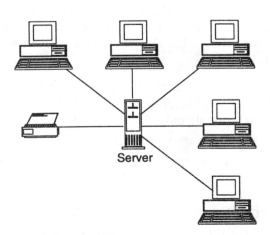

Figure 4.6 A star system

In a tree network, large-scale processing is done by a mainframe or minicomputer, and lower-level processing by minicomputers or PCs. At the end of the scale is a series of PCs or even dumb terminals. Tree networks are more commonly encountered as wide area networks, with the physical siting of each layer being designed to minimise data transmission costs. Figure 4.3 of a distributed processing system earlier in this chapter shows a typical tree network.

Why have LANs become so popular?

Local area networks have been successful for a number of reasons. Networks have been made available to computer users at a fairly low price. Some computer users who could not afford a mainframe or minicomputer with terminal links have been able to afford a LAN with PCs.

Networks provide important advantages for the computer user.

(a) Data files can be shared by all the PCs in the network. With stand-alone PCs, each computer would have its own data files, and there might be unnecessary duplication of data. A system where everyone uses the same data helps to improve data processing and decision making. The value of information increases with its availability.

(b) Each PC in a network can do the same work. If there were separate stand-alone PCs A, B and C, A might do job 1, B might do job 2 and C might do job 3. In a network, any PC (A, B or C) could do any job (1, 2 or 3). This provides flexibility in sharing workloads. In a peak period for job 1, say, two or more people can share the work without having to leave their own desks.

(c) Peripheral equipment can be shared. For example, in a LAN, five PCs might share a single on-line printer, whereas if there were stand-alone PCs, each PC would need its own separate printer.

(d) LANs can be linked up to external services via a communications server, thus adding to the processing capabilities in an office.

Activity 6

Assume that a network is set up so that any user can read and work on files created by any other user. Give two reasons why this could sometimes be a disadvantage instead of an advantage.

Wide area networks (WANs)

Wide area networks (sometimes called long haul networks (LHNs)) are networks on a wide geographical scale. WANs often use minicomputers or mainframes as the 'pumps' which keep the data messages circulating, whereas LANs normally use PCs for this task. A wide area network is similar to a local area network in concept, but the differences are as follows.

(a) The *geographical area* covered by the network is wider.

(b) WANs will send data over *telecommunications links*. LANs, in contrast, will use direct cables for transmitting data.

(c) WANs will often use a *larger computer* as a server.

(d) WANs will often be larger than LANs, with *more computers linked* to the network.

4.4   The Internet

One of the benefits of the drive to open systems is that with the standardisation of communication protocols in theory any computer can connect with any other.

The Internet is an attempt to do just that. It is based on the TCP/IP protocols developed to provide the US military with a redundant communications network. TCP stands for *transmission control protocol* and is the part of the system that ensures that message are delivered completely and correctly. IP stands for *Internet protocol* and is responsible for actually carrying the message through the network. It has a logical structure independent of the medium actually used for transmission.

Internet protocol

Internet protocol is based on a system of 32 bit IP addresses; the first part of the address corresponds to the network address, the rest to the host address or to a specific computer on that network. Some machines pass messages between networks. They are called *bridges* when they close the gap between networks, and *routers* when they control the path taken by messages to get to their destination. For security purposes some routers act to inhibit unwanted message traffic and are referred to as firewalls.

The choice of 32 bit addresses was sufficient for the time the Internet was designed and has in fact allowed it to grow to the enormous size that it has. However, the limit is now being reached and, until a new standard is accepted, the allocation of new addresses is strictly rationed on a basis of need.

Domain names

Numeric addresses are all well and good for computers, but for easier use a more user friendly means of naming is required. A solution to this was to give names to each of the host machines, and also to group the machines into logical structures called domains. Some of the machines on the network act to provide a domain name service (DNS) translating these names into IP addresses and back again.

The domain name is built up with the last part representing the highest level.

.com	a commercial company
.edu	an educational establishment
.gov	a government institution
.net	an organisation providing services to the net
.mil	a military institution
.org	a non commercial organisation

For example, the domain name of the world wide web server at Microsoft (a commercial company) is

www.microsoft.com

The expansion of the Internet outside the US has added a further layer of country code, with each country using its own codes to delimit various forms of activity. For example, in the United Kingdom the *Daily Telegraph* website is www.telegraph.co.uk, and Kensington and Chelsea College, an academic institution, is www.kcc.ac.uk.

Since the system requires that names be unique to the business user, having the right to a domain name reflecting the name of your organisation within your sphere of activity is very important, and there has been a 'gold rush' to register names before someone else lays claim to them. For example, Guardian Insurance could not use Guardian.co.uk as this belongs to the *Guardian* newspaper.

To increase the namespace available, a new set of names has been ratified for international use.

.firm	for businesses, or firms
.store	for business offering goods to purchase
.web	for entities emphasising activities relating to the WWW
.arts	for entities emphasising arts and entertainment activities

.rec   for entities emphasising recreation/entertainment activities
.info   for entities providing information services
.nom   for those wishing individual or personal nomenclature

Domain name registration used to be free, and organised by an organisation called INTERNIC, but the work involved grew so rapidly that this was no longer possible. It is now provided by commercial organisations which charge for the service. There is a market for names and hence the more desirable .com domain names are more expensive than the newer names, or names specific to a country or geographical area.

The world wide web

The most notable application of the Internet to date is the world wide web, designed by Tim Berners-Lee of the CERN laboratory in Switzerland. The hypertext transfer protocol http: enables a multi-layered information structure to be easily browsed using suitable software. The hypertext markup language (HTML) allows authors to link their text to documents or images on any other service in the network.

This network, since it was originally developed on UNIX servers, has a similar style of conceptual file system of uniform resource locators/identifiers (URL or URI) which uses the following format:

protocol://server.name:port/virtual/directory/path/filename.type

protocol://	the method of data transmission to be used
server.name	the name of the server or its IP address
port	the socket number the service is handled by (typically port 80 for http)
/virtual/directory/path/	the path to the data from the virtual server 'root'
filename.type	the file name of the resource with an extension to denote the type of information it contains, eg .txt for text, .htlm for hypertext, .gif for images etc.

To a business user the world wide web seems to offer unbounded scope for marketing. However, to date, success has been limited to companies whose target is the technophile already interested in them. The web is not like television, or newspaper advertising, which goes out to customers; customers have to come to you and will need a reason to do so. They will also need a reason to keep coming back, because your competitors are only a few key strokes and a mouse click away.

Value of the internet

The real value of the Internet to a business person is that there is now the means for anyone to have a relatively inexpensive virtual wide area network. Given the existence of the Internet as infrastructure, the need for long leased lines or having to make expensive telephone calls is diminished. The line, or call, need go no further than the local node of your Internet service provider (ISP).

The standardisation of the network has led to the proposal, by Larry Ellison of Sun Microsystems, of a return to the concept of dumb terminals/large mainframe with, in this case, a semi-intelligent browser machine and an intelligent network ('the network is my computer'). This will use Java, a language system which is supposed to be capable of running on any platform.

To put it in perspective, think how hard it would be to run a modern business without the telephone network. The Internet will give the same boost to your computer systems.

4.9 Processing methods

There are many different ways in which data can be processed, and we will end this chapter by considering the main ones. Different methods make different demands on communications links. The most frequent distinction made in commercial data processing is between batch and *real-time*, but other variants are possible.

Batch processing

Much *bulk volume* routine processing is done on a batch processing basis.

Definition

Batch processing is the processing of a group of similar routine transactions in a single operation. The input transactions might be entered into the computer system all at once, or over a period of time, but computer processing does not begin until they have all been collected together in a transaction file.

Payroll work for salaried staff, for example, will usually be done in one operation once a month. To help with organising the work, the payroll office might deal with each department separately, and do the salaries for department 1, then the salaries for department 2, and then department 3, and so on. The batch processing would be carried out by dividing the transaction records into smaller batches, one batch per department.

Some delay in processing the transactions must be acceptable for batch processing to be used. For example, in a purchase ledger system it must be possible to pay invoices once a month (say) without provoking complaints from creditors.

Batch input allows for better control over the input data, because data can be grouped into numbered batches. The batches are dispatched for processing and processed in these batches, and printed output listings of the processed transactions are usually organised in batch order. If any records go missing – for example, get lost in transit - it is possible to locate the batch in which the missing record should belong. Errors in transaction records can be located more quickly by identifying its batch number. A check can be made to ensure that every batch of data sent off for processing is eventually received back from processing, so that entire batches of records do not go missing.

Demand processing

Demand processing (also called transaction processing) is carried out when batch processing would be inconvenient or undesirable and the user wants to process transactions on demand. It requires that the input device is on-line to the computer, that is connected to it and under its control.

Transactions for processing might arise infrequently, and so it would take too long to build up a batch for processing at the same time. Alternatively, the user might not be prepared to accept the delay implicit in batch processing. For example:

(a) if a final demand to pay an invoice is received, perhaps because the invoice had been overlooked, it might be decided to pay it at once;

(b) if a manager asks for some information from the data files, such as a statement of monthly sales figures for the past year, he will usually expect to have the work done on demand.

Activity 7

A company makes several sales on credit each day. The input documents are batched and processed at the end of each week, when invoices are printed and posted. Customers are allowed 30 days from the invoice date (which is the same as the date of printing) to pay. Why might the company prefer this method to daily batch processing or demand processing, despite the longer credit period allowed to customers who buy early in the week?

Interactive processing

Interactive processing is a form of demand processing where:

(a) data is input to the computer;

(b) the data is processed immediately by the computer;

(c) the computer produces processed output.

An example of interactive processing is as follows.

(a) An operator inputs details of a transaction into the computer from a remote terminal.

(b) The computer processes the transaction and then outputs the results of the processing, usually on to a visual display screen.

(c) The operator notices an error in the output, or decides that some further processing is needed on the data, and so inputs more data.

(d) The computer processes the new input or amendment and displays the results, and so on until the operator is satisfied that the transaction has been fully and correctly processed.

Another example of interactive processing is a situation in which an operator wants to carry out several data processing operations on some input data, and the processing is divided into small stages. After each stage of processing, the computer will show the operator the results so far and sometimes even ask the operator in a message on the screen what he or she wants to do next. In effect, the processing is carried out by means of the operator and the computer talking to each other, and this form of interactive processing dialogue is referred to as conversational mode of data processing.

Real-time processing

Real-time processing is a form of interactive processing.

A data processor who wants to process transactions one at a time, and receive output information from the processing, might simply want to get the job over and done with and may not need the processed output straightaway.

In other situations, however, the data processor might want the output so that the information can be used at once. The information would have an immediate effect on what is done next. There is real-time processing when the computer's response affects the immediate situation.

Examples of real-time systems

Real-time systems are invariably expensive, and the larger the system and the faster the response times required, the more expensive it is going to be. However the use of real-time systems is rapidly increasing and examples include the following.

(a) The *British Airways Booking System* (BABS), which is operated by a central computer at Heathrow linked to British Airways agents in the UK and overseas via a communications network (telephone and satellite). An intending passenger may enquire at an airline office or travel agent for a flight to a particular place on a certain day. The reservation clerk is able to ascertain immediately if there is a vacancy, and then make a booking if required to do so. If no seats are available the computer will indicate possible alternatives for the customer's consideration. Thus the response to the original enquiry is received sufficiently quickly for the customer to await it, and make a decision based on that response. Hardware required includes keyboards for data input, banks of fixed disk drives and disk controllers, VDUs to provide output, a powerful processor which can poll the lines to allocate time slots to each terminal, a central operations console to monitor faults, usage, etc and communications hardware.

(b) *Stock control in shops*. As a sale is made and details are recorded (perhaps by reading a bar code), the stock records are updated in real time. Any customer wishing to buy a product can be informed as to whether the item is available or not (if not, an alternative might be offered). Although the stock files are maintained in real time, other files (such as a sales analysis or a file of debtors) may be batch processed at a later stage with the accumulated sales details from each terminal. The computer can automatically order goods from suppliers should stocks fall below replenishment level.

Activity 8

How might a customer of a bank use an automated teller machine in a way which would be an example of real-time processing?

Chapter roundup

- Data transmission occurs whenever data is sent from one data processing device to another.
- Communications links may include electrical cables, fibre optic cables and microwave and satellite links.
- Packet switching methods may be used to ensure efficient use of the available transmission media.
- A link may be simplex, half duplex or full duplex. Data may be transmitted synchronously or asynchronously, depending on the sending and receiving computers.
- Modems may be used to change the form of data before transmission.
- PCs may need to be modified before they can communicate with mainframe computers.
- In a multi-user system, dumb terminals cannot do their own data processing but PCs can.
- In distributed processing, data processing can be done by several computers.
- In a local area network, there are several computers linked to each other and to a server computer.
- Possible network topologies include buses, rings and stars.
- Wide area networks are spread over a large area, and generally use fairly large computers as servers.
- Distributed processing reduces data transmission and makes a system less vulnerable to breakdown, but it can lead to unnecessary duplication of data.

> ## Chapter roundup (*continued*)
>
> - Batch processing involves a delay in processing individual transactions, unlike demand processing.
> - Interactive processing involves the computer promptly processing input and producing output.
> - In real-time processing, output affects the immediate decisions of the computer user.

Quick quiz

1 How does a public line differ from a private line?
2 Why is the bandwidth of a telecommunications link important?
3 What is packet switching?
4 What type of transmission requires start and stop bits, and why?
5 Why are modems needed?
6 What is a stand-alone computer?
7 What are the advantages of multi-user systems?
8 What is an emulation board used for?
9 What is a server computer?
10 What is a bus structure?
11 How can a network enable work to be distributed more efficiently?
12 What is conversational mode?
13 What is a URL and how is it structured?
14 What is an Internet domain name?
15 Which communications protocol is used to underpin the Internet?

Answers to activities

1 (a) A would be more likely to use a leased line.

   (b) B would be more likely to use bit serial transmission.

2 The first six bits of '5' are the same as the last six bits of 'j'. Thus it is necessary to know exactly where each ASCII character starts, either from a start bit or because sender and receiver know that they are in step, so that '5' and 'j' are not confused.

3 There might be, say, 200 terminals but the processor might only be designed to handle 100 terminals at any one time. If all terminals were in use at once, the processor would have too much to do. A rationing system, in which some users are denied access to the computer at peak times, might be needed.

4 Hardware: modems, multiplexors, emulation boards. Software: emulation program.

5 Some processing can be done by the PCs themselves, thus reducing demands on the central mainframe and on the communication links.

6 Some files would be confidential. One user might be unaware that another user has altered the contents of a file.

7 The cost of the extra credit period might be greater than the extra cost of daily processing.

8 The customer could request his or her account balance, and then based on that balance decide how much cash to withdraw.

Further question practice

Now try the following practice questions at the end of this text.

Multiple choice questions   **25 to 31**

Exam style question   **3**

Chapter 5

SOFTWARE

Introduction

A computer operates under the control of instructions normally collected in a program. All programs used by computers are known as software. Some software is built into the computer's ROM memory. Other software must be loaded into the computer's RAM memory from elsewhere, for example, from a disk.

In this chapter, we provide an introduction to the main types of software which you are likely to encounter. We identify three separate categories. Programming and translation software is the category you are least likely to come across in practice, so it is dealt with in outline only. You may of course wish to, or need to, write programs for certain applications, but packages are available to support most commercial activities and for anything major you would employ professional programmers anyway. Still, an understanding of the terminology is useful and you may need to write a program to process results at your local Sunday football league or at your sailing club.

Next, we look at the operating system. You should certainly know something about this. It provides the link between hardware and applications software, and it controls the human-computer interface, or HCI. An understanding of the operating system is key to an appreciation of graphical user interfaces. Furthermore, the OS is no longer just something supplied automatically with a processor, but a piece of software on which you may have to make choices which will affect the whole way in which you use a computer.

The third, and largest, category is applications software. This covers everything from specially written software to control train timetabling and signalling on the London Underground to the Locoscript word processing package on an Amstrad home computer. In the two chapters following this one, we will introduce a range of applications software.

Your objectives

After completing this chapter you should:

(a) understand the need for programming languages;

(b) be able to distinguish between low level and high-level languages;

(c) know the names of several languages, and the main uses of some high-level languages;

(d) understand why programs in high-level languages need to be compiled or interpreted;

(e) understand the role of fourth generation languages;

(f) know what tasks are performed by an operating system;

(g) be able to give a list of utilities normally provided with an operating system;

(h) understand the benefits of multitasking and multiprogramming;

(i) understand the concept of open systems, and be aware of the main features of UNIX;

(j) be aware of recent developments in PC operating systems;

(k) know the difference between applications software and general purpose software.

1 PROGRAMMING AND LANGUAGES

1.1 Programming and translation software

Programming languages are the various languages that programs are written in. There are many different languages. A programming language is neither the normal written language of human beings, nor is it usually the strings of 1s and 0s used by processors. This might seem odd. Why is it necessary to invent new languages for programming a computer?

A computer can only deal with data and program instructions which are in binary form (the 1 and 0 corresponding to the 'on' and 'off' states of an electronic component). So every program must be in a computer's machine code (which only uses 1s and 0s) before the computer can do anything with it. Writing in machine code is difficult, because it takes a long time to learn, and is therefore usually restricted to programs developed by the computer manufacturers themselves. A program in a programming language can be translated into machine code. The programming language is easier for humans to use, being more condensed and displaying a logic that human beings can understand.

Source programs and object programs

The program written in a programming language is called the source program or source code. The translation into machine code is done by a specialised translation program. The translated program in its machine code (or machine language) version is called the object program or object code.

1.2 Machine code

A program instruction in machine code defines a particular machine operation that the computer can obey. A typical machine code instruction consists of two parts:

(a) an operation code, which states what operation should be carried out on the data; and

(b) one or more address fields, which specify the addresses in the computer's memory where the data can be found.

The programmer writing in machine code has to know the operation codes used in the particular computer, and the physical locations in store and physical lengths of data items. Because the machine code is determined by the computer hardware design, machine codes are said to be machine specific. Machine code application programs could be written, but this would normally be too complex and time consuming.

1.3 Assembly languages

Assembly languages (also known as low-level languages) are a development from machine code. They are also machine specific, but the task of learning and writing the language is made easier than with machine code because they are written in symbolic form. Instead of using machine code operation numbers, the programmer is able to use easily-learned and understood operation mnemonics (for example, ADD, SUB and MULT), and symbolic data locations (names allocated by the programmer and used to refer to particular data areas in the program) instead of addresses.

For the most part one instruction must be written in an assembly language program to create one instruction in machine code, but this is not always necessary. There are some *macro instructions* in any assembly language which, when translated into machine code, become several machine code instructions. Macro instructions make programs written in an assembly language shorter than machine code programs.

Assemblers: translation programs for assembly languages

The assembly language must be translated into machine code. Computer manufacturers will supply an assembler program which translates the operation mnemonics and replaces the symbolic data locations by the addresses reserved for them. The assembly language source program is thus assembled into the machine code object program, the process involving translation, the allocation of storage space and the detection of errors in the program. Once the source program has been assembled into the object program in machine code it is on file and can be used for data processing. The program has to be assembled only once.

An assembly language for a computer is designed to make full use of the particular computer's processing capabilities and so is designed to give the most efficient coding to each part of a computer program.

Activity 1

Why would a computer manufacturer be unable to write an assembler program in assembly language?

1.4   High-level languages

To overcome the low-level language difficulty of machine dependency, high-level (or machine independent) languages were developed. Such programming languages with an extensive vocabulary of words and symbols are used to instruct a computer to carry out the necessary procedures, regardless of the type of machine being used. The main purposes of a high-level language are as follows.

(a) It improves the *productivity* of programmers. An instruction written in a high-level language may produce many machine code instructions when it is translated into machine code. There is no clear visible relationship between a high-level language program and the machine code that it eventually becomes. High-level language source programs are shorter than low level language source programs, and programs can be written comparatively quickly.

(b) New programmers can be *trained* more quickly as they need only learn the language, not the detailed layout of the processor.

(c) Programs can be used on *different types of computer* without having to re-write them. A program written in COBOL, for example, can be moved from one make of computer to another simply by re-translating the source program into a new object program. This is not the case with low-level languages, because each low-level language is specific to a particular make or range of computers.

(d) It speeds up *testing* and *error correction*.

(e) It makes programs *easier to understand*.

Some high-level languages are said to be problem-oriented, because they have been created to deal with particular types of data processing problem. Thus FORTRAN is designed for scientific applications and COBOL for commercial applications. Some high-level languages are more general purpose, and have been developed simply to make the task of programming easier (for example, BASIC). When a high-level language is problem-oriented, it will handle other types of problem (for which it was not designed) inefficiently or not at all.

The following are examples of high-level languages. They are also known as third-generation languages.

(a) COBOL, used for business data processing.

(b) BASIC is designed for beginners, particularly on microcomputers. Several enhanced versions of BASIC are available.

(c) FORTRAN is a scientific language.

(d) CORAL is a language well-suited to on-line real time systems.

(e) PASCAL is well-suited to the structured programming technique.

(f) C is a language developed for the UNIX operating system which combines high-level language capabilities with the ability to address hardware (like an assembly language).

(g) C++ is an object orientated version of C.

The main disadvantage of using a high-level language as opposed to a low-level language is that high-level languages cannot usually take advantage of specific facilities on individual machines. Programs written in high-level languages are therefore unlikely to be as efficient in terms of processing speed and the use of memory as programs written in machine code or in assembly language. However, with recent falls in the cost of memory and improvements in processing speed, this disadvantage is becoming less significant.

Compilers: translation programs for high-level languages

As with a program in assembly language, a high-level language program has to be translated into machine code before it can be used. This is done by a *compiler program*, supplied by the manufacturer as software which *compiles* the source program into the object program. Once compiled and tested the object program is ready for operational use. As with the assembly process, once a source program in a high-level language has been compiled, the object program in machine code is filed and can be used whenever it is required for data processing. The source program has to be compiled only once.

An *interpreter* does the same sort of job as an assembler or compiler, but in a different way. It takes a program written in a high-level language and executes it, instruction by instruction, during the running of the program. With an interpreter, there is no need for a compiler to produce machine code in advance. On the other hand, the program must be interpreted afresh each time it is run.

The *advantage* of an interpreter over a compiler is that it is suitable for *interactive work*, where the programmer wishes to test (or amend) the program segments on-line, as the results can be seen immediately.

The *disadvantages* of an interpreter are as follows.

(a) It is slower.

(b) It uses up more memory, because although the high-level language program in memory is shorter than its machine code equivalent, the interpreter program must also be in memory at the same time.

(c) Mistakes may not be found until they are encountered.

An interpreter is useful for those who wish to write small programs for their own use. BASIC is interpreted rather than compiled.

Activity 2

A company wishes to write its own (large) program to prepare detailed weekly management accounts, and then to recoup the cost of writing the program by selling copies of it to other companies. Why would COBOL be a better choice of programming language than either BASIC or an assembly language?

1.5   Programming aids and fourth generation languages

Programming aids or programming tools are programs which are provided to help programmers to do their work.. Examples of programming tools are:

(a) *program development systems* which help users to learn programming, and to program in a high-level language. Using a VDU and keyboard terminal under the direction of an interactive program, users are helped to construct application programs;

(b) a *program generator* or *applications generator*. This is a program which assists users to write their own programs, by expanding simple statements into full programs;

(c) *RAD* (rapid applications development) tools.

Definition

The term *tools* is a fairly recent one, and is used loosely to mean any software productivity aid for programmers

Fourth generation languages

Fourth generation languages, or 4GLs, are intended to help computer users or computer programmers to develop their own application programs quickly and cheaply. A 4GL, by using a menu system for example, allows users to specify what they require, rather than describe the procedures by which these requirements are to be met. The 4GL produces a program in a high-level language to meet the user's needs, and that program can then be compiled.

A 4GL is therefore a *non-procedural language*. The programmer decides what he or she wants, but does not specify the procedures to achieve the desired result.

4GLs arose partly in response to the *applications backlog*. A great deal of programming time is spent maintaining and improving old programs rather than building new ones. Many organisations therefore have a backlog of applications waiting to be developed. 4GLs, by speeding up the process of application design and by making it easier for users to build their own programs, help to reduce it.

Object-orientated programming languages shift the focus from how a program performs its task to the data which is being processed.

By putting the data and its related processes (or methods) together inside an object, a technique referred to as encapsulation, the model the programmer constructs to represent the system is much closer to the real world.

These objects may be extended by inheriting the behaviour of existing objects. This allows programs to be changed to adapt to new requirements, extending the original code without actually rewriting it (which is prone to creating errors).

Object-orientated programming is hoped to be a solution to the problem of program maintenance, a problem brought into focus by the need for computer systems to cope with dates before and after the year 2000.

RAD tools provide the backbone of a program architecture and allow the program to focus on the specific task.

Modern operating systems have a vast overhead in managing the GUI front end, which means it is far too complex for programmers to develop their own routines to handle tasks. What programmers do is to use the application development environment to patch their requirements into the operations systems application programming interface (API).

Popular tools for this are Microsoft's visual programming tools (Visual C++ and Visual Basic) or Borland Delphi. Sometimes the visual front end of a program can be coded with an RAD tool such as Visual Basic, while a more efficient program language such as C++ would be used to program the process intensive back end.

Activity 3

A user of a 4GL may get a computer to achieve the desired results without understanding the procedures the computer uses to do so. Could this be a disadvantage of the use of 4GLs?

2   OPERATING SYSTEMS

As computer systems developed over the years, and processors became more powerful and operated at higher speeds, it became apparent that inefficient use was being made of processors by human operators. The problems arose because of the set-up times required to load the peripheral units (with tapes, paper and so on), the manual intervention required to investigate problems and the slowness of peripheral units in comparison with processors. It became apparent that the handling of most computer operations could best be done by means of stored programs. A whole package of control programs makes up an operating system (OS). An operating system provides the interface between the computer hardware and both the user (via the keyboard and VDU) and the other software. Leading operating systems include MS-DOS and UNIX.

2.1   Functions of an OS

An OS will typically perform the following tasks.

(a) Initial set-up of the computer, when it is switched on. This is achieved by the boot (or bootstrap) program , which is normally resident in ROM. It summons the rest of the OS from backing storage into RAM.

(b) Checking that the hardware (including peripheral devices) is functioning properly.

(c) Calling up program files and data files from external storage into memory.

(d) Opening and closing files, checking file labels and so on.

(e) Assigning program and data files from memory to peripheral devices.

(f) Maintaining directories in external storage.

(g) Controlling input and output devices, including the interaction with the computer user.

(h) Controlling system security (for example, monitoring the use of passwords).

(i) Handling interrupts (responding to hardware events).

(j) Applying checkpoint procedures. If there is some catastrophe, the entire contents of memory can be recorded (*dumped*) in a storage device and printed for investigation. Sometimes checkpoint programs will be implemented dumping memory contents onto a disk as a matter of routine, so that if processing is interrupted, it can be continued from the most recent checkpoint.

(k) Managing multitasking and multiprogramming (see below).

(l) *Spooling*. This means collecting data which is waiting to be processed or waiting to be output (for example, printed) in a storage device, until it can be processed or output. Thus spooling is a form of buffering, but instead of (for example) sending output into the printer's own buffer memory, it is kept within a storage device under the processor's control. When the printer is free, it is taken from that storage device by the processor and sent to the printer.

Software companies writing software packages (such as word processing programs) must write each software package for a specific operating system. A PC user must be aware of what operating system his PC uses in order to establish whether a particular software package will run on it. More packages have been written for MS-DOS than for other operating systems. However, the more popular off-the-shelf software packages are available in different versions, one for each of the leading operating systems.

2.2 Utilities

A utility program does routine jobs which frequently arise. Whilst strictly speaking a utility is not part of the OS, utility programs are usually provided with OS software. MS-DOS, for example, includes a number of utilities. Examples of utilities include:

(a) file conversion (transferring data or program files from one output or storage medium to another);

(b) file copying (producing back-up files). MS-DOS, for example, allows you to copy files from hard disk to tape;

(c) memory dumping, as part of a checkpoint program;

(d) listing files;

(e) comparing the contents of two disks, if one has been copied from another;

(f) deleting files;

(g) sending files to a printer or other output device;

(h) renaming files;

(i) sorting data by key field sequence.

2.3 Multitasking and multiprogramming

As the processor works much faster than any peripheral device, processor time is wasted to the extent that processing times depend on the speeds of these peripheral units. Wasted processor time can be reduced by the simultaneous use of more than one peripheral device (simultaneity), so that the processor can be receiving some input A from one peripheral device, processing data B and sending output C to another peripheral device all at the same time. In spite of simultaneity, a computer's processor is still idle for a large part of the time. Multitasking and multi-programming enable several programs to share the use of the processor and take up the under-used capacity.

In multitasking, one user does more than one thing simultaneously (for example, print one document while editing another). In multiprogramming, the processor runs several programs at once, executing bits of each in turn.

Some programs will be *peripheral bound*, requiring considerably more input/output time than processor time, while others will be processor bound , requiring more processor time than input/output time. The programs used in a multiprogramming or multitasking operation should ideally comprise a mix of peripheral bound and processor bound programs which can be put in an order of priority. With a large number of programs and peripheral units, the processor can be kept occupied for almost 100% of the time. This needs a suitable operating system, whose functioning in turn requires:

(a) sufficient *memory* to hold all programs and the data to be processed by each program;

(b) *memory protection* (a user must not be allowed access to parts of memory not allocated to his program and data);

(c) a *priority rating* for each program. The highest priority program (usually the most peripheral bound) is allowed to use the processor whenever it can (for example, after an input/output transfer). When the program can no longer use the processor, the operating system allocates processing time to the next program in line. Whenever a higher priority program is ready to use the processor, the operating system interrupts the lower priority program and gives processor time to the higher priority one.

2.4 Operating systems and the user interface

The operating system controls how the user relates to the computer system and the processing operation.

Readers familiar with DOS will be aware of the fact that the user interface is based on a series of commands, and in most DOS manuals a long list of commands can be found to enable the user to manipulate the system, access the utilities provided with the system software and so forth. For example, if you are using a PC with a hard disk that is called drive C and you wish to delete a text (or document) file named MTI.DOC, then after the prompt C> you will type in DELETE MTI.DOC and then press return.

This type of screen dialogue is being overtaken by more user-friendly techniques, as we have seen, including the graphical user interface. IBM's operating system designed for 32-bit PCs uses Presentation Manager as its graphical user interface. Microsoft Windows can be used with MS-DOS, and is now also available as an operating system in its own right. Machines using the UNIX operating system can be run with X Windows. Apple computers tend to have their own graphical user interfaces, as the Apple operating system is only used by Apple computers.

Activity 4

A computer runs two programs for two different users at once. Program A requires 15 seconds of processor time and five minutes of printer time. Program B requires one minute of processor time and one minute of printer time. In both cases, some of the printing can be done when only part of the program has been executed by the processor. Which of the two programs should be given priority if both of them request processor time simultaneously?

2.5 Developments in operating systems

Operating systems in a network environment

So far, the discussion of operating systems has been limited to consideration of the interaction between one processor and the peripheral devices attached to it. An OS is also needed to control the interaction and communication between the various computers and peripherals in a LAN or WAN. There are two approaches to this problem.

(a) A separate networking operating system can be put in charge of the operating systems of the individual computers. As MS-DOS was designed purely for personal computing, this is the solution necessary when machines using MS-DOS are to be linked. An example of network OS is Novell's Netware.

(b) An operating system in which networking facilities are an integral part of the design can be used. An example of such an operating system is UNIX.

Open systems

Open systems aim to ensure compatibility between different makes of equipment and software, enabling users to choose on the basis of price and performance.

It is arguable that in the PC market there is already a sort of de facto open systems arrangement, given that there are so many makes of PC using MS-DOS. However, while MS-DOS is ideal for stand-alone PCs, it has a number of drawbacks, in that:

(a) it has limitations when it comes to multitasking;

(b) it is basically single-user;

(c) it was developed originally for the IBM PC, and it may not be powerful or flexible enough to make full use of the more recent 32-bit PCs.

Until recently many computer users have not given a great deal of thought to their operating system. Purchasers of mainframes and PCs are supplied with a proprietary system by the hardware manufacturer and that is usually the end of the story. IBM users have OS/VS, ICL users have VME and each machine will only run on its own system. Recently, the market has changed. Mainframe and mini users are talking of UNIX and PC users, instead of accepting MS-DOS, can choose the new systems OS/2 or Windows NT. Suddenly, there is consumer choice in an area where users have traditionally had to use what they were given.

UNIX

The UNIX operating system was developed by AT&T in 1969 as a multitasking operating system that could be used on computers with different architectures. It is an example of an open system. It first gained popularity in universities, where many computer science students needed to be able to work at the same time, but was seen as lacking in user-friendliness and uneconomic by commercial suppliers and users. However, its popularity among those who used it ensured that it survived and by the 1980s it had been developed far enough for commercial users to take an interest in it.

UNIX works equally well in a network environment as in a multi-user system. Particular areas where UNIX has already demonstrated its capabilities are communications, where the ability to accommodate other operating systems in the UNIX environment supports the use of electronic mail, and engineering, where UNIX's capabilities are suited to running high-resolution graphics systems.

The strategic decision is whether, in the long term, an organisation should change to open systems. In principle, there seems little to be said against it. It has government support. The UK Department of Trade and Industry is encouraging firms to take an interest. It might also be noted that ICL, the UK's major indigenous computer company, (now owned by Fujitsu of Japan) took the open systems route many years ago. The European Union is also encouraging open systems. The hardware is reputedly cheaper and much easier to upgrade than that of most proprietary systems.

UNIX is perhaps best able to satisfy another trend towards managerial workstations. UNIX allows a user to carry out a number of tasks concurrently, at the same terminal (a different window appearing for each task), or to use computing resources on other machines in the network.

On the other hand, many users have already invested large amounts in other systems. If these are working well, there is little point in changing over, at least in the short term.

Open systems may be a sensible choice for an organisation which:

(a) is contemplating a major change in its computer systems in any case;

(b) is contemplating a substantial increase in the use of information technology throughout the organisation;

(c) requires multi-user, multi-tasking computers.

Activity 5

A company decides to change to an open system. Why is the change likely to be of greater benefit to managers than to staff carrying out routine data input?

PC operating systems

Just as UNIX looks set to become the standard choice for mainframes and minicomputers, Microsoft is trying to make Windows, in one form or another, the standard for PCs.

Modern PCs are powerful enough to perform as servers themselves, and there are versions of UNIX designed for the x86 architecture, such as SCO UNIX or the Free Software Foundation (LINUX).

IBM's first attempt to replace DOS foundered because too many DOS programs failed to work on OS/2 1.x. Their second attempt did not succeed as Microsoft had a runaway success with Windows which they wished to build upon to create their own server product, Windows NT.

Windows NT is a POSIX compliant operating system designed to take on UNIX as a multi-platform, multi-tasking operating system to run on x86, Dec alpha and RS6000.

The Windows shell placed over DOS has been transformed by Windows 95 into a single user operating system performing true multi-tasking. The new version of Windows expected in late 1997 will bring NT server and Windows 95 capabilities together, incorporating an Internet browser style interface.

DOS is not dead yet and many of its features such as 8.3 filenames are themselves hangovers from an older system, CPM. Many thousands of DOS applications 'aren't broke yet', and users will see no need to 'fix' them until absolutely necessary.

Activity 6

Explain how a finance director preparing a report for the board of directors might benefit from the multitasking facilities offered by Windows.

Chapter roundup

- A computer can only execute instructions in machine code, which is unintelligible to most people.
- To bridge the gap between everyday language and machine code, programming languages are used.
- Assembly languages are low-level, machine specific languages.
- High-level languages, which can be used with several makes of computer, include BASIC, COBOL and FORTRAN.
- Programs must be assembled, compiled or interpreted in order to convert them into machine code instructions.
- Fourth generation languages enable users to specify their requirements, which are then automatically converted into programs in high-level languages.

Chapter roundup (*continued*)

- An operating system is in overall charge of a computer, supervising the execution of programs and the running of peripheral devices.

- Utilities operate on files as a whole, without regard to their contents, performing commonly required tasks.

- Multitasking and multi-programming are responses to the fact that peripheral devices work much more slowly than processors.

- Open systems are designed to allow users a free choice of hardware and software, and facilitate networking.

- Recent developments in PC operating systems include OS/2 and Windows NT.

Quick quiz

1   Why is an assembly language easier to use than machine code?

2   Give some examples of problem-oriented high-level languages, and the corresponding types of problem.

3   How does a compiler differ from an interpreter?

4   Why are fourth generation languages described as non-procedural?

5   List the tasks typically performed by an operating system.

6   What utilities are commonly supplied with an operating system?

7   What tasks must an operating system perform in order to allow multiprogramming?

8   In what situations might an organisation do best to change to open systems?

9   What are the significant features of Windows?

Answers to activities

1   An assembly language program cannot be assembled into a form which a computer can use until an assembler program has been written. The assembler program must therefore be written in machine code.

2   COBOL is compiled whereas BASIC is interpreted, so COBOL is better for large programs. COBOL is machine independent (unlike assembly language), so copies of the program could be sold to users with other types of computer.

3   Yes: someone who does not understand how a program works may fail to understand its limitations.

4   Program A should have priority, because it is the more peripheral bound.

5   Routine data input requirements are likely to change only slowly, and the work done by the staff can be standardised. Managers, on the other hand, often want new ways of analysing and presenting information, and want good communication links to each others' computers.

6   The finance director might type some text, draw up a table and prepare a graph. On looking at the graph he might decide to change the text, and then amend the table. Thus several different types of job would need to be done in quick succession.

Further question practice

Now try the following practice questions at the end of this text.

Multiple choice questions   **32 to 38**

Exam style question   **4**

Chapter 6

GENERAL PURPOSE PACKAGES

Introduction

A distinction can be made between general purpose software and applications software. *General purpose software* can be used for processing of a general nature, but the software can be applied to a variety of specific uses to suit the computer user's choice. Spreadsheets are an example. *Applications software* will carry out a specific processing application: for example, sales ledger software would enable a computer user to do sales ledger processing work and payroll software would be specific to payroll processing.

General purpose packages provide ready-made general purpose software. *Applications packages* are ready-made programs written to perform a particular job. The job will be common to many potential users, so that the package could be adopted by all of them for their data processing operations.

As an alternative to using packages, software of either type can be specially written. However, specially written applications software is far more common than specially written general purpose software.

In this chapter we will look at general purpose packages, and in the next chapter we will look at applications software.

There are several types of package usually classified as general purpose packages. They can be tailored by the user for a wide range of applications. In this chapter we will examine the features and uses of spreadsheets, word processing (WP), desk top publishing (DTP), graphics and modelling packages.

Your objectives

After completing this chapter you should:

(a) know how a spreadsheet is used for financial calculations;

(b) appreciate the use of spreadsheets in sensitivity analysis;

(c) be aware of additional features available with some spreadsheet packages;

(d) appreciate the usefulness of word processors;

(e) be aware of word processing facilities which can enhance the appearance of documents;

(f) appreciate the sophisticated presentation facilities available in desktop publishing;

(g) know the ways in which data can be presented graphically by a computer;

(h) know the main output devices for computer graphics;

(i) appreciate the uses of financial modelling packages.

1 SPREADSHEETS

A spreadsheet is a type of software package for financial modelling. The computer's VDU displays a sheet divided into rows and columns, and figures or text can be inserted into the boxes on the sheet. Examples of spreadsheets are Lotus 123 and Excel.

1.1 Uses of spreadsheets

Some of the more common uses of spreadsheets are:

(a) cash flow analysis/forecasting;

(b) inventory records;

(c) job cost estimates;

(d) market share analysis and planning;

(e) profit projections;

(f) tax estimation.

What all these uses have in common is that they all involve data processing with:

(a) numerical data;

(b) repetitive, time-consuming calculations;

(c) a logical processing structure.

The great value of spreadsheets derives from their simple format of rows and columns of data, and the ability of users to have direct access themselves to their spreadsheet models via their own PCs. For example, accountants can construct cash flow models with a spreadsheet package on a PC in their office; they can create the models, input the data, manipulate the data and read or print the output directly. They also have access to the models whenever they are needed.

1.2 What does a spreadsheet look like?

When a blank spreadsheet is loaded into a computer, the VDU monitor will show lines of empty rows and columns. The rows are usually numbered 1, 2, 3 ... and the columns lettered A, B, C. Each box in the table, for example column A row 1, column A row 2 or column B row 1, is referred to as a cell.

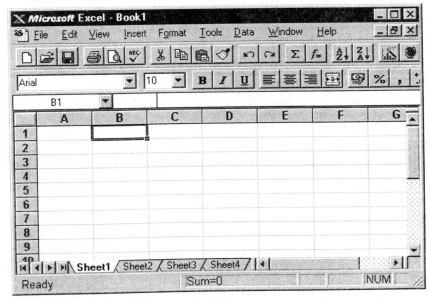

Figure 6.1 A blank spreadsheet

The screen will not be able to show all the columns and rows. The spreadsheet will 'scroll' in any direction when the user operates the cursor keys on the keyboard, to find the rows and columns that the user wishes to look at. If the user wishes to look at two different parts of a spreadsheet on the screen at the same time, there is a command in all spreadsheet packages which enables the user to split the screen. It is usually called a 'window' command, and enables two separate parts of a large spreadsheet to be viewed at the same time on the screen.

A spreadsheet, then, consists of a large number of cells, each identified by a reference such as A4, D16 or AA20. (After Z, we have AA, AB and so on.) The screen cursor will highlight a particular cell: in Figure 4.1 above, it is placed over cell B1. At the top or bottom of the screen, the spreadsheet program will give information such as:

(a) the reference of the cell where the cursor lies;

(b) the width of the column where the cursor lies (you can alter column widths to suit yourself, up to about 100 characters, without changing the total number of columns available on the spreadsheet);

(c) the contents of the cell where the cursor lies, if there is anything there.

The contents of any cell can be one of the following.

(a) Text. A text cell, or label cell, contains words or numerical data that cannot be used in computations (such as a date) providing it is so designated. Lotus 123 requires you to insert an apostrophe before a number if that number is to be read as an item of text.

(b) A value. A value is a number that can be used in a calculation.

(c) A formula. A formula refers to other cells in the spreadsheet, and performs some sort of computation with them. For example, if cell C1 contains the formula =A1-B1 this means that the contents of cell B1 will be subtracted from the contents of cell A1 and the result displayed in cell C1. If the amount in A1 is changed, the amount in C1 will change as well. (The = sign before A1 indicates that cell A1 contains a number or a formula, and is not a text cell.)

(d) A macro. Macros are automated commands (see below).

Activity 1

In a spreadsheet, cell A1 contains the number 2. Cell A2 contains the formula +A3-A1. Cell A3 contains the formula +A2 − A4. Cell A4 contains the number 5. What is wrong with this spreadsheet?

1.3 Spreadsheets in practice

The user constructs a model in rows and columns format, by:

(a) identifying what data goes into each row and column and inserting text, for example, column headings and row identifications;

(b) specifying how the numerical data in the model should be derived. Numerical data might be:

(i) inserted into the model via keyboard input;

(ii) calculated from other data in the model by means of a formula specified within the model itself (the user must insert these formulae into the model); or

(iii) occasionally, obtained from data on a disk file.

Suppose you wanted to set up a simple profit and loss account in such a way that you could use it to estimate how the net profit will change in total when any individual item is altered. You know that cost of sales is 40% of sales, but that distribution expenses do not vary over a reasonable range of sales.

Inserting text

The first job is to put in the various headings that you want. It is usually convenient to start at row 1 and column A, although this is not essential.

At this stage, your screen might look as follows.

	: A	B	C
1:			
2:		£'000	£'000
3:			
4:	Sales		
5:	Less cost of sales		
6:	Gross profit		
7:			
8:	Administration expenses		
9:	Distribution expenses		
10:	Finance expenses		
11:	Total expenses		
12:			
13:	Net profit		

Figure 6.2 A part-completed profit and loss account

The 'A' column has been widened so that long titles will fit into it and not spill over.

Inserting formulae

The next stage in constructing a model is to put in the calculations you want the computer to carry out, expressed as formulae. For example, referring back to our example, in cell C11 you want total expenses, so you put in the formula + B8 + B9 + B10 (Lotus 123) or = B8 + B9 + B10 (Excel). This could also be written as @SUM(B8..B10), or =SUM(B8:B10) respectively.

Other formulae required for this example are as follows. Again, in Excel each format is preceded by an equals sign instead of a plus sign.

(a) in cell C5:   +C4 * 0.4 (* is used for multiplication)

(b) in cell C6:   +C4-C5

(c) in cell C13: +C6-C11

Unlike the text, these formulae will not be shown on the spreadsheet itself, but at the top or bottom of the screen (in an 'edit' bar) when the cursor is over the relevant cell. So at this stage, the spreadsheet looks just the same as it did after setting up the headings, except that when the cursor is on a cell where a formula has been input, that formula is shown at the top or bottom of the screen.

Our example only uses plus and minus functions and multiplication, but most spreadsheets offer several functions including:

(a) division;

(b) multiplication of items by a constant factor;

(c) square roots;

(d) logical functions (such as true or false);

(e) financial analysis (such as discounted cash flow);

(f) statistical functions (such as standard deviation).

Inserting numerical data

The last stage in setting up a spreadsheet is to input data. In our example, suppose sales are £17m. This would be input as a figure into cell C4 and the computer would automatically show the cost of sales in cell C5 and the gross profit in cell C6, using the formulae already specified in the model. Other data would be input to cells B8, B9, and B10.

The completed profit and loss account might look like this.

	: A	B	C
1:			
2:		£'000	£'000
3:			
4:	Sales		17,000
5:	Less cost of sales		6,800
6:	Gross profit		10,200
7:			
8:	Administration expenses	600	
9:	Distribution expenses	1,200	
10:	Finance expenses	800	
11:	Total expenses		2,600
12:			
13:	Net profit		7,600

Figure 6.3 A completed profit and loss account

Using a spreadsheet model for sensitivity analysis

Whenever a forecast or budget is made, management should consider asking 'what if' questions, and so carry out a form of sensitivity analysis.

With our example, 'what if' questions for sensitivity analysis might be:

(a) what if the cost of sales is 43% of sales?

(b) what if administration expenses rise by 25%?

Using the spreadsheet model, the answers to these questions, and others like them, could be obtained simply and quickly, using the editing facility in the program. Managers could then work out what changes might lead to budgeted profit not being achieved.

Activity 2

Returning to the above example of a profit and loss account, suppose you want to show in cell C15 the sum of the cost of sales and the administration and distribution expenses. What formula would you put in that cell?

1.4 Features of spreadsheets

Spreadsheets are versatile tools. Different spreadsheets will offer different facilities, but some of the more basic ones, which should feature in all spreadsheet programs, are as follows.

(a) *Print* commands. You should be able to print the contents of the spreadsheet in total or in part, with or without the spreadsheet row and column labels.

(b) *File* commands. You should be able to save the spreadsheet model for further use as a file on your disk, either all of it or just part of it. Other file commands allow you to combine data from another spreadsheet model with the present one (for example, the prior year's profit and loss account could be inserted alongside the current year's).

(c) *Cell editing facilities*. The program should allow alteration of anything shown on the spreadsheet. This is particularly useful for 'what if?' calculations. For instance, in our example, you might want to know what net profit would be if the cost of sales were 43% of sales. Using the editing facility, you would only have to change the formula in cell C5 to = C4 * 0.43, then ask the computer to recalculate the entire spreadsheet on the basis of the new figures.

(d) *Facilities to rearrange the spreadsheet*, for example, to insert a row or column at a desired spot. For example, you might wish to split finance expenses into overdraft interest and long term loan interest. The insert command facilitates this, and the formulae in the spreadsheet are adjusted automatically. Alternatively, you might wish to move or copy a cell, row, column or block of cells elsewhere or delete a row or column altogether.

(e) *Sort*. A spreadsheet package will usually provide a facility for sorting data alphabetically or numerically.

(f) Copy a formula. For example, suppose you wanted to have a cumulative total of a list of numbers, as follows.

	A	B	C
1:			
2:	9	9	
3:	10	19	
4:	14	33	
5:	3	36	
6:	86	122	
7:	9	131	

The numbers in the A column are data. The cumulative numbers in the B column are calculated from the formulae B2 = A2; B3 = +B2 + A3; B4 = +B3 + A4 and so on. Clearly it would take a long time to input all these formulae individually, and so to save time it is possible to input +B2 + A3 in the B3 cell, and then copy the formula down the column. It is usually possible to copy downwards or sideways throughout the spreadsheet, and the computer will automatically change the formula to give the right cell addresses, in this instance the cell above plus the cell to the left. This is described as treating the cell addresses in the formula as relative cell addresses. Absolute cell addresses can also be specified, so that when a formula is copied into another cell the cell addresses do not change.

(g) *Format.* This command controls the way in which headings and data are shown, for example by altering column widths or changing the number of decimal places displayed. You can format a selected range of cells, or the whole spreadsheet.

(h) Spreadsheets offer a *graphics* facility, so that data can be displayed as bar charts or pie charts.

(i) *Macros.* Many spreadsheet facilities are provided as *commands* in a menu. Some procedures require a number of commands to be executed. This is often time consuming. For example, if you wish to print some or all of your spreadsheet, you will first execute the print command. You may then see a menu which asks you to specify, for example, what part of the spreadsheet you wish to print and the length of the pages you are using in the printer, what you wish the size of the margins to be and so forth. Several commands must be executed before the spreadsheet is printed and you will have to repeat them each time you wish to print the spreadsheet. Spreadsheets provide a macro facility. This allows the user to automate a sequence of commands, 'recording' them and then executing them by pressing two keys.

(j) Spreadsheets offer a *search* and *replace* facility to highlight and alter individual formulae.

(k) Spreadsheets offer a *protect* facility, to ensure that the contents of a specified range of cells (for example, the titles in column A of the example on the previous page) cannot be overwritten.

Three-dimensional spreadsheets

One of the problems with using spreadsheets for financial modelling is that spreadsheets work only in two dimensions (columns and rows). Combining information in three dimensions is difficult. For example, you might wish to produce financial statements for a number of companies in a group, as well as the consolidated results for the group as a whole, analysed over a number of months. In a normal two-dimensional spreadsheet you would have, say, the months across the top as columns, and the income and expenditure down the side as rows. If there is more than one company involved you would have to repeat this design separately for each company.

Lotus 123 and Excel both have a facility that permits working in three dimensions, as multiple related sheets can be held in memory at one time. A filing cabinet is perhaps a good analogy, as the user can flip between different sheets in a file. Cells in one sheet may refer to cells in another sheet. In our example, the front sheet would be the consolidated results, and the other sheets the results for the constituent companies. The formulae in the cells in the front sheet could refer to the cells in the spreadsheets behind it.

In addition to macros, Excel has its own programming facility. Visual Basic for Applications (VBA) allows complex tasks/operations to be designed in a structured manner.

This programming language is to be standardised across Microsoft Office products to make it easier to transfer skills between applications.

Activity 3

In a spreadsheet, the formula in cell D8 is @SUM(A2..A6)*(+B4-C2) [or alternatively =SUM(A2:A6)*(B4-C2)]. All addresses are relative. This formula is copied to cell G22. What will the resulting formula in cell G22 be?

2 WORD PROCESSING (WP)

2.1 What is a word processor?

Word processors are computers which provide a system for storing letters and text on disk, recalling them at a later time and possibly amending them so as to reproduce them with slight variations (such as a change of name and address on a letter). Corrections are easily keyed in. Word processors may be dedicated machines, for word processing only, or may be general purpose computers (normally PCs) using word processing software packages. Leading packages include Word and WordPerfect.

Certain features of word processing are worth emphasising.

(a) Text which is keyed in can be merged with other text already held on a file (such as common text for standard letters). The facility to merge some keyed-in text with text on file enables the user to produce personalised standard letters quickly and with few keying-in errors.

(b) Word processing enables the person preparing the text to check the input visually on the VDU screen as it is being keyed in, and to correct errors immediately (some spelling checks can be built into the word processing software).

(c) The user can easily make amendments to the original text.

   (i) If the contents of the text are discussed and as a result of these discussions, changes are agreed, the changes can be made quickly and simply. For example, contracts under negotiation can be amended in this way.

   (ii) Text can be held on file and subsequently updated. For example, a company might hold its rules and procedures books, or its price lists on a file and update them just before they are to be reprinted. Updating can be done quickly and with a low error rate.

2.2 Using WP

Different word processing packages have been developed with different design philosophies as to the user interface.

(a) Some packages use a system of commands whereby the operator remembers a number of keystrokes (or consults a list of commands in a help facility) and uses them appropriately.

(b) Some packages use a menu system, whereby, at the top or bottom of the screen, a number of options are listed. Some packages operate several menus.

(c) Finally, some packages employ a WIMP interface (for example, using an icon of a pair of scissors for 'cut and paste' editing). Some packages are available in versions which run with Microsoft's Windows. They can be identified by their titles, for example Word for Windows and WordPerfect for Windows.

The WYSIWYG (what you see is what you get) facility is another helpful feature for users who wish to see on screen exactly the format and typeface they will get on paper. Thus italics would actually appear on screen as italics rather than being indicated by a code.

Document creation

When saved onto backing store, a word processed letter, for example, is a file of data like any other file. So creating a document requires giving it a name and setting it up as a file. In some word processors, setting up a document may also involve filling in a formatted screen giving basic details about the document (such as the originator, the destination or the date).

There is a limit to the number of characters which can be held in the processor's memory at any one time. When the document is longer than memory allows, part of it must be saved on disk as a file in its own right, rather like a chapter in a book. However it should be relatively easy to move between these subdocuments.

The word processor screen is first of all given all the characteristics of a sheet of paper. The operator is able to specify the *width* and *length* of the area the text is to cover on the page, taking into account desired margins when the text is printed on paper. If the text area is larger than the screen can accommodate, the operator can scroll up and down or pan from side to side in order to view a page.

Editing

Once the text in its basic form has been keyed in, the editing facilities of the software come into their own. The functions of *erasure*, *correction* and *insertion* are all available on screen. Text can be *moved* or *duplicated*. Moreover, text can be *justified* (given straight left and right hand edges) automatically within preset margins.

Single characters, words, lines or specified blocks of text can be removed from the screen, erased, replaced, or moved elsewhere. Keying-in can be set to *type over* existing text, or to insert text immediately to the left of the cursor.

Repeated errors or items for updating can be found, and corrected automatically if desired, using a *search and replace* function, for example 'search for *typewriter* ... replace with *word processor*'. The *search* facility is also useful for moving quickly to required points in the text.

Layout can be altered with equal ease.

Commands to indent, tab, centre, right align, close up or widen vertical gaps can be inserted into a block of text.

All adjustments entailed by the move will be carried out automatically.

Blocks of text can also be either moved from their original positions to specified points in the document, or copied to one or more positions.

Activity 4

Give some examples of business letters, other than those used in direct mail selling, which would be worth saving on disk for re-use with changes of detail.

2.3   Features of WP packages

Other valuable aids in producing documents include the following.

(a) *Page headers* (such as chapter headings) can be keyed in only once, but inserted by the program at the top of every page.

(b) *Footers* can be added at the foot of each page. An 'input' point may be inserted so that the appropriate page number within the document will be printed automatically.

(c) A *spell-checker* program can check a specified word, page or file against its own dictionary and call attention to any word it cannot recognise: the operator then has the choice of ignoring the word (if it is unfamiliar to the machine, but correctly spelt), adding it to the dictionary (if it is unfamiliar, correctly spelt and much used) or correcting the error (by substituting a word offered by the machine from its dictionary, or by typing afresh).

(d) *Typescript variations* can be used for emphasis or appearance. These are entered as controls in the text, or selected from a menu, as instructions to a printer, and may or may not appear on screen as they will on paper. For example:

Underlining, *italics*, **emboldening**, different type sizes and type faces.

(e) *Proportional spacing* is available with most packages. This means that each character is printed in a space proportional to its size. Letters like 'i' take up less room than 'w' or 'm', and so would have too much space around them if all the characters, for example in a word like wimp, were given 'm'- or 'w'-sized spaces.

(f) Tables can be set up for the presentation of figures. *Calculation facilities* may be included, including automatic totalling of columns and rows of figures. The calculator program may also be used to check and correct paragraph numbering. A code is entered with each number, and the calculator can then be asked to check and match sequences.

(g) Form design and graphics software packages are increasingly added to basic word processing. Graphics facilities enable lines to be drawn on screen (directed by cursor movement from the keyboard or by means of a mouse), areas to be shaded, points to be plotted and even colour to be applied in advanced graphics systems.

For users of word processors, perhaps the most useful application of a graphics-related program is in the design of forms and documents of camera-ready quality for bulk printing and use.

Lines and boxes, which can be moved and/or duplicated as required, can be 'drawn' on screen, with a mouse or by marking relevant points with the cursor. Lines can be of varying density and areas can be shaded in various tones. Operations are usually selected from a series of easily-assimilated menus, offering options such as draw, edit, move, copy, shade or delete, within which there are further options, such as shade 1, 2, 3 or 4.

Once a graphic format has been designed to the user's satisfaction, it can be 'downloaded' or overlaid onto a separate text file (with the form headings, document contents and so on) which has been appropriately laid out: the two are printed together to create the finished document.

(h) *Work flow management* is facilitated by 'background printing' which allows the operator to continue keying in and editing material while the printer carries on printing documents put into its own memory. This also allows for queuing of tasks: an urgent printing task may override routine or held-back tasks, which are made to queue up in order of importance.

(i) *Communications* facilities are important. Any computer running a particular package should be able to communicate with other computers running the same or compatible software: they may be close enough to be linked by a cable, or they may be linked by telephone using a modem. This means that documents or disk files can be sent or read across from one computer to another, with complete confidence that the text will be sent and received correctly.

(j) Some word processing packages allow tables of figures taken directly from spreadsheets to be included in a text without re-typing. Graphs prepared using other software (*graphics packages*) may also be added to documents.

(k) *Macros* are automated sequences of commands which can be executed with single keystrokes, menu choices or toolbar choices. If a text editing function is repeated over many pages, it can be automated and executed easily.

(l) *Stylesheets* enable a selected font and page layout to be given a name and stored for later use.

(m) Many packages enable *pagination* to be achieved, especially useful for long documents.

Three of the most valuable specialist applications often included in packages are:

(a) record keeping (indexing of all correspondence);

(b) mailing (preparation of address labels);

(c) indexing.

Activity 5

A long report on a new project is to be prepared, incorporating text, graphs and tables of figures. The report must be attractively presented, because it is to be shown to external providers of finance for the project. Which features of a sophisticated word processing system would be particularly useful in the preparation of the report?

3 DESKTOP PUBLISHING (DTP)

3.1 What is desktop publishing?

Desktop publishing is the use of office computers to implement computerised typesetting and composition systems. A desktop publishing package has at its root a word processing package, but it is more sophisticated than a word processing package. A word processing package produces high quality text, suitable for letters and some reports. However, if the text so produced is to be embellished with, for example, graphs, diagrams, photographs or tables, the text may require further (manual) manipulation prior to publication. A DTP package allows pages to be made up on screen and printed in the required format. The need for a messy cut-and-paste exercise is avoided and the package will produce pages of the type found in books, magazines or newspapers. It is used to produce output which is well finished, professional and above all well designed. With time, DTP and word processing have moved closer together as word processing becomes more sophisticated.

These capabilities mean that organisations wishing to produce a wide range of documents no longer require outside typesetters. Annual reports, sales catalogues, marketing brochures, reviews of the business, newsletters, press releases and other documents for which a high quality finish is required can be produced in-house. The only equipment required is a PC and a laser printer. DTP packages are becoming increasingly user friendly, so that any operator can learn how to use a package without difficulty. The lead time necessitated for sending documents to external typesetters is eliminated and documents can be produced to extremely tight deadlines.

3.2 DTP software packages

Desktop publishing software packages vary in complexity. Some are suitable for the general user producing an occasional document; others are appropriate for specialist DTP departments, producing brochures, company reports and advertisements, with sophisticated photography and artwork for output on professional typesetting printers.

The finished page can be made to resemble any newspaper, magazine or brochure page, with boxes, ruled lines and frames delineating or emphasising areas of text. Text can be spread right across the page, or in two or more columns; it can be wrapped round diagrams or presented in blocks. However, with one or two exceptions, DTP programs are not good programs with which to create text or graphics.

DTP's main function is that it enables the page, both graphics and text, to be seen as the 'artwork' image for editing and production. A space for a picture can be moved around the page, like 'cut and paste' artwork.

DTP software should:

(a) offer WYSIWYG: what appears on the screen should look like what will be printed;

(b) support PostScript for output;

(c) be able to import text from a wide variety of word processing and graphics software, including high quality graphics;

(d) support colour output;

(e) provide standardised style sheets for typeface and layout, which can save time in determining the look of a document;

(f) be able to work with a document scanner for the input of photographs and diagrams.

DTP is likely to need a powerful computer, as it requires lots of memory and processing.

It is important that the user does not get carried away with the features of DTP for its own sake. This kind of package can become addictive and an end in itself, rather than a means to an end. Discipline is required; many organisations experience a flurry of beautifully designed but relatively unimportant memos and notices after the acquisition of DTP. Similarly, users must be aware of what constitutes good design. The positioning of illustrations, the size of headlines, the choice of fonts and the overall 'feel' of the made-up page can have a large effect on how the finished product is received. The 'cropping' of photographs to emphasise important subjects is a technique commonly used in newspaper publishing and can be adopted in DTP.

Activity 6

Which features of desktop publishing might make it the best way to produce a staff magazine for a large organisation?

---

4 COMPUTER GRAPHICS

One use of computers is the production of information in the form of pictures, diagrams or graphs (collectively known as graphics).

4.1 Graphics software

Graphics software comes in a variety of forms and may provide any of the following facilities (in ascending order of sophistication):

(a) the facility to interpret and present data in graphical form;

(b) presentation graphics;

(c) free-form graphics (in which any required output can be drawn, even if it is not in the form of a recognised type of graph).

4.2 The presentation of data in graphical form

Some programs with a graphics facility allow the user to display data in graphical form, as:

(a) line graphs (for example, a time series graph, perhaps showing profits over time);

(b) bar charts;

(c) pie charts;

(d) scattergraphs which plot the value of one item against the corresponding value of a second item, for a number of pairs of data;

(e) maps;

(f) time series charts;

(g) architectural drawings;

(h) organisation charts.

Most graphics programs are menu-driven, allowing the computer user to select the type of graph required. The numerical data must be input or produced by other parts of the program's operations. The software then produces a graph automatically.

4.3 Presentation graphics

Programs for presentation graphics allow the user to build up a series of graphical displays or MS images which can be used for presentation. With additional hardware, this type of software can be used to produce 35mm slides for an on-screen slideshow or storyboard (which can be synchronised with a sound track). The Powerpoint software package is an example: this includes a large library of icons, symbols and images for inclusion in presentations.

4.4 Graphics hardware: processor, input and output equipment

All graphics packages accept commands from the standard keyboard terminal, but other useful input devices are a light pen, a mouse and a digitiser. A powerful processor and a colour monitor are essential for implementation of an advanced graphics package.

For a computer to be able to produce graphics, it must have the appropriate processor hardware. With a PC, a *graphics card* can be inserted into the PC (there are monochrome graphics cards and colour graphics cards). This hardware is used with suitable software to produce graphics.

4.5 Types of graphics

Graphics, like letters and numbers, can be displayed on a VDU screen by lighting up tiny dots called pixels (which stands for picture elements). The quality of the graphics (whether high or low resolution) depends on the size of the individual pixels. A program can instruct the VDU screen to light up a pixel on any x and y co-ordinate, and this is how computer graphics are formed on a screen.

(a) *Line graphics* are created on screen by specifying two points on the screen and instructing the computer to light up all the pixels between them. In this way, several lines can be created to build up a full line drawing.

(b) *Animated graphics* simulate motion by creating a whole series of 'frames'. By deleting one frame and replacing it with the next in quick succession, the impression of movement is given. You only have to think about all the home computer games you have seen or played to get an idea of animated graphics.

(c) *3-D graphics* give the illusion of a three-dimensional object. One way of doing this is to create a 'wire frame drawing' in which all the lines which make up the picture are shown even if they would be hidden if the object were really solid.

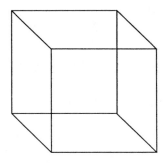

Figure 6.4 An example of 3-D graphics

(d) *CAD* stands for computer aided design, which is the use of computer graphics to help professional designers in industry in their design of new products.

Activity 7

A presentation (to be shown on VDU screens) is being prepared for the board of directors of a company which is considering relocation of its head office. The presentation is to be about a new office building, and is to include drawings of the overall space available and of individual rooms. The presentation will also include graphs of costs, divided between rent, business rates, gas, electricity and so on, and projected over the next five years. Explain how computer graphics might be used in the presentation.

4.6 Hard copy output of graphics

A graphics software package will be of limited value if the images it produces can only be displayed on a VDU screen. There ought to be a way of producing the image either on paper or on photographic film.

Dot matrix printers can be used to print graphics, using the pins on the print head to build up a picture in dots. Higher quality graphics are available from the newer dot matrix printers with 24×24 pins on the print head (instead of the 9×9 pins on many printers). These printers can print in monochrome (black on white paper) but colour options are available for them, even though not many graphics software packages currently support colour printing options. Not every make of dot matrix printer is compatible with a particular graphics software package, because not all printers obey the same set of commands.

Laser printers can produce graphics output more quickly and of better quality than dot matrix printers.

Plotters are output devices which actually draw on paper or transparencies, using pens held in a mechanical arm. Unlike dot matrix printers, they can draw unbroken straight lines, and so are particularly useful for computer aided design work. They can be very slow output devices, so they are often unsuitable for normal office applications.

Photographic output is often useful. Graphs on a VDU screen can be photographed, but the quality of picture that this produces is variable. A fairly recent development is a special item of hardware, the Polaroid Palette, which can be used to make 35mm slides by taking data from the graphics program itself rather than from the image on the screen.

Improvements in the quality of computer graphics

There have been some significant improvements in the quality of colour display graphics recently. Some graphics packages provide the following facilities.

(a) Different *colours* can be used, either chosen from a fairly limited selection or generated by mixing the desired colours from a palette. ArtWorks Paint offers in theory 16 million colours.

(b) *Multi-level masking* enables images to be superimposed on each other, with the image behind still visible.

(c) *Colour cycling* allows colours to be animated to suggest movement, such as water flowing through a pipe.

(d) *Video feed* enables pictures from a video tape to be displayed on screen with computer graphics at the same time.

(e) The stages of image creation can be saved and replayed as a *sequence*.

(f) Images can be drawn freehand, using a mouse. Alternatively, some packages offer stencils to help you draw. A 'rubberband' feature might be offered, so that circles or ovals can be pulled to the required shape.

(g) Three dimensional graphs with shading can be generated automatically.

Activity 8

Why might a graphics package suitable for an engineer be unsuitable for an advertising agency?

5 FINANCIAL MODELLING PACKAGES

5.1 Purpose

The purpose of a financial modelling package is to allow the computer user to develop a model for financial forecasting. For example, credit terms, interest rates and the rate of inflation can be projected across a forecast time period to see how variations in these will affect company performance. Such forecasts help managers to make decisions, so financial modelling packages are often referred to as decision support systems.

Financial models can be developed using spreadsheets, and often are. But a spreadsheet is a blank matrix of cells into which the user inserts formulae and data. All the instructions for column formats and titles, all the formulae to compute the values in given cells and all the original data are keyed into the blank matrix. In contrast, with a financial modelling package, there is a spreadsheet for holding the data, but:

(a) there are *command files* which contain the program instructions about entering, manipulating and formatting the data; for example, there will be commands for the column headings and row titles and for the formulae (specified by the user when the model is first set up) for calculating data values (on a *logic file* or job file). There will also be a *report generator* file of commands to format output reports;

(b) other data might be extracted from a *data file* (whereas with a spreadsheet model the data would usually have to be keyed in). Packages may well use data which has been extracted from a database onto a data file, for example. On the other hand, input data may be keyed in, just as with a spreadsheet package.

Examples of financial modelling packages are:

(a) Micro FCS (for PCs);

(b) Microfinesse (for minicomputers);

(c) EPS (which has a PC version and a mainframe version);

(d) Plusplan (a financial modelling package for accountants).

5.2 Financial modelling packages and spreadsheet packages

Although financial modelling packages often include built-in 'what if?' functions for sensitivity analysis, they do not work interactively with the computer user. In this respect, they differ from spreadsheet packages where the user can key in 'what if' questions and receive answers more or less immediately.

Financial modelling packages have an advantage over spreadsheet packages, however, in that they are better suited to the creation of large and complex models with many different formulae, for example, models which consolidate divisional accounts and budgets. The problem with spreadsheets is that formulae have to be entered into each cell individually.

The other advantages of financial modelling packages over spreadsheet packages are as follows.

(a) They have more complex programming capabilities.

(b) More sophisticated reports can be produced.

(c) They can be used by several different users. Spreadsheets are single-user models for PCs.

Financial modelling packages such as Micro FCS can be linked in easily to other packages, such as a database or a word processing package. Output can be written onto a text file rather than being output to a printer or screen. The text file can then be fitted into other text in a word processing operation, or used as input to a database or statistical package. This can be a big advantage, for example, when there is a need to add explanations to figures in a report. There are also some, but not many, packages which provide a spreadsheet with database and word processing facilities, for example Lotus Symphony.

5.3 Forecasting packages

Software packages that prepare forecasts from historical data are available for all sizes of computer, from mainframes to PCs, varying in complexity and cost. These packages take historical data fed in by the computer user, and conduct correlation analysis and regression analysis to produce forecasts and information about the degree of confidence that can be placed in them.

Some packages include a Box-Jenkins model, which analyses source data and produces a forecasting model which best fits the historical data. A firm might use a package to forecast future results from past trends.

5.4 Risk analysis packages

Spreadsheets and financial models are not particularly good at dealing with uncertainty. 'What-if' analyses are unwieldy if the number of variables becomes large, as the number of possibilities increases. For example, assume you are manufacturing a product whose profitability depends on four variables:

(a) materials cost, which can be high or low, depending on the market;

(b) exchange rates, which can be high or low;

(c) the market which can be tough or easy;

(d) the world economy which can be good or bad.

You would need $2^4 = 16$ models to analyse every situation.

Risk analysis software aims to cope with this uncertainty, by using a probability distribution. Rather than using a large number of separate models, these situations are represented on a graph.

Predict!, a package developed in the oil industry, is used by the Post Office Counters Division to simulate arrival patterns of customers. Service demands, and so appropriate staffing levels, can be planned in advance.

With such a package, not only is factual uncertainty dealt with, but it is also possible to build in the potentially conflicting objectives of a number of different strategies.

Activity 9

A company is considering the future profitability of an existing product, which has been sold for the past five years. Increases in both the selling price and production costs are possible, and competitors might enter the market. List the data you would expect to be needed by a financial modelling package in order to predict the product's future profitability.

Chapter roundup

- A spreadsheet package effectively gives the user a large worksheet, on which text and numbers may be entered.
- Calculations may be performed automatically, and reperformed if any numbers are changed, by the use of formulae.
- Facilities available with spreadsheet packages include cell editing, rearrangement of the spreadsheet, copying of formulae, formatting and macros.
- Word processing is a sophisticated form of typing with many additional facilities.
- Word processing facilities include editing of existing documents, headers and footers (with page numbers if required), variations in typescript and shading.
- Macros, stylesheets and communication between computers may also be available with word processing packages.
- Desktop publishing offers more sophisticated presentation techniques than word processing, including the preparation of complete page layouts with both text and photographs.
- Computers can present data in a variety of graphical formats, and can output graphs to VDU screens, to paper or to photographic slides.
- Financial modelling packages can build up models using historical data, probability distributions and other statistical methods. They can predict different outcomes and the risks involved.

Quick quiz

1 Why are window commands useful when working with spreadsheets?
2 What mathematical functions are commonly available with spreadsheets?
3 How do relative cell addresses differ from absolute cell addresses?
4 What sorts of user interfaces are used in word processing packages?

5   How is a spell-checker used?

6   What, in a word processing package, is a macro?

7   What are the important features which desktop publishing software should have?

8   What are graphics cards used for?

9   What is CAD?

10 How does a plotter work?

11 What does a command file in a financial modelling package contain?

12 What are the advantages of financial modelling packages over spreadsheet packages?

Answers to activities

1   The computer cannot work out the value in A2 until it knows the value in A3, and it cannot work out the value in A3 until it knows the value in A2. Furthermore, the value in A2 must be 2 less than the value in A3, but the value in A3 must also be 5 less than the value in A2, which is impossible.

2   +C5+B8+B9, or = C5 + B8 + B9

3   @SUM(D16..D20)*(+E18-F16), or = SUM (D16: D20) * (E18 - F16)

4   Requests for suppliers' catalogues; letters to confirm appointments; contracts for major sales; debt collection letters

5   Typing facilities, including spell-checking, correction of text, typescript variations and proportional spacing; page headers and footers; the ability to incorporate tables of figures taken from spreadsheets, and to perform simple calculations; graphics facilities and the ability to incorporate graphs prepared using graphics packages

6   The magazine could be produced quickly and entirely under the organisation's control; pictures (for example, of staff sports teams) could be incorporated easily; contributions from throughout the organisation could be submitted on disk and incorporated directly, thus avoiding re-typing.

7   There would probably be a wire frame drawing of the whole building, and then line graphics plans of individual floors and rooms. Overall costs over five years could be shown on a line graph or a bar chart. Such graphs could also be used for individual items of expenditure (such as rent over the next five years). Pie charts could be used to show the elements in the total cost for each year.

8   Engineers require precisely drawn lines, but usually only need drawings in one colour. Advertising agencies need to be able to use photographs, in full colour.

9   Sales data for the past five years; expected inflation rates for selling prices and costs; expected changes in the size of the market; expected changes in the company's share of the market.

Further question practice

Now try the following practice questions at the end of this text.

Multiple choice questions   **39 to 45**

Exam style question   **5**

Chapter 7

APPLICATIONS SOFTWARE

Introduction

In this chapter, we will look at software for specific business applications. Before we do so, however, we need to identify the different areas of a business which might need applications software.

Your objectives

After completing this chapter you should:

(a) be able to analyse a business into subsystems by function;

(b) appreciate the effect of integrating the data processing parts of subsystems;

(c) appreciate how computers can be used in the marketing function;

(d) be able to list the files, input and output for a typical computerised sales ledger;

(e) appreciate the uses of computers in the production function;

(f) be able to list the files, input and output for a typical computerised purchase ledger;

(g) know the main features of computerised stock control and payroll systems;

(h) be aware of the functions of the nominal ledger and of budgeting systems.

1 SUBSYSTEMS BY FUNCTION

A business consists of many parts or subsystems, and each part will be divided into further smaller parts, or sub-subsystems. Each subsystem or sub-subsystem should be:

(a) clearly distinguishable as a recognisable unit, function or operation; and

(b) related to other subsystems within the overall system, so as to achieve good co-ordination and co-operation between all the subsystems.

Co-ordination between subsystems will be achieved by the flow of relevant information between them.

Subsystems analysed by function include:

(a) sales and marketing;

(b) production, including purchasing and stock control;

(c) personnel, including payroll;

(d) finance and administration.

The data processing part of each subsystem may be integrated with those of the others, so that data entered in one subsystem will be passed automatically or by simple operator request through into any other subsystem where the data is of some relevance.

For example, if there is an input into the invoicing subsystem authorising the despatch of an invoice to a customer, there might be automatic links to:

(a) the sales ledger, to update the file by posting the invoice to the customer's account;

(b) the stock subsystem, to update the stock file by:

    (i) reducing the quantity and value of stock in hand;

    (ii) recording the stock movement;

(c) the nominal ledger, to update the file by posting the sale to the sales account;

(d) the job costing subsystem, to record the sales value of the job on the job cost file;

(e) the report generator, to update the sales analysis and sales totals which are on file and awaiting inclusion in management reports.

2 THE SALES AND MARKETING FUNCTION

Marketing is not simply the task of selling goods which are produced or services which are offered; it is a means of trying to ensure in advance that the goods produced or services offered are what potential customers want and will buy. Selling is only one aspect of the marketing process. Marketing is concerned with events before the act of selling (such as research and product development) and after the act of selling (after-sales service).

2.1 Functions

The principal functions of marketing management are market research, advertising and sales promotion, public relations, selling, servicing and methods of payment and credit. The organisation of marketing management is fairly standard across industry. A marketing director will usually report directly to the chief executive or managing director. Reporting to the marketing director there may be a sales manager, a merchandising manager (responsible for advertising and public relations) a market research manager and a service manager.

2.2 Data requirements

Many of the data processing needs of the marketing function are suitable for computerised methods. Typical data requirements within the department would include:

(a) data for market research, including the results of surveys, needed to determine marketing strategy. Widely used databases to giving information on potential customers include Mosaic and Acorn.

(b) data relating to the success or failure of advertising. You may yourself have been asked where you heard of a product or service which you have ordered;

(c) data relating to sales and distribution. This may include:

(i) customer orders and enquiries;

(ii) sales made by each salesperson and commission earned;

(iii) sales per outlet, per geographical area or per product;

(iv) comparisons with budget;

(d) data relating to after-sales service and warranty work.

2.3 Use of systems in marketing

A typical use of computer systems in marketing and market research would be a *customer database*. Details of customers would be accessed based on a variety of different criteria, such as age. This means that various types of customers can be targeted for direct mail. To reach a small market by direct mail is much cheaper than advertising on television. Knowing who your potential customers are is likely to save money in the long run.

Activity 1

What criteria might be used to select customers from a database for a direct mail campaign?

3 THE SALES LEDGER

3.1 Purpose

While a marketing system ensures sales are made, there should always be a system to record and process them, and to ensure that invoices are correct and that customers pay up. The sales ledger system:

(a) keeps the sales ledger up to date;

(b) produces output such as statements, sales analysis reports and responses to customer file interrogations. The output might be produced daily (day book listings), monthly (statements), quarterly (sales analysis reports) or as required (responses to file interrogations, or customer name and address lists printed on adhesive labels for despatching catalogues).

3.2 Features

The input data must be sufficient to allow the user to keep the sales ledger file up to date and, together with the data on this file, it must be capable of producing the desired output. The file data, output and input might be as follows.

(a) *The sales ledger file*

(i) *Standing data for each record (one record for each customer)*

(1) Customer account number

(2) Customer name

(3) Address

(4) Credit limit

(5) Account sales analysis code

(6) Account type (open item or balance forward)*

* Where the number of invoices for a customer each month is small, and the customer usually pays promptly, the customer's account may be processed by the balance forward method. With this method, there is no attempt to identify individual invoice debts; instead, the customer's balance is maintained in total. The only check on the customer is that he does not exceed his total credit limit. In contrast, the open item method identifies specific invoices, and credits individual payments against specific invoices. Late payments of individual invoices can be identified and chased up.

(ii) *Variable data relating to transactions*

(1) Transaction date

(2) Transaction description

(3) Transaction code

(4) Debit

(5) Credit

(6) Balance

(b) *Output*

(i) *Day book listing*: a list of all transactions posted each day. This provides an audit trail. Batch and control totals will be included in the listing.

(ii) *Invoices.*

(iii) *Statements*, produced monthly for customers.

(iv) *Aged debtors list.* Probably produced monthly.

(v) *Sales analysis reports.* These will analyse sales according to the sales analysis codes on the sales ledger file.

(vi) *Debtors reminder letters.* Letters can be produced automatically to chase late payers when the due date for payment goes by without payment having been received.

(vii) *Customer lists* (or perhaps selective lists). Lists might be printed onto adhesive labels, for sending out circulars.

(viii) *Responses to enquiries*, perhaps output onto a VDU screen rather than as printed copy.

(ix) *Output onto disk file for other modules.*

(c) *Input data*

(i) *Amendments*

(1) Amendments to customer details, for example changes of addresses or credit limits

(2) Insertion of new customers

(3) Deletion of old customers

(ii) *Transaction data*

    (1) Sales transactions, for invoicing

    (2) Customer payments

    (3) Credit notes

    (4) Adjustments (debit or credit items)

Activity 2

Which other parts of a computerised accounting system might receive data directly from the sales ledger?

4 THE PRODUCTION FUNCTION

The function of the production director is to provide an agreed volume of products within an agreed delivery plan and at a pre-planned cost and level of quality, and also to achieve a planned return on assets employed.

Production systems involve the following.

(a) The organisation and operation of the manufacturing department and assembly department.

(b) The provision of a production engineering capability to plan manufacturing methods, the use of tools, the design of machine tools and so on.

(c) The provision of a purchasing activity capable of buying the raw materials, components, tools and equipment necessary for manufacturing.

(d) The provision of a quality control department to ensure adequate quality commensurate with cost, by inspection at various stages of manufacture and assembly and by testing finished products.

(e) The provision of a production control department. The problems of economic machine loading and the satisfaction of customers' requirements is one of the most complex in modern factory management. Most large companies now handle this complicated activity with the help of computers.

(f) Maintaining the efficiency of the company's plant, buildings and tools by establishing and controlling a maintenance department.

(g) The provision of economic and efficient storage of consumable goods, raw materials and components, with records capable of ensuring that quantities held in stock are within the predetermined budgets.

Production management information systems provide information to help with the planning and control of production. Computer systems are being used in a number of contexts in advanced manufacturing environments.

Just-in-time (JIT) systems are used to monitor, in detail, the flow of stock and components through the system, to minimise inventory levels. This is done to reduce the costs (such as warehousing costs) of high stock levels. *Material requirements planning* (MRP) systems are used to plan backwards from expected output to materials and subassemblies required, taking into account purchase delivery and production lead times. *Computer integrated manufacture* (CIM) is the integration of a number of manufacturing systems so that stock control is integrated with process control.

Computer aided design (CAD) is the use of advanced computer graphics in product design. In particular this reduces the amount of time needed to be spent on technical drawing.

Activity 3

Outline how computers could be used in production planning by a printing company, which has several presses and receives orders for a wide variety of sizes and numbers of copies of books.

5 THE PURCHASE LEDGER

5.1 Purpose

Purchasing is one of the necessary support services provided by the accounting function to the production function. At the same time, management of creditors is important in managing an organisation's working capital. If creditors are not paid, then they might cease to make supplies. If they are paid too soon, this might cost overdraft interest.

5.2 Features

The simplest purchase system is one where the computer is used to maintain the purchase ledger and produce a purchase analysis. The file data, input and output might be as follows.

(a) *Purchase ledger file*

   (i) *Standing data for each record (one record for each supplier)*

      (1) Account number

      (2) Name

      (3) Address

      (4) Credit details

      (5) Bank details

      (6) Cash discount details, if appropriate

  (ii) *Variable data relating to transactions*

      (1) Transaction date

      (2) Transaction description

      (3) Transaction code

      (4) Debit

      (5) Credit

      (6) Balance

(b) *Input data*

   (i) *Amendments*

      (1) Amendments to supplier details, for example, changes of addresses

      (2) Insertion of new suppliers

      (3) Deletion of old suppliers

  (ii) *Transaction data*

      (1) Purchase transactions and invoices received

      (2) Payments made

      (3) Credit notes received

      (4) Adjustments (debit or credit items)

(c) *Output*

   (i)   Lists of transactions posted, produced every time the system is run.

   (ii)   An analysis of expenditure for nominal ledger purposes, may be produced every time the system is run or at the end of each month.

   (iii) A list of creditors' balances together with a reconciliation between the total balance brought forward, the transactions for the month and the total balance carried forward.

   (iv) Copies of creditors' accounts.

   (v)   Details of payments to be made, for example:

      (1) remittance advices (usually a copy of the ledger account);

      (2) cheques;

      (3) credit transfer listings.

   (vi) Other special reports for:

      (1) costing purposes;

      (2) updating records about fixed assets;

      (3) comparisons with budget.

Activity 4

A foundry works on a small number of different projects, all specifically ordered by customers, at any one time. How might information from the production planning system be used to check the accuracy of information on the purchases ledger?

6   STOCK CONTROL

6.1   Purpose

Computerised stock control systems vary widely. The simplest types involve just updating a stock file from movement records. In a manufacturing company it is necessary to distinguish between different categories of stocks (raw materials, work in progress, finished goods and consumable stores) and appropriate internal movement documents will be required. In on-line computer systems it would be possible to give customers up-to-date information on stock availability. A good stock control system should reduce working capital that would otherwise be tied up in stocks.

6.2   Features

The main features of a simple stock control system are:

(a) inputs, which would include data about:

   (i)   goods received notes;

   (ii)   issues to production;

   (iii) production to finished goods store;

   (iv) despatch notes;

   (v)   adjustments;

(b) outputs, which would include:

   (i)   details of stock movements, produced every time the system is run. Summary movements listings may also be produced less frequently as management reports;

(ii) stock balances produced as required, perhaps weekly;

(iii) stock valuation lists, produced at the end of each accounting period;

(c) files used. The main file is the stock ledger. There would be a record on file for each stock item, and record fields might include:

(i) stock number;

(ii) description;

(iii) standard cost;

(iv) quantity in stock.

If summary movements schedules are produced it will also be necessary to maintain the appropriate details on file.

Another important role common to many stock control systems is the identification of slow moving items. A print-out will be obtained of all materials and products whose turnover has failed to reach a predetermined level over a specified time.

It is also normal for the results of physical stock counts to be matched against the stock file so that a list of differences can be printed out. This should be done as often as necessary to enable wastage and pilferage to be identified and to allow the stock files to be corrected.

Stock control systems can be automated so that stock movements are recorded by bar codes. Bar code readers used in shops can alter stock files as transactions occur. Shops depend on good stock control systems to ensure that they are able to respond swiftly to changes in consumer requirements.

7   OTHER SYSTEMS

7.1   Payroll

The main features of a payroll system are:

(a) inputs, which include:

(i) clock cards or time sheets (sometimes both are used). Details of overtime worked will normally be shown on these documents;

(ii) amounts of bonus or appropriate details if the bonus is calculated by the computer;

(iii) annual salary, where appropriate.

(b) outputs, which include:

(i) payslips;

(ii) the payroll;

(iii) a payroll analysis, including an analysis of deductions (tax, national insurance and so on) and details for costing purposes;

(iv) a note and coin analysis, cheques or credit transfer forms as appropriate;

(v) in some cases, a magnetic tape, cassette or floppy disk with payment details, for despatch to the bank and payment through the BACS system;

(c) files used. The master file will hold two types of data in respect of each employee:

(i) standing data, including personal details, rates of pay and details of deductions (including a tax code);

(ii) transaction data, including gross pay to date, tax to date and pension contributions.

Activity 5

When a new employee joins a large organisation, why should it not be possible for the ordinary payroll clerks to add the employee's details to the payroll master file?

7.2 The nominal ledger

The nominal ledger is the nucleus of any accounting system. It contains details of assets, liabilities, capital, income and expenditure, and consequently profit or loss.

Some nominal ledgers are structured as stand-alone systems, so that every transaction or group of transactions has to be input as a separate process. Others are posted automatically from related accounting subsystems.

7.3 Budgeting

The budgeting process is a key activity in any organisation. It is usually co-ordinated by the finance department. Larger organisations might set up a budget committee.

The budget committee does not *prepare* budgets. This is done by functional departments, with the finance function usually taking responsibility for central costs. The traditional approach to budgeting starts by assuming that last year's activities will continue at the same volume, and that next year's budget can be based on last year's costs and revenues amended to allow for expected expansion, contraction and other factors like inflation.

Budgets prepared at departmental level are consolidated centrally, in the same way as actual results are consolidated at the end of each management or financial reporting period.

Activity 6

What inputs and outputs would you expect to find in a budgeting system?

Chapter roundup

- The data processing parts of a business's subsystems may be integrated, so that transactions need only be entered once.
- Computers can be used to conduct market research, to design products to meet customers' requirements and to facilitate the distribution of promotional literature.
- The sales ledger keeps track of sales made and payments received. A record is kept for each customer, and the master file is updated with transactions data.
- Computers can be used to schedule and control production, to ensure that raw materials are available when needed and that finished goods are ready when required by customers, and to design new products.
- The purchase ledger keeps track of purchases and payments made for them. A record is kept for each supplier.

> ## Chapter roundup (*continued*)
>
> - A stock control system both records stock movements and provides the information needed for managers to control stock levels.
> - A payroll system records details for each employee and computes the amounts to be paid on each payday.
> - The nominal ledger collects together all the information on income, expenses, assets and liabilities and thus enables the business's profit or loss to be calculated.

Quick quiz

1   List some functional subsystems of a business.
2   What sorts of data will a marketing department collect?
3   What fields are likely to be contained in records for individual customers in the sales ledger?
4   What is MRP?
5   List the typical outputs from a purchase ledger system.
6   List the typical inputs to a stock control system.
7   List the typical outputs from a payroll system.

Answers to activities

1   Age, area of residence, likely cost of house or flat, whether a car owner, likely income, credit cards held and so on.
2   Stock control, so that goods which are selling well are re-ordered; cash recording, so that payments by customers can be followed through to the company's bank account.
3   The company will want to keep all its presses busy, or at least not have work waiting to be done while a press is idle. A computer could maintain a work schedule for each press. On being given details of a new book, it could search the work schedules for a space on an appropriate press, taking into account the customer's deadline.
4   Goods should only be bought for particular orders. Thus it should be possible to relate all purchases (as shown in the purchases ledger) to products recorded in the production planning system.
5   If it were possible, the clerks could use the same procedure to add fictitious employees to the payroll, diverting the net pay into their own bank accounts.
6   *Inputs*

Last year's actual results; last year's budgets

Estimates of changes in sales volume

Estimates of changes in selling prices

Estimates of changes in costs

Outputs

Detailed budgets for separate departments

An overall budgeted profit and loss account

Further question practice

Now try the following practice questions at the end of this text.

Multiple choice questions   **46 to 52**

Exam style question   **6**

Chapter 8

MANAGEMENT INFORMATION SYSTEMS

Introduction

In the last chapter we examined a range of transaction processing, or data processing, systems; these could be said to represent the lowest level in an organisation's use of information systems. They are used for routine tasks in which data items or transactions must be processed so that operations can continue.

Transaction processing systems provide the raw material which is often used more extensively by management information systems. In other words, transaction processing systems might be used to produce management information, such as reports on cumulative sales figures to date, total amounts owed to suppliers or owed by debtors, total stock turnover to date, value of current stock-in-hand, and so on, but the main purpose of transaction processing systems is operational, as an integral part of day-to-day operations.

The term management information system (MIS) can be defined in a number of different ways. One definition is that it is a system to convert data from internal and external sources into information and to communicate that information, in an appropriate form, to managers at all levels in all functions to enable them to make timely and effective decisions for planning, directing and controlling the activities for which they are responsible.

The scope of an MIS, potentially, is to satisfy all the informational needs of management. A good MIS will provide good information to those who need it. Whether this is possible will depend to some degree on the nature and type of information provided. An MIS is good at providing regular formal information gleaned from normal commercial data. It may be less efficient at presenting information which is relatively unpredictable, or informal, or unstructured.

In this chapter, we look at management information systems and then develop the discussion into a study of specific types of MIS: decision support systems, executive information systems and expert systems.

Your objectives

After completing this chapter you should:

(a) know the differences between strategic, tactical and operational information;

(b) know the differences between planning, control and operating information;

(c) appreciate how management information systems for the different levels of information differ;

(d) be aware of the general characteristics of information;

(e) be aware of the different ways in which management information can be presented;

(f) know the features of decision support systems, executive information systems and expert systems;

(g) appreciate the different roles of the different types of management information system.

104

1 INFORMATION

Management information systems (MIS) are systems to gather, process and distribute information within an organisation, in order that management can take informed decisions. The development of information technology means that management information can be provided quicker and more cheaply than before, and that managers can have greater involvement in information production and report design.

1.1 Levels of information

Information within an organisation (as distinct from information provided by an organisation to external users, such as shareholders, the general public, pressure groups, competitors, suppliers and customers) can be analysed into three levels.

(a) *Strategic information* is used by senior managers to plan the objectives of their organisation, and to assess whether the objectives are being met in practice. Such information includes overall profitability, the profitability of different segments of the business, future market prospects, the availability and cost of new funds, total cash needs, total manning levels and capital equipment needs. Much of this information must come from outside sources, although internally generated information will always be used. Strategic information is used in *strategic planning*.

(b) *Tactical information* is used by middle management. Such information includes productivity measurements (output per man hour or per machine hour), budgetary control or variance analysis reports, and cash flow forecasts, manning levels and profit results within a particular department of the organisation. A large proportion of this information will be generated from within the organisation and is likely to have an accounting emphasis. Tactical information is usually prepared regularly, perhaps weekly or monthly (whereas strategic information is communicated irregularly) and it is used in *management control*.

(c) *Operational information* is used by 'front-line' managers such as foremen or head clerks to ensure that specific tasks are planned and carried out properly within a factory or office. In the payroll office, for example, operational information will include each employee's hours worked each week, rate of pay per hour, details of deductions and, for the purpose of wages analysis, details of the time spent on individual jobs during the week. In this example, the information is required weekly, but more urgent operational information, such as the amount of raw materials being input to a production process, may be required daily, hourly, or in the case of automated production, second by second. Operational information is used in *operational control*.

The amount of detail provided in information is likely to vary with the purpose for which it is needed, and operational information is likely to go into much more detail than tactical information, which in turn will be more detailed than strategic information. What is information to one level of management or one department may be raw data (needing to be processed) to another. Supervisors, for example, will check the output of each worker within the area of their responsibility but their superiors may only wish to know about the performance of sections as a whole.

Data and information

In normal everyday speech the terms data and information are used interchangeably. However, in the context of data processing and information systems the terms have distinct meanings.

(a) *Data* relates to facts, events, and transactions and so forth.

(b) *Information* is data that has been processed in such a way as to be meaningful to the person who receives it.

Definition

Data is the raw material for data processing

An example might make things clear. Many companies providing a product or service like to research consumer opinion and employ market research organisations to do so. A typical market research survey employs a number of researchers who request a sample of the public (or the target market) to answer a number of questions relating to the product. Several hundred questionnaires may be completed. The questionnaires, which contain data, are input to a system. Once every questionnaire has been input, a number of processing operations are performed on the data. A report which summarises the results and discusses their significance is sent to the company that commissioned the survey. The processing operations carried out to obtain the results include classifying, sorting, calculating and summarising.

Individually, a completed questionnaire would not tell the company very much, only the views of one consumer. In this case, the individual questionnaires are *data*. Once they have been processed, and analysed, the resulting report is *information*: the company will use it to inform its decisions regarding the product. If the report revealed that consumers disliked the product, the company would scrap or alter it.

The quality of source data affects the value of information. Information is worthless if the source data is flawed. If the researchers filled in questionnaires themselves, inventing the answers, then the conclusions drawn from the processed data would be wrong, and poor decisions would be made.

1.2 Planning, control and operating information

Another way of categorising information is into planning, operating and control information. This overlaps with the previous analysis by level.

(a) *Planning information* is information needed to formulate plans and consider alternative courses of action. It will include forecasts (such as demand forecasts or forecasts of increases in prices and wages) and estimates of environmental conditions, such as likely actions by competitors or possible legislation.

Planning information may be based on historical data, but is essentially forward-looking and so, inevitably, it will be subject to uncertainty. When plans depend on environmental information, there is also likely to be some difficulty in obtaining all the relevant information.

(b) *Control information* is information which provides a comparison between actual results and the plan. Control information cannot exist without a plan or target. *Feedback* is the key concept in the use of control information. The value of control information in an organisation will depend largely on the qualities of the information – its relevance, accuracy, comprehensiveness, timeliness and who receives it. Frequent criticisms of control information are that it arrives too late to be of any use and that it contains information about matters outside the control of the person who receives it. Sometimes the person receiving it does not rely on it, perhaps suspecting it of being inaccurate or incomplete.

(c) *Operating information* is information which is needed for the conduct of daily operations. It includes much transaction data, such as data about customer orders, purchases, cash receipts and payments. Operating information must usually be consolidated into totals in management reports before it becomes management control information.

Activity 1

How would you classify each of the following pieces of information as strategic, tactical or operational?

(a) 27 cars were painted yesterday morning.

(b) The company will need to raise £5m in new capital over the next two years.

(c) 2,000 cars should be sold next month.

Control

A system must be controlled to keep it steady or enable it to change safely, in other words each system must have its control system. Control is required because unpredictable disturbances arise and enter the system, so that actual results (outputs of the system) deviate from the expected results or goals. Examples of disturbances in a business system would be the entry of a powerful new competitor into the market, an unexpected rise in labour costs, the failure of a supplier to deliver promised raw materials, or the tendency of employees to stop working in order to chat. A control system must ensure that the business is capable of surviving these disturbances by dealing with them in an appropriate manner.

To have a control system, there has to be a plan, standard, budget, rule book or some other sort of target or guideline towards which the system as a whole should be aiming.

Control is dependent on the receipt and processing of information. Information is processed for human beings by the biological senses of sight, sound, taste, smell and touch. Within organisations, information may be received from a variety of sources, which include the following.

(a) Formal sources within the organisation, designed by managers of the organisation.

(b) Informal sources within the organisation.

(c) Formal sources outside the organisation, ie from the environment.

(d) Informal environmental sources.

Business information is needed to plan or make rules. It is also needed to compare actual results against the plan, so as to judge what control measures, if any, are needed.

Feedback

Feedback is information. In a business organisation, it is information produced from within the organisation (for example, management control reports) with the purpose of helping management and other employees with control decisions.

Definition

Feedback is the return of part of the output of a system to the input as a means towards improved quality or correction of error.

Feedback may be defined as modification or control of a process or system by its results or effects, by measuring differences between desired and actual results. Feedback forms the link between planning and control.

2 MIS AND LEVELS OF MANAGEMENT

2.1 Operational level MIS

We have seen that operational decisions are essentially small-scale and programmed, and that operational information is often highly formal and quantitative. Many operational decisions can be made automatically by computers.

At operational level, management information systems are used for processing transactions, updating files and so forth. The inputs will be basic transaction data, and outputs will be simple reports, which have sorted or listed the input data, or documents as records of transactions, or further instructions.

2.2 Tactical level MIS

A variety of MIS can be used at the tactical level, and there may be a greater reliance than at operational level on:

(a) exception reporting;

(b) informal systems;

(c) investigation and analysis of data acquired at operational level;

(d) externally generated data.

Tactical information may be generated in the same processing operation as operational level information. For example, tactical level information comparing actual costs incurred to budgeted costs can be produced by a system in which those costs are recorded.

Functional MIS at tactical level are typically linked to other functional MIS. Information from the sales MIS will affect the financial accounting system, for example.

2.3 Strategic level MIS

At strategic level the MIS is likely to be informal, because it is not always possible to quantify strategic information and much of the information will come from outside sources. The MIS will, however, obtain summary level data from transactions processing.

2.4 A comparison of the three levels

The table shows typical inputs, processes and outputs at each level of a management information system.

	INPUTS	PROCESS	OUTPUT
Strategic	Plans	Summarise	Key ratios
	Competitor information	Investigate	*Ad hoc* market analysis
	Market information	Compare	Strategic plans
		Forecast	
Tactical	Historical data	Compare	Variance analysis
	Budget data	Classify	Exception reports
Operational	Customer orders	Update files	Updated files
	Stock control levels	Output reports	Listings
	Cash receipts		Invoices

In a finance subsystem, to take just one example, the operational level would deal with cash receipts and payments, bank reconciliations and so forth. The tactical level would deal with cash flow forecasts and working capital management. Strategic level financial issues are likely to be integrated with the organisation's commercial strategy, but may relate to the most appropriate source of finance (such as equity or long-term debt).

3 CHARACTERISTICS OF GOOD INFORMATION

Information has certain other general characteristics.

3.1 Purpose

Information must have a purpose, otherwise it is useless. It might have an immediate purpose or it might be filed away for future use, even if it is just being held because it might be needed one day.

When information is used, it should be good enough to fulfil its purpose. Whether information fulfils its purpose adequately will depend on:

(a) whether it is *relevant*;

(b) whether it is *complete*;

(c) how *accurate* it is;

(d) whether it is *clear* to the user;

(e) whether the information user has *confidence* in the information or is inclined to mistrust it.

Since information should have a purpose, the information users ought to be identifiable. The information should be designed for their needs.

3.2 Volume

The information available to an information user might vary in volume as well as scope. It is difficult for manual data processing systems to cope with very large volumes of information. In many systems, control action works on the principle of reporting by exception.

3.3 Timeliness

Information might be communicated when it is needed, or it might be delayed. Some information is needed at once whereas other items of information are not needed for some time and so must be filed away until later.

3.4 Channel of communication

Information can be communicated in a number of different ways. A path or medium by which information is transmitted is known as a channel of communication. Some examples are:

(a) written reports;

(b) graphs or visual displays;

(c) sheets of figures;

(d) telephone conversations;

(e) management meetings;

(f) informal discussions;

(g) transfers of data by computer;

(h) information obtained simply by looking around to see what is happening;

(i) TV or videos;

(j) broadcasting or announcing systems;

(k) factory noticeboards;

(l) company journals;

(m) the Internet.

3.5   Cost

Data costs money to collect and process. Information costs money to communicate and file away. The cost of having information is therefore an important characteristic of an information system because each feature or part of an MIS should not cost more than it is worth.

Activity 2

A computer sales company, which employs representatives who visit clients in their offices, uses a computer system to record all sales made by its representatives. What output from this system would you expect to see as:

(a) operational information;

(b) tactical information?

3.6   Exception reporting

The principle of exception reporting is the idea that if no decisions or actions are necessary, then a situation does not have to be reported. This means that managers can direct their attention to exceptional items and situations as a means of maintaining control.

Definition

Exception reporting is a system of reporting based on the exception principle which focuses attention on those items where performance differs significantly from standard or budget.

Slight variations between actual results and the plan may be considered acceptable, and corrective action is only applied when results exceed certain established tolerance levels. For example, a factory has six production departments and the production manager uses efficiency ratios as tolerance limits in the scheme of control. If the efficiency ratio for any department is below 95% or above 110% each week, the reasons for the low or high performance are investigated in order to decide whether control action is needed. In one week, the production manager might receive the following report (assuming that reporting by exception did not exist).

Department	Efficiency ratio	Comments
1	99	Acceptable ...
2	103	Supplier discounts were ...
3	94	Machine failure caused ...
4	106	Large production runs ...
5	98	Set-up time was ...
6	102	Acceptable ...
Overall	100	

The manager would only be interested in the poor performance of department 3. Time and effort would be saved in preparing the report, as well as for the manager, if reporting by exception were used.

Department 3 had an efficiency ratio of 94

Reasons: Problems with machine B led to ...

In the example shown, there is only a very simple control system using one measurement of performance. As a system gets larger, the volume of data being processed also increases, and the principle of exception reporting becomes more efficient and more necessary. Exception reporting is a very important element of a good management information system.

3.7 The presentation of management information

One of the qualities of good information is clarity. This has implications for MIS design, in that modern technology has greatly expanded the techniques for displaying management information. Management information can be presented in a number of ways.

(a) *Computer printouts*. Management information can be presented in printed computer reports. For relatively simple information these are cheap and easy to prepare. Once the information becomes complicated, rows of figures become harder to use.

(b) *Desktop published*. More advanced printing technology has greatly expanded the flexibility of visual presentation of management information. Graphs, charts, maps and so on can be used.

(c) *On a VDU*. Much management information is computer generated. Managers can access information with a VDU and keyboard. The advent of powerful graphics software means that the information can be manipulated, converted into graphical format and made easier to understand.

(d) *Orally*. Remember that management information, especially of the more unstructured nature, can be distributed on the grapevine.

Some management information can be presented in a group context.

(a) If senior management wish to communicate, say, a change in strategy to middle management, this can be achieved by group presentations. Videos, for example, can be used to present this type of information. Moreover, some computer graphics packages are able to manipulate video-based information so that a combination of graphics and pictures can be prepared.

(b) Another source of information is the computerised 'bulletin board' so that managers can communicate information to all their colleagues. This is a good way of sharing ideas. Computers are arranged in a network, and everybody has access to the bulletin board, which any user can put messages on.

(c) Videoconferencing can be used. PCs can be supplemented by video cameras and special hardware and software, so that managers in separate offices (perhaps in several countries) can discuss issues and can see each other on their PC screens.

(d) Intranet. The use of world wide web technology to 'publish' data on a private network.

4 DECISION SUPPORT SYSTEMS

Decision support systems (DSS) are a form of management information system. Decision support systems are used by management to aid in making unstructured decisions where it is not obvious how to work out the answer.

These complex problems are often very poorly defined with high levels of uncertainty about the true nature of the problem, the various responses which management could make or the likely impact of those actions. These highly ambiguous environments do not allow the easy application of many of the techniques or systems developed for more well-defined problems or activities. Decision support systems are intended to provide a wide range of alternative information gathering and analytical tools with a major emphasis upon flexibility and user-friendliness.

The term 'decision support systems' or DSS is usually taken to mean computer systems which are designed to produce information in such a way as to help managers make better decisions.

(a) They are now often associated with information 'at the touch of a button' on a manager's PC.

(b) DSS can range from fairly simple information models based on *spreadsheets* to *expert systems* which review data and themselves suggest solutions.

Decision support systems do not make decisions. The objective is to allow the manager to consider a number of alternatives and evaluate them under a variety of potential conditions. A key element in the usefulness of these systems is their ability to function interactively. This is a feature, for example, of spreadsheets. Managers using these systems often develop scenarios using earlier results to refine their understanding of the problem and of possible responses.

Some decision support computer systems are composed of three elements.

(a) A language subsystem used by the manager to communicate interactively with the decision support system.

(b) A problem processing subsystem which provides analytical techniques and presentation capabilities.

(c) A knowledge subsystem which holds internal data and can access any needed external data.

Many decision support systems have been developed so that they can be implemented on a wide range of hardware: fully featured systems require mainframe or minicomputers while less powerful or specialised applications may quite comfortably be used on PCs. The most common implementation is on distributed processing systems with all types of hardware so that several users may easily use the system.

A decision support system integrates many of the functions supplied by information systems so that managers may use them more easily and on a wider range of both structured and unstructured problems.

Activity 3

In which subsystem of a decision support system would you find each of the following?

(a) Monthly sales figures for the past six months

(b) Software to translate instructions such as 'compute budgeted profit' into machine code

(c) Software to compute probabilities of different outcomes

---

5 EXECUTIVE INFORMATION SYSTEMS

An executive information system (EIS) is a type of management information system, and takes the form of PCs on executives' desks linked to the organisation's other computer systems. An EIS is likely to have the following features.

(a) Provision of summary-level data, taken from the organisation's main systems.

(b) A facility which allows the executive to 'drill down' from higher levels of information to lower levels (for example, from total sales to sales of particular products).

(c) Data manipulation facilities, such as comparison with budget or trend analysis.

(d) Graphics, for user-friendly presentation of data.

(e) A template system. Using this, the same type of data (such as sales figures) is presented in the same format, irrespective of changes in the volume of information required.

A good EIS should adhere to the following design philosophy.

(a) It should be easy to use, as it may be consulted during a meeting, for example.

(b) It should make data easy to access, so that the EIS describes the organisation from the executive's point of view, not just in terms of its data flows.

(c) It should provide tools for analysis (including ratio analysis, forecasts, what-if analysis and trends).

(d) It should provide presentational aids so that information can be conveyed in a readily comprehensible form.

Many of the features described can be provided by spreadsheets. However, an EIS is not only a tool for analysis, but also a tool for interrogating data (drilling down, as mentioned above).

6 EXPERT SYSTEMS

An expert system is a program with access to a large amount of specialised data, for example on legal, tax, engineering or medical matters. The user keys in certain facts and the program uses its information on file to produce a decision about something on which an expert's decision would normally be required. For example:

(a) a user without a legal background can obtain guidance on the law without having to consult a solicitor;

(b) doctors can use an expert medical system to arrive at a diagnosis.

Definition

Expert systems are computer programs which allow users to benefit from expert knowledge and information, and also give advice.

Applications of expert systems include:

(a) locating the most relevant data from a database;

(b) identifying the causes of problems, for example in production control systems or in medical applications;

(c) credit scoring.

Expert systems can be written from scratch, in specialised artificial intelligence programming languages such as PROLOG or LISP. Alternatively, an expert system can be bought off-the-shelf as a 'shell', that is a package which is empty of information but with a rule structure already in place.

An expert system has four parts.

(a) The *knowledge base* contains facts (such as 'a rottweiler is a dog') and rules (such as 'if you see a dog, then run away').

(b) The *knowledge acquisition program* is a program which enables the expert system to learn new facts and rules.

(c) The *inference engine* is the software which executes the reasoning. It needs to discern which rules apply, and allocate weights to different factors.

(d) The *user interface* is the means by which the expert system communicates with the user. The expert system may be designed to accept enquiries in something very close to everyday English.

Activity 4

How might an expert system be useful to a credit controller?

7 MIS AND DECISION MAKING

Problems requiring decisions can be: structured, semi-structured or unstructured.

7.1 Structured decision

A *structured* decision can also be described as a programmable decision, in that unambiguous decision rules can be specified in advance. Many structured decisions are automated, although they do not have to be. Structured decisions can often be characterised as routine and frequently repeated. Little or no human judgement is required. An organisation can prepare a decision procedure for a structured decision. This consists of a series of steps to be followed, and may be expressed in the form of, for example, a flowchart or a decision table. Examples of structured decisions include stock re-order formulae and rules for granting credit to customers.

7.2 Unstructured decision

An *unstructured* decision is said to be non-programmable. It cannot be pre-planned in the same way that a structured decision can be. It will usually occur less frequently and will be non-routine. There is no pre-prepared decision procedure for an unstructured decision, either because it does not occur frequently enough to warrant one or because it is too complex. Data requirements cannot be fully known in advance and so data retrieval may include *ad hoc* requests. Unstructured decisions usually involve a high degree of human judgement.

7.3 Semi-structured decision

A *semi-structured* decision falls somewhere between the two categories described. It is likely to involve an element of human judgement and to have characteristics of standard procedures with some programmed elements.

7.4 Strategic, tactical and operational levels of information

You will also recall the division into information at strategic, tactical and operational levels.

Given that the aim of any management information system is to provide managers with information, we have to assess how well a formal MIS can do so.

Strategic information is:

(a) derived from both internal and external sources;

(b) summarised at a high level;

(c) relevant to the long term;

(d) concerned with the whole organisation (although it might go into some detail);

(e) often prepared on an '*ad hoc*' basis;

(f) both quantitative and qualitative;

(g) incapable of providing complete certainty, given that the future cannot be predicted.

Tactical information is:

(a) derived from a more restricted range of external sources, so is thus primarily generated internally;

(b) summarised at a lower level – a report might be included with summaries and raw data as backup;

(c) relevant to the short and medium term;

(d) concerned with activities or departments;

(e) prepared routinely and regularly;

(f) based on quantitative measures.

Operational information is:

(a) derived almost entirely from internal sources;

(b) highly detailed, being the processing of raw data;

(c) relevant to the immediate term;

(d) task-specific;

(e) prepared constantly, or very frequently;

(f) largely quantitative.

A management information system cannot realistically provide for all the information needs of management, but tools for decision support can be provided in the format of a computer system.

(a) Executive information systems are used at strategic level, for *unstructured* problems, or perhaps even to identify problems rather than solve them.

(b) Decision support systems are not often used by top executives, being less user friendly and requiring more expertise. They are used by middle managers for routine modelling, but also to analyse unstructured problem situations for senior executives.

(c) Normal MIS provide structured information from transactions data, for all levels of management.

Chapter roundup

- Strategic information is used in strategic planning, tactical information in management control and operational information in operational control.

- Planning information is used in planning, control information in comparing plans with actual outcomes and operating information in conducting daily operations.

Chapter roundup (*continued*)

- Management information systems for different levels of information differ in their inputs, processes and outputs.
- For any information, we can consider its purpose, its volume, its timeliness, its cost and the channel of communication used.
- Management information may be communicated on paper, on VDU screens or orally.
- Decision support systems provide information in a form which helps managers to make decisions.
- Executive information systems give the user access to data at all levels, and allow that data to be analysed.
- Expert systems have their own knowledge bases and methods of inference, and can make recommendations.
- In selecting an appropriate management information system, it is important to distinguish between structured, semi-structured and unstructured decisions.

Quick quiz

1 Where is strategic information likely to be obtained?
2 List some frequent criticisms of control information.
3 What are the typical outputs of strategic, tactical and operational management information systems?
4 List some channels of communication for information.
5 For what decisions are decision support systems appropriate?
6 What are the main features of an executive information system?
7 What are the main components of an expert system?
8 How do semi-structured decisions differ from unstructured decisions?

Answers to activities

1 (a) Operational
  (b) Strategic
  (c) Tactical
2 (a) Sales made each day by each representative
  (b) Sales made each month by each representative, in each geographical area and by the company as a whole.
3 (a) The knowledge subsystem
  (b) The language subsystem
  (c) The problem processing subsystem
4 It could consider a defaulting customer's recent payment record, and suggest whether an ordinary statement, a reminder letter or a letter threatening legal action is most likely to lead to prompt payment. It could also consider financial information about a prospective customer, and suggest how much credit, if any, should be allowed to him.

Further question practice

Now try the following practice questions at the end of this text.

Multiple choice questions   **53 to 59**

Chapter 9

DATABASES

Introduction

A database is an example of a general purpose system. The concept is based on considering what information can be provided and then suiting that to the needs of particular applications, rather than beginning with the needs of particular applications. A typical accounting application package processes only one sort of data. A payroll file processes only payroll data and a stock file only stock data. The database overcomes the problems and inefficiencies inherent in such an approach.

Your objectives

After completing this chapter you should:

(a) be able to distinguish between application specific files and databases;

(b) be able to state the advantages and disadvantages of a database system;

(c) be aware of some of the uses of the database approach;

(d) understand the concepts of data independence and data redundancy;

(e) know how a database is administered and operated;

(f) be able to distinguish between the three different types of database;

(g) be aware of some of the general features of database packages.

1 APPLICATION SPECIFIC FILES VERSUS DATABASES

Any organisation will keep a large amount of information in files, whether manual or computerised. If an organisation uses a system of application specific files, this means that there is a set of files dedicated to each business function, with each set being accessed by a separate program. For example, the sales function will use its own files to process orders and record sales, the stock control department will maintain its own files and the purchasing department will maintain purchase ordering and bought ledger records.

These files are likely to have some data in common. This is called data redundancy.

(a) The sales files will have customer details, despatch notes and invoices.

(b) The stock control files will have details of goods despatched, customers and goods inwards.

(c) The purchasing files will contain details of goods ordered and goods received.

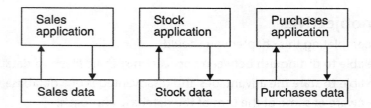

Figure 9.1 The application specific file approach

Application specific files are common where computerisation is patchy or not approached in a systematic way. With 'islands of automation', application specific files will develop inevitably. They are found where information technology is widely used in an organisation, but where there are a variety of competing systems, perhaps using incompatible hardware and/or software, and where the use of stand-alone computers has encouraged the growth of application specific files. The main problems with such files are as follows.

(a) Different functions of the organisation are kept artificially separate.

(b) They are not easily accessed by other applications.

(c) Two files which should contain the same data might come to contain different data.

In the *database* approach, there is only one set of data, which is accessed by all applications.

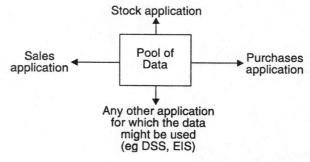

Figure 9.2 The database approach

Activity 1

Give some examples of how two application specific files could come to contain conflicting data.

2 DATABASES FOR MANAGEMENT INFORMATION

The database approach can be used for a wide variety of functions. A database is built up, updated and accessed using a program called a database management system (DBMS). Access is a leading DBMS for PCs, and Oracle is one for larger systems.

2.1 The advantages of database systems

The advantages of database systems are as follows.

(a) Unnecessary duplication of data is avoided. Data can be used for many purposes but only needs to be input and stored once. For example, the code number and name of each raw material item will be input and stored once, instead of several times for a stock control system, a production control system and a purchase ledger system. The *drawback* to single entry input is that one department must accept responsibility for the accuracy of the input.

(b) A database provides data for the organisation as a whole, not just for individual departments. The database concept encourages management to regard data as a resource that must be properly managed just as any other resource. The installation of a database system encourages management to analyse data, relationships between data items and how data is used in different applications.

(c) The organisation of data into a database, rather than into separate files, encourages the integration of data and makes data more widely available.

(d) Because each item of data is only held in one place, it is easier to ensure that it is up to date, so that no department in an organisation uses out-of-date data, or data that differs from the data used by other departments.

(e) Data is independent of the user programs that access the data. This allows greater flexibility in the ways that data can be used. New programs can be easily introduced to make use of existing data in new ways. A database can also be easily extended and then more user programs can be developed for these additions, without affecting existing application programs. In other words, a database can be evolved as the user's data needs evolve.

(f) Developing new application programs with a database is easier than developing them without one, because the programmer is not responsible for the data organisation, which is already taken care of by the DBMS software.

(g) 'Off-the-shelf' DBMS software packages can be obtained, and so the cost of installing a database can be reduced.

2.2 The disadvantages of database systems

The disadvantages of database systems are being reduced as DBMS become more sophisticated. Current disadvantages are as follows.

(a) There are problems of data security and data privacy. Forms of control include control of terminal access, user identification and restrictions on access by certain users to certain programs or certain parts of the database. However, because of the widespread access by a variety of users to the same database, the potential for unauthorised access to data creates a serious problem. Problems of data security are increasingly handled by DBMS software. Even so, administrative procedures for data security must supplement software controls.

Definition

Data security is preserving data from alteration by unauthorised people. *Data privacy* is preserving the confidentiality of certain data.

(b) Since there is only one set of data, it is essential that the data should be accurate and free from corruption. The responsibility for ensuring the integrity of the data might have to be delegated to a data administration manager.

(c) Since data is held once, but its use is widespread, there are potential problems of recovery of data in the event of a system failure. DBMS software increasingly looks after data recovery, but management must consider the consequences of a system failure, how serious these consequences might be and how the damage could be minimised.

(d) A database implies a central store of data, but access might be required over a wide geographical area. The data itself could be spread around several computers on a single network system (a *distributed database*) , but this might add to the problems of access. A system that has users over a wide geographical area must rely on a communications network, which can be both expensive and unreliable.

2.3 Using the database approach

The database approach can be used at strategic, tactical and operational level. Just as a single database system contains data relating to, say, sales and purchase applications, so, too, information relevant to strategic, tactical and operational decisions may be contained on a single database system. This does not necessarily mean that all data is available to every user, as there can be restrictions on access to parts of the database.

Databases can be used to provide strategic information. A database cannot hope to capture all the necessary information, but it is very useful for analysing and abstracting data from current operations. An *executive information system* can only really be useful if the executive can 'drill down' into the company's database to analyse those bits of information which are of interest.

An organisation's use of databases need not be limited to the databases created by the organisation itself. Some organisations make it their business to provide information to their subscribers or to the general public. These *public databases* are becoming more common, and may provide useful strategic information.

A database approach makes it possible to produce more management control information, useful at both tactical and operational levels for the following reasons.

(a) The database can be used to provide key indicators about performance as a matter of routine.

(b) The database can be used to present the information it contains in new ways. For example, it would be a relatively easy task to change a report in a sales database from debtors analysed by size of debt, to debtors analysed by region. There is flexibility in the way that existing data can be presented. This means that new indicators can be developed, or new relationships established between variables.

(c) Many databases, especially the more advanced ones, can easily be amended, so that additional categories of information can be added. This flexibility means that management can ensure that its control measures maintain their relevance.

(d) Because databases can filter information in any way required, they are increasingly being used as part of the marketing function. For example, airlines have built up profiles of 'frequent fliers' which include their hobbies, sports and preferred reading. This enables direct and appropriate targeting of potential and actual customers.

However, when using databases for marketing purposes two points should be borne in mind.

(i) The requirements and restrictions of the Data Protection Act 1984.

(ii) The success of any marketing operation depends on the quality of the information being filtered, and how up-to-date this information is. Use of the database is supplementary to, not a replacement for, standard market research procedures.

Databases can introduce flexibility into the *identification* of possible control information, the *presentation* of that information and the *updating* of the control measures used.

The banks use a database approach in marketing. They used to operate data processing on an *account* basis. This meant that it was not really possible for the information system to give information about *customers*: a customer who had a current account and a mortgage would appear on two accounting systems, with different codes. Barclays' Customer Information System takes a database approach to address this problem by ensuring that a financial profile of the customer can be drawn up by the computer. This is a valuable aid to marketing.

Activity 2

In a database system, might there be reasons for preventing senior executives from having access to operational information?

2.4   Data independence and data redundancy

Two important and related concepts in database design are *data independence* and *data redundancy*.

Suppose you wish to store four records (A, B, C and D) in a storage device which has a maximum storage capacity of four records. This means that there are only four positions (1, 2, 3 and 4) where records can be stored.

You wish to access the records in alphabetical order. If this is the case, on a sequentially organised file, record A would be stored in position 1, B in position 2 and so on. On a non-sequential file, however, the records could, for example, be stored with C in position 1, B in position 4, A in position 2 and D in position 3. However, as far as you, the user, are concerned, this makes no difference at all, as you can still access the data in the logical order by providing the software used to access records with an index to where records A, B, C and D are stored. Even if you decide to change the order in which you wish to use the data (perhaps to D, C, B, A) this need not affect their physical position on the storage medium.

The point of this example is to indicate the difference (which is particularly important in the design of databases, although not exclusive to them) between *logical data structures* and *physical data structures*. The logical relationship between items of data need have no bearing on where they are physically stored.

The independence of logical structures from physical structures, and the independence of data items from the programs which access them, is referred to as *data independence.*

Additionally, you might wish to use information from several records. Where this is the case, it is desirable to create *logical records* that access the relevant data but avoid having to duplicate it within separate physical records. The use of logical records then permits data to be organised and manipulated without disturbing the physical records.

The use of *database systems* has permitted programmers and users to focus on the logical relationships which are of importance in using information. The database system takes over the mechanics involved in handling the physical storage of data and accessing it as needed.

With application specific files, data items are likely to be duplicated in, for example, separate sales, stock control and purchases system. This duplication of data items is referred to as *data redundancy*. It can have damaging effects if two records referring to the same transaction are inconsistent. This problem is generally avoided by a database system, using logical records to avoid duplicating data for different applications.

Activity 3

A company keeps all accounting records in a single database. The credit control department decides that it would like to have information on debts arranged by size of debt, instead of (as hitherto) by time since the invoice was issued. However, the finance director still wants to be provided with the information arranged by time since the invoice was issued. Explain why the database approach is particularly helpful in a case like this one.

3 DATABASE SYSTEMS

3.1 The objectives of a database system

A database system should have four major objectives.

(a) It should be *shared*. Different users should be able to access the same data in the database for their own processing applications, and at the same time if required. This removes the need to duplicate data on different files. Database systems need not be multi-user (multi-access) systems, but they are much more useful if they are. A database on a stand-alone PC can only be used by one person at a time.

(b) The *integrity* of the database must be preserved. This means that one user should not be allowed to alter the data so as to spoil the database records for other users. However, users must be able to update the data.

(c) The database system should provide for the *needs of different users*, who each have their own processing requirements and data access methods.

(d) The database should be capable of *evolving*, both in the short term (it must be kept updated) and in the longer term (it must be able to meet the future data processing needs of users, not just their current needs).

3.2 Administration of the database

The contents of the data records will be continually changing, and the types of data and the relationship between the items will also occasionally change. The DBMS will automatically re-index the records according to the changes made and provide the interface with the application programs which use and update the database. The application programs should be independent, as far as is possible, of the actual organisation of the database. The DBMS has to protect data from unauthorised access and from corruption during processing. By keeping a record of data items accessed, the DBMS can identify redundant items that should be removed from the database.

A *database administrator* (DBA) will often be appointed to look after the structure, physical storage and security of the data in the best interest of all users. The database administrator is responsible for:

(a) maintaining the database, including setting out procedures for the addition of new data (liaising with users, the systems analysts and programmers) and ensuring that there is no duplication;

(b) maintaining a *data dictionary* describing the data items;

(c) maintaining manuals for users telling them how to use the facilities of the database;

(d) overseeing the security of the database and ensuring that individual privacy is not eroded;

(e) ensuring that the requirements of the Data Protection Act 1984 are complied with.

Data dictionary

Definition

A *data dictionary* is a form of technical documentation which is simply a list or record of each data store in the system, showing what data items each contains.

It is easy for different users to give different names to the same data item; for example, *stock number*, *part number* and *stock code* might be used interchangeably. The data dictionary defines each data item and assists in maintenance and other accesses to the data.

3.3   Operating a database system

The four main operations in using a database are:

(a) creating the database structure, that is the structure of files and records;

(b) entering data on to the database, and amending and updating it;

(c) retrieving the data, manipulating it and using it in a variety of applications;

(d) producing reports.

Creating a database structure

The database user must begin by specifying what records (entities, such as employees) will be held in the database, what fields (items of data about the entities, such as salaries) they will contain and how many characters there will be in each field. The fields must be named, and the characteristics of particular fields (such as all-numeric or all-alphabetic) should be specified.

Entering and amending data

When the database structure has been established, the data user can input data and create records. The data must be kept up to date, which means there will be subsequent insertions of new records, deletions of unwanted records and amendments to existing records.

Another amendment function allows the same field in every record, or all records with certain characteristics, to be amended in the same way by means of a single command. For example, a single command could arrange for all customers whose accounts have never been settled late to have their credit limits raised by 5%.

The retrieval and manipulation of data

Data can be retrieved and manipulated in a variety of ways.

(a) Data can be retrieved by specifying the required parameters. For example, records of all employees in the sales department who have been employed for over 10 years and are paid less than £12,000 a year could be extracted. If certain search and retrieve parameters are used regularly, they can be stored on a search parameters file for future use.

(b) Retrieved data can be sorted on any specified field (for example, for employees, sorting might be according to grade, department, age, experience or salary level).

(c) Some calculations on retrieved data can be carried out, such as calculating totals and average values.

Report production

Most database packages include a report generator facility which allows the user to design report structures so that information can be presented on screen and printed out in a format which suits the user's requirements and preferences. Report formats can be stored on disk, if similar reports are produced periodically, and called up when required.

Activity 4

Give some examples of calculations a human resource manager might want to carry out on employee records selected from a database.

4 DATABASE SOFTWARE PACKAGES

The scope for many organisations to construct and use database systems has been considerably enhanced by the availability of database software packages. A user of the software package can insert data into a database framework that the package contains, and then use the database.

There are three broad categories of database package: hierarchical databases, network databases and relational databases.

4.1 Hierarchical databases

A hierarchical database has a simple tree structure. For example, a database of students at a university might have a record for each faculty (Business School, Sciences, Arts). A faculty record would be linked to a record for each course within that faculty (so the Business School record might be linked to a record for the Accounting course, a record for the Economics course and so on). Each course record would be linked to records for the individual students on that course.

The hierarchical model requires each member record to have *one* owner record. In a customer database, for example, the hierarchical model might be used to show customers and customer orders. Thus, an extract from a parts department database might be structured as in Figure 9.3.

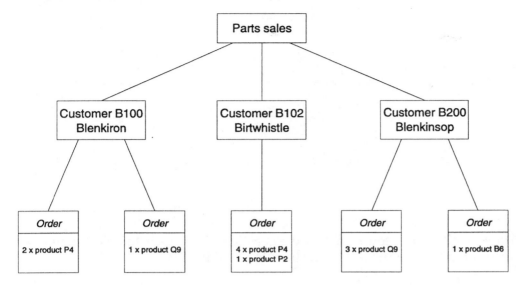

Figure 9.3 Structure of a hierarchical database

The biggest drawback to a file organised in hierarchical data structure is that the user is limited in the number of ways records can be looked for because the file organisation makes it much easier to search for certain items in the file records than for others. In this second example, to access an order record it is necessary to specify the customer to which it belongs, which is straightforward. However, let us imagine that you wish to obtain a listing of all customers who have ordered a particular part number. This would require a search of each customer record; a long process. If the hierarchical model had been structured so that *products* were superior to *orders* and each order contained customer data instead of product data, this would be simpler, but the *first* process would be harder!

This asymmetrical character of the hierarchical model makes it unsuitable for many applications, especially where there is not a true hierarchical relationship between the data.

4.2   Network databases

In a network database, each record may be linked to other records, but in a more flexible way than the tree structure required in a hierarchical database. Thus, using our example of a university, there might be a record for courses with an information technology element, linked to both the computer science course in the sciences faculty and the business studies course in the business school. A user could thus obtain access to the records for all students studying information technology.

Whereas a hierarchical data structure only allows a one-to-many relationship between data items, a network database is a database in which the logical data structure allows many-to-many relationships.

Using the same data as in Figure 9.3, Figure 9.4 shows how a network database might be structured.

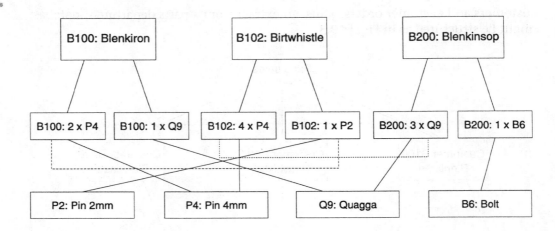

Figure 9.4 Structure of a network database

There is still some redundancy of data at the order level, although the problems inherent in the hierarchical model have been eliminated.

4.3 Relational databases

In a relational database, all records are effectively arranged in a table, with columns for the different fields and a row number for each record. Any record may be identified by its row number, and records meeting any specified criteria may be selected (for example, in a database of customers, all customers who spent over £15,000 last year and who are entitled to a 2% discount on the company's normal prices this year). The structure of the data inside the database (as opposed to what the user sees) may be made more sophisticated than the table, to reflect the relations between different field values. For example, if all customers who spent between £20,000 and £29,999 last year are entitled to a 4% discount this year, and all customers who spent £30,000 or more last year are entitled to a 5% discount this year, a table of amounts spent and discount rates could be drawn up. The records of the individual customers would then only need to record the amounts they spent last year, and not the discounts they are now entitled to. If the system were to be called upon to display full details of a customer, it could use the table of discount rates to look up what discount rate to display.

Taking the original example a step further, Figure 9.5 shows how the same data might appear in a relational model.

Customer table	
B100	Blenkiron
B102	Birtwhistle
B200	Blenkinsop

Product table	
B6	Bolt
P2	Pin 2mm
P4	Pin 4mm
Q9	Quagga

Order table		
B100	P4	2
B100	Q9	1
B102	P4	4
B102	P2	1
B200	Q9	3
B200	B6	1

Figure 9.5 Structure of a relational database

The redundant data in the network model, ie the customer number and part number in the order relation, has been eliminated. Any data element can be recognised by its record number or field name. The primary key is used to identify a record.

All three models are used in commercial packages. The hierarchical model is popular because of its simplicity, and because IBM's IMS (information management system) uses it. Network databases allow a more direct connection between data items at the various levels; examples are IDMS and Total. Relational databases require more storage space; examples are Ingres and Oracle.

Hierarchical and *network* databases require a transaction to 'navigate' through other data in the system before the required record is reached. The structure of the file is contained in the data items themselves, as it is contained in a pointer system. In a *relational* data structure, the structure of the file is independent of the actual data. The relationships between different entity types have been determined at the outset, and are not embodied in the records themselves. Thus, a relational database does not require a transaction to navigate through other data before reading the required record.

Activity 5

Give another example of how a relational database package might set up a subsidiary table, showing the relationship between two variables, so as to reduce the amount of information which has to be stored in the records for the individual entities.

4.4 General features of a database software package

Definition

Database software is software that sees to the administration and use of the database files, providing a bridge between the data files and the user's application programs.

All database packages ought to have certain basic features. The recent trend in database software has been away from the traditional complex software to user-friendliness, with pull-down menus, graphical user interfaces and other features that make them easier to learn and use.

(a) For interrogating the files, DBMS should allow the user to construct queries, either single queries or multiple queries chained together. Queries are put to the DBMS in a *query language*, for example structured query language (SQL).

(b) The database must be capable of being restructured and reorganised without losing data. The DBMS should automatically re-index records according to changes that are made.

(c) The package must allow the user to print out information, for example onto address labels or in reports.

(d) Report writers enable users to define and format the output.

(e) Security features are needed if data is to be shared.

Different database packages have other features which vary from package to package.

(a) Some packages limit the number and size of the fields that are permitted in records. For example, an address field might be limited to 60 characters. Others allow much more flexibility in the number of fields, and also allow variable length fields.

(b) Some packages limit the number of allowable key fields, that is fields which are used to speed up sorting and searching.

(c) Some packages allow the user to update records in batches.

(d) Packages vary in the way they handle and store data, and in the degree of control the user has in retrieving information.

(e) Some packages allow a database to be multi-user, that is accessible from several terminals. Others do not.

(f) For data security, some packages offer a system of passwords for restricting access to specified records or fields.

(g) Some packages allow users to define their own menus and help screens.

Chapter roundup

- Application specific files are not shared between different applications. With a database, all applications use the same set of records.

- A database ensures that all applications use the same data, and avoids duplication of data.

- Holding all an organisation's data in one database can be risky.

- A database can provide all levels of information, and can provide a wider variety of control information than application specific files.

- In a database, the logical structure of the data is independent of its physical structure.

- The integrity of a database should be protected, while allowing its widespread use within the organisation.

- A database administrator is responsible for maintaining a database, although several users will be able to enter and update data.

- There is normally great flexibility in the ways data may be retrieved and manipulated and reports prepared.

- Hierarchical databases use a tree structure, whereas network databases are more flexible.

- Relational databases can take account of the relationships between values in different fields.

- Database software offers the ability to put queries in various forms to the database and to restructure the database.

- Other facilities include report writing, passwords to limit access and user-defined menus.

Quick quiz

1 In what sorts of organisation are application specific files likely to be found?

2 Does the fact that data need only be entered once in a database system have any disadvantages?

3 How may databases can be used for marketing purposes?

4 What is data redundancy?

5 What are the duties of a database administrator?

6 Give some examples of commands for entering and amending data in a database.

7 Distinguish between a hierarchical database, a network database and a relational database.

8 What is a query language?

Answers to activities

1   Cash received from a customer who bought goods on credit might be recorded in the cash control system but not in the sales ledger.

Goods received might be recorded in the stock control system but not in the system for payment of suppliers' invoices.

2   Yes: some information, such as salaries, might be confidential; and it might be better to prevent senior executives from getting immersed in detail, so as to encourage them to focus on broad strategic issues.

3   Only one record is needed for each debt. The DBMS can take information from these records in order of size of debt for the benefit of the credit control department, or in order of time since the invoice was issued for the benefit of the finance director, without disturbing the records themselves.

4   Average length of service
Average basic pay
Total cost of overtime
Percentage of hours worked which are overtime hours

5   Products for sale might be subject to any one of several different delivery charges, including fixed charges (say £10 per delivery) and variable charges (say 3% of selling price). These charges could be given names (say charge A, charge B and so on), and the record for each product would just record the name of the appropriate charge. A table would show what charge each name referred to. If the £10 charge were increased to £12, only the table would need to be amended, not the records for all the products subject to that charge.

Further question practice

Now try the following practice questions at the end of this text.

Multiple choice questions   **60 to 66**

Exam style questions   **7 and 8**

Chapter 10

THE ELECTRONIC OFFICE

Introduction

In this chapter we set out some specific applications of information technology. The most widespread uses of IT are probably in basic data processing and, increasingly, in the provision of information to management. However, IT is being used increasingly to underpin a wide range of office activities.

In the first part of the chapter, we will examine some internal applications of IT, considering ways in which it can be used within an organisation. Specific applications supported by general purpose software packages, such as spreadsheets, have already been described and here we are more concerned with what could loosely be termed office administration.

Your objectives

After completing this chapter you should:

(a) understand the scope of office automation;

(b) be aware of modern techniques for handling correspondence;

(c) understand the document image processing technique;

(d) know several different ways of communicating information electronically;

(e) know how funds may be transferred electronically;

(f) be aware of the main electronic public information services;

(g) appreciate the effects on business of office automation.

1 WHAT IS OFFICE AUTOMATION?

Office work is generally a matter of information handling and information processing. In spite of the widespread use of the telephone, and even early developments in computer technology, office work has always been associated with paperwork. However, the advance of information technology has brought nearer the coming of the *electronic office*, in which paper is less central than it used to be.

Technology has developed to the point where an office might have a PC on every desk, with data processed and transmitted by cable links rather than by means of paper and internal mail. 'Workstation' is a term sometimes used to described an office manager's desk which has its own PC, together with readily available application software. However, automation means more than simply having a PC on every desk. For example:

(a) a number of PCs can be linked in a small *local area network*;

(b) office switchboards and *telephone systems* might offer sophisticated features. Private Automatic Branch Exchanges (systems) provide features such as automatic message switching, automatic dialling and call repeating (when a line is engaged) and conference calls;

(c) office users can access information provided by an information-supplying organisation using, for example, the Prestel service of British Telecom;

(d) office automation software (such as IBM's Officevision) combines electronic mail and word processing applications.

The development of the electronic office has meant that office workers do their jobs in a different way. Technological change has brought about job changes and changes in organisational structure. These in turn affect the way that office workers communicate with each other. The social life of office workers and the group behaviour of office workers are also changing.

2 CORRESPONDENCE AND FILING

The old fashioned office in which correspondence is typed has been superseded by more modern methods of preparing and transmitting correspondence.

(a) *Word processing* makes it easy to produce high quality correspondence.

(b) Some correspondence may not need to be on paper at all. It might be appropriate to hold much information on computer, whether in word processed form or as part of a *document image processing* system which allows a user to read a document by calling it up onto a VDU screen. Alternatively, records can be held on *microfilm* or *microfiche*.

(c) *Fax machines* allow correspondence to be sent instantaneously;

(d) Inter/Intranets allow web 'publishing' of information.

2.1 Electronic mail (e-mail)

The term *electronic mail* describes various systems of sending data or messages electronically via the telephone network or other data network. It has the advantages over paper correspondence of:

(a) speed (transmission, being electronic, is instantaneous);

(b) economy (there is no need for stamps);

(c) security (access can be restricted by the use of passwords, although a committed hacker might breach access controls);

(d) the ability to retrieve documents from or store them in word processing packages;

(e) document files may be attached to the e-mail message.

One form of electronic mail popular in the office environment is a system of sending messages (letters, information etc) over a telecommunications network. Messages are 'posted' by the senders to a central computer which allocates disk storage in the form of 'mailboxes' to recipients. The messages then stay in the mailboxes until the recipients 'collect' them. This sort of service is also called a *message handling service*.

Each user typically has password-protected access to a personal mailbox. The system allows letters and other texts to be prepared and edited using word processing, and mail can be sent using standard headers and identifiers to an individual or to a group of people on a prepared distribution list.

2.2   Facsimile (fax)

Facsimile transmission or fax involves the transmission by data link of exact *duplicate copies* of documents. An original is fed into a fax machine, which scans it and converts it into electronic form so it can be transmitted over a telephone line. It is printed by the recipient's fax machine. PC fax systems do not even require the document to be input in *hard copy* form to the sender's fax machine. The computer communicates directly with the receiving fax machine.

It was thought that fax might be particularly beneficial to the legal profession, because speed in sending documents (with signatures) might reduce the time needed to make contracts or settle cases. However, the service has much more widespread appeal and the use of fax is growing rapidly.

Activity 1

A report on a company's Manchester branch is prepared locally. It is then amended by a manager at the head office in Cardiff, and finally incorporated into a report on prospects for the north of England being written by the marketing director at the head office. Explain how modern techniques for document handling might be used to facilitate this process.

2.3   Document image processing (DIP)

Document image processing is an electronic form of filing. In a DIP system, a document is passed through a *scanner* and a *digitised image* is then stored on a storage device (perhaps an *optical disk*). This can then be retrieved at will and shown on a computer screen. The image of the document can include handwriting and diagrams. The process is the same as that employed in fax machine technology. That is, the image is recorded but the system does not identify the marks on the paper as letters or numbers. A scanner scans a whole page of input and records and stores a pattern of dots, according to whether areas of the paper original are black or white.

An example of a DIP system is Philips' Megadoc. As an indication of the power of DIP systems, one manufacturer has indicated that one optical disk could contain 60,000 pages of A4.

Some DIP systems not only store the electronic image of a document, but also allow stored documents to be used in other office systems. It might be possible to display, on a VDU, both a scanned document and keyed-in text commentary (which can be stored with a file, for example, of a subsequent telephone conversation about a dispute referred to in a letter).

The advantages are that:

(a) reduced storage space is needed;

(b) the same document can be viewed by different users simultaneously;

(c) documents cannot be lost as the image is on disk.

The main cost savings from using DIP are in storage and retrieval, as the time taken to hunt for a paper file is eliminated. In order for these savings to be achieved, documents must be scanned as soon as they are received by the mail room.

Applications of DIP include:

(a) handling written customer enquiries;

(b) desktop publishing by enabling photographs or other images to be stored;

(c) the management of accounting transactions. All the documentation relating to an accounting transaction can be referenced to the ledger record: an entry in the sales ledger for example, could be accompanied by images of all the related paperwork.

A possible disadvantage of DIP is that a lot more information is stored than is strictly necessary. So, companies installing a DIP system should bear in mind the following.

(a) The *importance* of the documents, if their loss would be a major disaster.

(b) How often documents are *accessed*. If a document or file is greatly in demand, document imaging might be a useful technology.

(c) The *volume* of documents involved: small volumes of documents probably do not justify the expense of a DIP system. Large volumes, which would otherwise cost a lot in storage space and handling time, almost certainly do.

An example of a company which uses DIP is National Westminster Bank, which has three image scanners in its card services centre. Letters are read by scanner, processed overnight and are ready for use by the following morning. Typically 18,000 to 20,000 items might be processed every day. The introduction of credit card annual fees together with the marketing of financial products from the card services centre means that a lot of correspondence is received at the centre.

The customer's file can be on-screen within seconds. Previously any caller's letter would have to be retrieved from filing and the customer then called back. This incurred additional costs for the bank. NatWest's use of DIP is an example of the introduction of information technology making office procedures simpler, cheaper and quicker.

Activity 2

Why could a DIP system not, on its own, read the address on a letter received and start a draft reply incorporating that address?

3 COMMUNICATION

In spite of the increasing popularity of e-mail, the telephone is still the most important method of communication in the office and, even in this area, there have been major advances in technology, for example, in mobile communications (cellular radio telephones and telepoint phones) and office switchboards (PABX).

3.1 Telex

Telex is a service which enables users to transmit and receive printed messages over a telephone line. Users have to be telex subscribers, with their own telex equipment and code number, in order to send or receive messages. The telex service started in the 1930s, and from the mid-1970s it developed significantly as an international message transmission system.

As a communication system, it has certain disadvantages. Data transmission speeds are very slow compared with other methods such as leased telephone lines, and only a restricted set of characters can be used in messages. However, the great strength of telex is the number of telex users, around 100,000 in the UK and 2,000,000 worldwide. Advances in telex technology have made it possible for a telex user to connect PCs to the telex system. A user's PC can also:

(a) store a large number of commonly-used telex addresses;

(b) store messages for transmission at a predetermined time;

(c) re-dial numbers automatically if the addressee's line is busy;

(d) send the same message to a large number of users.

Telex, in spite of earlier predictions to the contrary, therefore continues to be an important communication facility for businesses. BT and Mercury are investing in a digital telex network. However, telex is likely to be superseded by fax machines where the quality of communications links permits (fax needs higher quality links than telex).

3.2 Voice mail

Definition

Voice mail is a system allowing the caller's spoken message to be recorded at the recipient's voice mailbox (similar to a mailbox in an e-mail system).

The main advantage of voice mail is that it only requires a telephone to be used; no typing or keying in is necessary. Compared with cellular radio or mobile communications, it is relatively cheap. On the other hand, it cannot be used for two-way conversations.

Voice mail can be used:

(a) to leave messages in departments in different time zones;

(b) in organisations where employees might be working away at a client's premises.

3.3 Computer conferencing (teleconferencing)

A computer conferencing system is similar to e-mail but more expensive, in that there is a large central mailbox on the system where all persons connected to the system can deposit messages for everyone to see, and in turn read messages which other people have left in the system. Computer conferencing can be appropriate for a team of individuals at different locations to compare notes. It becomes a way of keeping track of progress on a project between routine team meetings.

Computer conferencing systems can become organisation-wide *bulletin boards*, where members can leave messages of general import. A bulletin board system can be a way of re-establishing some of the social ties of office life which may suffer from computerisation. The management problem is recognising the importance to employee morale of informal communication systems outside the management hierarchy or chain of command. A bulletin board might encourage new ideas to be developed informally, and so is a way by which companies can tap their employees' creativity and expertise.

3.4 Videoconferencing

Videoconferencing is the use of computer and communication technology to conduct meetings whereby several participants, perhaps in different parts of the world, are linked up via computer and a video system. Conference calls on a telephone system, whereby several people can converse at the same time, are a precursor of videoconferencing.

The most expensive videoconferencing systems feature a separate room with several video screens, which show the images of those participating in a meeting.

Although the technology might be expensive, it is arguable that it is far cheaper than the management time and air fares spent on business travel.

3.5 Video phones

The first video phones, also called 'picture phones' or 'view phones', are now coming on to the market in the UK. Each user has a terminal which consists of a telephone, a screen and a camera. The technology enables callers to see each other during the telephone conversation. The camera 'scans' the caller a certain number of times a second, and so an 'animated' image is transmitted frame by frame. Use of video phones may help to bridge the gap between office and telecommuter.

Activity 3

Which methods of communication would be suitable in each of the following cases?

(a) A company's head office and clients need to be able to leave messages for sales representatives who, although they have telephones in their cars, are often out of their cars and in other clients' offices.

(b) A company's regional managers in London, Paris and Berlin need to discuss business strategy for the coming year.

(c) Occasional, brief but urgent messages need to be sent to overseas offices which are often unstaffed for periods of up to an hour.

3.6 Electronic data interchange (EDI)

Electronic data interchange is a form of computer-to-computer data interchange. The general concept of having one computer talk directly to another might seem straightforward in principle, but in practice there are three major difficulties.

(a) Each business wants to produce documents (and hold records on file) to its own individual requirements. Thus a computer of X Ltd might not be able to transmit data to a computer of Y Ltd because the data transmitted might not be in a format to suit Y Ltd.

(b) Different makes of computer cannot easily talk to each other. The problem of compatibility between different makes of computer is a serious one, and some form of interface between the computers has to be devised to enable data interchange to take place.

(c) Businesses may work to differing time schedules, especially when they are engaged in international trade. For example, if a computer in London wants to send a message to a computer in San Francisco, the San Francisco computer might not be switched on and able to receive the message.

A way of ensuring that electronic communication is possible is to have an agreed format for electronic documents so that they can be recognised by all parties to the transaction. A standard which is widely adopted in the UK and Europe is *Edifact* (Electronic data interchange for administration, commerce and transport).

Joining an EDI network (there are several) is quite expensive. Many smaller companies are encouraged to do so by their suppliers and/or customers. Many of Marks and Spencer's suppliers use EDI. Tesco now has 400 trading partners across Europe connected to it by EDI. Alternatively, one or two low-cost services are offered, such as Ethosfax offered by INS for small companies dealing with the UK National Health Service. However, it is possible that these services could be challenged by the Public Data Network provided by the telecommunications companies.

In 1991 the five largest UK banks offered for the first time a *financial* EDI service for their corporate customers. This allows companies to send payment instructions electronically, along with electronic remittance advices to their bank, for onward transmission to companies with which they do business.

Until this development, payments (typically through cheques, CHAPS or BACS transfer) have been separated from remittance advices. The new service, called IDX, ties the payment instruction to the remittance advice. The certainty of payment and the saving in clerical time spent on reconciling incoming payments to invoices should bring considerable benefits to payee companies.

The advantages of EDI also extend to purely *internal* uses.

(a) If an organisation is decentralised, EDI can speed up internal billing.

(b) If an organisation's paperwork is intricate and complex, EDI can speed it up.

(c) EDI can be used to create files of historical information.

3.7 Electronic funds transfer (EFT)

In electronic funds transfer, a computer system is used to transfer funds, for example make payments to suppliers, pay salaries into employees' bank accounts or transfer funds from one bank account to another, by sending electronic data to a bank.

Since businesses keep most of their cash in bank accounts, electronic funds transfer must involve the banks themselves.

(a) A system for the electronic transfer of funds internationally between banks themselves is known as SWIFT II (the Society for Worldwide Interbank Financial Telecommunications; 'II' indicates that the current system is a replacement for the original system). If X Ltd in the UK wishes to make a payment to a company in, say, Germany, and if X Ltd's UK bank and the German company's bank are members of the SWIFT II network (all the UK clearing banks are members), the settlement between the banks themselves can be made through the SWIFT II system.

(b) Interbank settlements between clearing banks within the UK are also made by electronic funds transfer, using CHAPS (clearing house automated payments system). Many large companies now pay the salaries of employees by providing computer data to their banks, using the BACS (bankers' automated clearing house) or BACSTEL services. Originally, the banks could only process magnetic tapes sent by employers, but with the BACSTEL service, they can now process salary data sent by telecommunications link, and in addition will accept floppy disks or magnetic tape cassettes from customers.

Activity 4

What are the advantages of electronic funds transfer over more traditional methods of payment?

4   PUBLIC SERVICES

4.1   Teletext

There are a number of teletext systems in the UK. The most widely received are provided by the BBC (Ceefax) and the independent television companies (Teletext on 3, Teletext on 4). Users must have a television set with a teletext facility; otherwise they pay no fee for use of the service. The information is broadcast on pages as part of the television signal, and includes weather reports, news, sports reports, subtitles for certain television programmes, cooking hints and other items of general interest. Teletext on 3 and Teletext on 4 carry some advertisements.

4.2   Viewdata/Videotex

Definition

Viewdata is the name for systems which provide information through a telephone network to a television or terminal screen.

The most important feature of viewdata (also known as videotex), which makes it different from teletext, is that it is *interactive*. In other words, a viewdata customer can transmit information through the viewdata network as well as receive it.

In the UK the viewdata service provided by British Telecom is called Prestel. In the Prestel service most of the information is paid for by organisations that wish to provide the information. The Prestel service is provided over the telephone system and is therefore chargeable to the user at normal call rates. In addition, the user must pay a fee for consulting most pages of information (but not index pages and some other pages). This fee is paid to British Telecom, which then passes it on, less commission, to the information provider. The Prestel service is not widely used by the general public, but has found a niche with travel agencies.

The French viewdata system, Minitel, is far more widely used than Prestel. This is largely because telephone subscribers are provided with Minitel terminals free on request, and because services available on Minitel are widely advertised.

Viewdata systems, such as Prestel in the UK, have a much larger database than teletext systems such as Ceefax. The information is stored in a network of computers, with each computer serving a local area of customers but also capable of transmitting data to another computer in the network and so to customers in other areas.

4.3   Value Added Network Services (VANS)

VANS is a collective term for the range of computer services provided by external organisations, which are used in conjunction with the telephone network or another communications network. The term 'value added network services' derives from the idea that by combining a computer system with a communications network, the service is able to provide something extra (an added value) to the user, greater than the sum of the values of its components. Examples of VANS are:

(a) electronic mail (the added value here being the facility to hold messages in an electronic mailbox);

(b) services that provide financial information to subscribers, for example, on share prices, foreign exchange rates and interest rates;

(c) bibliographic database systems (in libraries of computerised information);

(d) viewdata services such as Prestel;

(e) electronic data interchange;

(f) Internet access;

(g) website hosting, providing companies with an internet presence.

Activity 5

What commercial possibilities are opened up by the scope to send viewdata messages to specific recipients and obtain responses from them?

5 MULTIMEDIA

Multimedia has been talked about for some time now, but has not yet made much of an impact in the office. The concept of multimedia is the delivery of text, sound and pictures through a single terminal, using communications and computer technology. It is not a type of system, but a *means* of communicating information.

In both the home and office environment multimedia is delivered via PC and is more likely to be based around CD-ROM technology. A standard has been developed for the multimedia PC, and a typical multimedia PC would meet the following specification.

(a) A 486SX processor.

(b) Memory of 4 megabytes.

(c) A 16-bit soundcard and an eight-note synthesiser.

(d) A 640 480 VGA monitor capable of displaying 65,536 colours (many are SVGA, which offer 1280 1024 or 1024 768).

(e) A 160 megabyte hard disk

(f) A double speed CD-ROM drive

(g) Speakers (a typical PC's internal speaker is not very sophisticated).

It should be noted that, although CD-ROM is an integral element of multimedia, CD-ROM and multimedia are *not* the same thing. CD-ROM is suited to storage of large volumes of data, whether encyclopaedias or archived transactions information. Multimedia is concerned with the way in which information is communicated.

It is not yet clear whether multimedia technology is going to prove more popular in the office or the home; the domestic systems are likely to be used as stand-alone while office systems will be used in communications networks. Examples of multimedia applications include the following.

(a) Provision of training, by use of interactive training materials and film demonstrations.

(b) Provision of computerised brochures and reports which could include audio introductions and video clips of personnel, products and processes.

(c) Enabling workgroup collaboration. If a camera is installed (as used in video phones), users can see each other but because a PC screen is used they can also share computer files on screen.

6 INTRANET

Definition

An *intranet* is a network which uses Internet protocols to distribute within the boundary of an organisation, the boundary being imposed logically not physically.

An intranet can actually use the Internet to connect satellite groups to it by encrypting and embedding messages between its sub-networks inside other messages, a technique known as *tunnelling*.

Effectively the web browser becomes the standard client. This software is freely available for almost any type of computer the company owns, and due to current aggressive marketing is available at very low expense. Microsoft's latest version of its desktop operating system, Windows 97, incorporates the browser as an integral part of the interface.

The real saving is in support costs as this software is very easy to use and maintain. Training costs are much reduced.

The focus of investment shifts to the server side. Web programming is a new discipline and the number of people who have mastered it is still small, but growing. Tools to make the Internet interactive are being developed for the mass market. Borland is selling a point-and-click tool (Intrabuilder) and Microsoft has integrated an Internet Information Server into Windows NT Server product, along with tools such as dBWeb.

Applications can include company telephone books, which could otherwise be out of date the moment they leave the printer, help manuals, updates to procedures and information resources. The information is literally a mouse click away.

7 OFFICE AUTOMATION'S EFFECT ON BUSINESS

Office automation has an enormous effect on business, in a variety of ways.

7.1 Routine processing

The processing of routine data can be done in greater volumes, at greater speed and with greater accuracy than with manual systems.

7.2 The paperless office

There might be less paper in the office (but not necessarily so) with more data processing done by keyboard. Data transmission is likely to shift from moving paper to moving data electronically. Files are likely to be magnetic disk files or microform files rather than paper files.

7.3 Staff issues

Office staff will be affected by computerisation. Office staff will need to show a greater computer awareness, especially in areas of the office where computerisation is most likely to occur first, such as the accounts department. Staff will need to learn new habits, such as the care of floppy disks and VDU screens, how to use keyboards and remembering to make back-up copies of files for security purposes.

7.4 Management information

The nature and quality of management information will change. Managers are likely to have access to more information. Information is also likely to be more accurate, reliable and up to date. The range of management reports is likely to be wider and their content more comprehensive. Planning activities can be more thorough, with the use of models (such as spreadsheets for budgeting) and sensitivity analysis.

Information for control should be more readily available. For example, a computerised sales ledger system should provide prompt reminder letters for late payers, and might incorporate other credit control routines. Stock systems, especially for companies with stocks distributed around several different warehouses, should provide better stock control. Decision making by managers can be helped by decision support systems.

7.5 Organisational structure

The organisation's structure might change. Stand-alone PCs allow local office managers to set up good local management information systems, and localised data processing. Multi-user systems and distributed data processing systems also put more data processing power into local offices, giving local managers access to centrally-held databases and programs. Office automation can therefore encourage the decentralisation of authority within an organisation.

On the other hand, multi-user systems and distributed data processing systems help head office to keep in touch with what is going on in local offices. Head office can therefore readily monitor and control the activities of individual departments, and retain a co-ordinating influence.

7.6 Change

Office automation commits an organisation to continual change. The pace of technological change is rapid, and computer systems, both hardware and software, are likely to be superseded after a few years by something even better. Computer maintenance engineers are often unwilling to enter into maintenance contracts for hardware which is more than a few years old, and so organisations are forced to consider a policy of regular replacement of computers.

7.7 Customer service

Office automation, in some organisations, results in better customer service. When an organisation receives many telephone enquiries from customers, the staff who take the calls should be able to provide a prompt and helpful service if they have on-line access to the organisation's data files.

7.8 Telecommuting

Consider the following facts.

(a) Office space is expensive.

(b) Many people feel that time spent commuting between their homes and their offices is time wasted.

(c) For practical purposes, information distributed electronically takes no longer to travel 100km than 100m.

Telecommuting is a solution to problems (a) and (b) by applying fact (c). It is now quite possible, technically, for employees of many descriptions to work from home.

PCs in the home enable users to handle data just as if they were in the office, using spreadsheet and word processing packages. Links to the office provide a means of transmitting information and receiving new data. Links are provided by means of a modem at each end of the telephone line. A network allows communication with the office and with colleagues in their homes by e-mail.

Advantages of telecommuting include the saving of office space and the elimination of travelling time. A disadvantage is the loss of face-to-face contact, which can be very important in meetings and negotiations and is not fully compensated for by e-mail or by telephone calls. A means of overcoming this is videoconferencing.

Activity 6

In what sort of organisation would office automation not be worth the expense?

Chapter roundup

- In the electronic office, PCs are linked in a network and communications with people and computers outside the office use electronic methods.
- Electronic mail can be a substitute for correspondence on paper.
- Document image processing avoids the need to pass incoming letters from the mail room to the addressees on paper.
- Telex is a way to send typed messages. Voice mail avoids the need to type messages, and videoconferencing allows discussions to be held between people in widely dispersed locations.
- Fax machines enable text and diagrams to be transmitted electronically. Electronic data interchange enables computers to communicate with each other directly.
- Electronic funds transfer is a means of transferring money between bank accounts.
- Teletext and viewdata systems make data publicly accessible.
- Office automation can bring greater management control, and can improve customer service. It also makes telecommuting feasible.

Quick quiz

1   What are the advantages of electronic mail over paper correspondence?
2   What are the advantages of document image processing?
3   What is the main strength of the telex system?
4   What is videoconferencing?
5   What are the main difficulties in setting up an electronic data interchange system?
6   What systems are used to transfer funds between banks?
7   What is the key difference between teletext and viewdata?
8   How might office automation affect an organisation's structure?
9   What is an intranet?
10 What are the advantages of standardising client software?

Answers to activities

1   The report could be prepared using a word processing package in Manchester, and then transmitted by electronic mail to Cardiff. The manager in Cardiff could amend the report on his PC, and then send it to the marketing director over the head office's local area network. The marketing director could use his PC to take extracts from the report and edit them for incorporation into the report on the north of England.

2   A DIP system records a picture of a piece of paper. It does not recognise the marks on it as letters and numbers, so it cannot use them in any sort of word processing.

3   (a)   Voice mail

   (b)   Videoconferencing

   (c)   Telex

4   It is faster and safer (cheques could be lost in the post), and it reduces the amount of paperwork needed.

5   Advertisements can be sent to selected people, and they can then place orders through viewdata.

6   In a very small business, where a certain number of full-time staff are needed anyway (perhaps to deal with customers) but those staff have enough free time to deal with administration using manual methods, there would be no point in investing money in office automation.

Further question practice

Now try the following practice questions at the end of this text.

Multiple choice questions   **67 to 73**

Chapter 11

THE COMPUTERISATION OF BUSINESS FUNCTIONS

Introduction

In the first half of this book we have been concerned primarily with the 'nuts and bolts' of IT, looking at hardware and software and giving examples of ways in which they function and are used within computer systems.

In the rest of the book, we will be focusing largely on the development and management of computer systems. We start in this chapter with an analysis of why an organisation might choose to develop a strategy for its use of IT and then describe the systems development life cycle.

Your objectives

After completing this chapter you should:

(a) appreciate the need for a strategy for information technology;

(b) know the stages in the systems development life cycle;

(c) know the purposes of a feasibility study;

(d) be aware of the likely costs and benefits of a computer system;

(e) know the main techniques of systems investigation;

(f) appreciate the role of systems analysis;

(g) understand the use of dataflow diagrams;

(h) appreciate the concept of entity modelling.

1 THE NEED FOR A STRATEGY FOR INFORMATION TECHNOLOGY

Information technology (IT) has a major impact on businesses. It is therefore important for management to have a clear strategy for selecting, developing and implementing computer systems. Michael J Earl (in *Management Strategies for Information Technology*) lists nine reasons justifying the case for a strategy for information technology. Information systems and information technology:

(a) involve high costs;

(b) are critical to the success of many organisations;

(c) are now used as part of a commercial strategy in the battle for competitive advantage;

(d) are required by the economic context;

(e) affect all levels of management;

(f) may mean a revolution in the way information is created and presented to management;

(g) involve many stakeholders, not just management, and not just within the organisation;

(h) make technical issues important;

(i) require effective management as this can make a real difference to successful IT use.

1.1 IT is a high cost activity

Many organisations invest large amounts of money in IT, but not always wisely. Much of the expenditure is on the leading technologies in end-user computing, and on high performance niche areas (such as expert systems and computer integrated manufacturing), rather than on traditional data processing. Despite all the expenditure, there may be a delay before the new facilities are exploited to the full. The benefits of IT expenditure might be delayed until the skills of users have improved.

1.2 IT is critical to the success of many organisations

IT functions in four ways in an organisation.

(a) As a *support activity* (providing *ad hoc* responses to queries), which is useful but not critical to organisational success.

(b) As a *production activity*, ensuring the smooth running of current operations.

(c) As a *turnround activity*, in which IT is used to open up new opportunities (for example, to enhance the flexibility of marketing and production of consumer goods).

(d) As a *strategic activity*, where without IT the firm could not function at all (for example, many financial services companies depend on computers, telecommunications and databases, just as a manufacturing company depends on raw materials).

In developing a strategy a firm should assess how important IT actually is in the provision of products and services. In the financial sector, many products or services would be inconceivable without IT.

1.3 IT as a strategic weapon

IT can be used as a strategic weapon in the following ways.

(a) It may give an organisation a competitive advantage.

(b) It can be used to improve productivity and performance, although some studies have concluded that broader changes to the work environment are also needed. Computer aided design (CAD) and computer integrated manufacturing (CIM) are two examples.

(c) It can be used to alter the management and organisational structure of the business (perhaps by using e-mail or telecommuting).

(d) It can be used to develop new businesses. For example, Reuters (the news and financial information agency) created an electronic market place where subscribers could trade in shares.

1.4 IT as required by the economic context

Earl argues that IT is an enabling technology, and can produce dramatic changes in individual businesses and whole industries, especially where there are other major forces for change. For example, when the US airline system was deregulated, it encouraged the growth of computerised seat reservation systems (such as SABRE as used by American Airlines, which always displayed American Airlines flights in preference to others). In short, IT can be both a cause of major changes in doing business and a response to them.

1.5 IT at all levels of management

IT can permeate all levels of management through management information systems. This trend is likely to continue, and so IT will become a routine feature of office life, a facility for everyone to use. IT is no longer a centralised technology.

1.6 IT and its effect on management information

Advanced executive information systems, decision support systems and expert systems can be used to enhance the flexibility and depth of MIS.

IT also has a longer term effect on the production processes about which information is collected. For example, having manufacturing controlled by computers changes the costs of many manufacturing processes. The era where manufacturing was a mass production exercise producing standardised products and employing a large labour force, so that wages were the predominant costs, is in some sectors over. A number of new costing systems have been developed to reflect this. In broad terms, the ingredients of product costs, and hence the techniques used to measure them, have been substantially altered by IT.

1.7 IT and stakeholders

A stakeholder is a person or organisation that has an interest in an enterprise. IT affects many stakeholders, as many parties both within and outside the organisation have an interest in IT. An organisation must take steps to manage these external stakeholders. Parties interested in an organisation's use of IT are as follows.

(a) Other business users (for example, when they want common standards for electronic data interchange). These can form into lobbying groups.

(b) Governments (for example, as telecommunications regulators, or as sponsors of research projects such as the Alvey program in the UK or the Esprit program for the European Union).

(c) IT manufacturers, who must often pioneer the development and use of new technology. Users need to make their voices heard so that they can influence what manufacturers do. The existence of competing standards is a problem.

(d) Consumers.

(e) Employees and internal users.

1.8   The importance of technology

Any strategic view of IT must take technical issues into account. Ignoring the technology-based choices in IT is rather like ignoring interest rates when you are borrowing money. An example from the financial services industry, which depends heavily on information systems, is provided by two UK building societies. Their merger was abandoned because of incompatibility between their computer systems.

1.9   The importance of management

It is argued that success or failure in implementing IT is a result not so much of the systems themselves as of the management effort behind them. For example, information systems will fail if:

(a) they are used to tackle the wrong problem (that is, the use of IT has not been thought through in the wider organisational context);

(b) senior management are not interested;

(c) users are ignored in design and development;

(d) no attention is given to behavioural factors in design and operation.

Activity 1

Give an example of an industry where the introduction of information technology by one large company to improve customer service may force other companies to introduce similar technology.

2   THE SYSTEMS DEVELOPMENT LIFE CYCLE

In the early days of computing, systems were developed in a fairly haphazard fashion. The consequence was poorly designed systems which cost too much and were not suited to users' needs.

The National Computing Centre in the 1960s developed a more disciplined approach to systems development, which could be applied almost anywhere. This was called the *systems development life cycle*. It contained the following stages.

(a) *Feasibility study*. Those conducting the study take a brief look at the present system and identify alternatives, one of which is recommended to management on the basis of its costs and benefits. A formal report is the result of the study which may include stages (b) and (c) below in some circumstances.

(b) *Systems investigation*. This is a thorough fact-finding exercise, using a number of methods to investigate current systems requirements and problems, volumes of data processed and so on. This may be largely conducted during the feasibility study.

(c) *Systems analysis*. Once facts about the present system have been established, the present system is analysed in terms of its problems, working methods, bottlenecks, inefficiencies and so on. Again, substantial analysis work may be conducted during the feasibility study.

(d) *Systems design.* The design is broadly based on that suggested during the feasibility study, but will go into considerable detail on inputs, outputs, files, security and so on. The main documentation produced here is the system specification.

(e) *Implementation.* This stage includes the writing of computer programs, testing and changeover to the new system.

(f) *Review and maintenance.* Maintenance involves keeping the system up to date, and the system should be subject to review to see that it conforms to the requirements identified in the feasibility study.

A final stage perhaps missing from this analysis is *identification of a new problem,* once the system is up and running which can lead to a new feasibility study to look at solutions to the problem. If we add this stage, we have a complete cycle of development.

In the remainder of this chapter, we will look at the first three stages in the systems development life cycle.

Activity 2

Why would it be a mistake to write programs for a new system before the systems design stage has been completed?

3 THE FEASIBILITY STUDY

A feasibility study, as its name suggests, is a formal study to decide what type of system can be developed which meets the needs of the organisation. Practice will vary between different organisations.

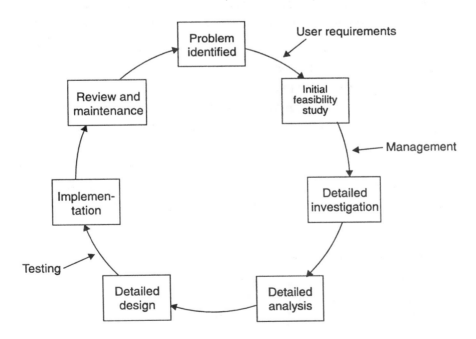

Figure 11.1 The systems development life cycle

Some of the reasons for having a feasibility study are that new systems:

(a) can cost a great deal to develop;

(b) can be very disruptive during implementation;

(c) can have far-reaching consequences in a way an organisation conducts its business or is structured.

3.1 The feasibility study group

A feasibility study team should be appointed to carry out the study (although just one individual might be given the task for a small project). Membership of the feasibility study team will probably be limited to a few individuals, including both managers from the user departments and individuals with technical knowledge of computer systems, including a *systems analyst*.

Definition

A *systems analyst* is a specialist in the analysis and design of whole systems.

At least one person must have a detailed knowledge of computers and systems design. In a small concern it may be necessary to bring in a systems analyst from outside.

At least one person should have a detailed knowledge of the organisation and in particular of the workings and staff of the departments affected. Managers with direct knowledge of how the current system operates can contribute enormously to the study. They will know what the information needs of the system are, and whether any proposed new system will do everything that is wanted. They are also likely to be in a position to recognise improvements that can be made in the current system.

3.2 The terms of reference of a feasibility study

The terms of reference of a feasibility study might consist of the following items.

(a) To investigate and report on an existing system, its procedures and costs.

(b) To specify objectives for the system.

(c) To define the system requirements.

(d) To establish whether these requirements are being met by the existing system.

(e) To establish whether these requirements could be met by a new system.

(f) To recommend the most suitable system to achieve the objectives.

(g) To prepare a detailed cost budget for the proposed system, within a set limit.

(h) To prepare a draft plan for implementation within a set timescale.

(i) To establish a detailed design, implementation and operating budget.

3.3 The costs and benefits of a proposed system

Cost-benefit analysis is an important part of a feasibility study. It means comparing all the costs and benefits of a proposal to see whether the benefits are likely to outweigh the costs. However, it is complicated by the facts that many of the system cost elements are poorly defined and that benefits can often be highly subjective in nature.

In general, the best cost estimates will be obtained for 'turnkey' systems bought as a whole from an outside vendor who provides a cost quotation against a specification. Less reliable cost estimates are generally made where the work is to be performed by the organisation's own employees.

The costs of a new system will include costs in a number of different categories.

(a) *Equipment costs* (capital or leasing costs) of:
  - (i) computers and peripherals;
  - (ii) ancillary equipment;
  - (iii) the initial system supplies (disks, tapes and stationery).

(b) *Installation costs*:
  - (i) a new building (if necessary);
  - (ii) the computer room (wiring, air-conditioning and so on).

(c) *Development costs*, or systems analysis, programming and changeover costs.

(d) *Personnel costs*:
  - (i) staff training;
  - (ii) staff recruitment or relocation;
  - (iii) staff salaries and pensions;
  - (iv) redundancy payments;
  - (v) overheads.

(e) *Operating costs*:
  - (i) consumable materials (tapes, disks and stationery);
  - (ii) maintenance;
  - (iii) accommodation costs;
  - (iv) heating, power, insurance and telephone costs;
  - (v) standby arrangements.

A distinction can be made between capital costs (incurred once) and revenue costs (incurred every year).

The benefits from a proposed new system may be of several types and must also be evaluated.

(a) Savings because the old system will no longer be operated. The savings should include:
  - (i) savings in staff costs;
  - (ii) savings in other operating costs, such as consumable materials.

(b) Extra savings or revenue benefits because of the improvements that the new system should bring, including:
  - (i) more sales revenue and so additional contribution;
  - (ii) better stock control and so fewer stock losses from obsolescence and deterioration;
  - (iii) further savings in staff time, resulting perhaps in reduced future staff growth.

(c) Possibly, some one-off revenue benefits from the sale of equipment which the existing system uses, but which will no longer be required. Secondhand computer equipment does not have a high value, however. It is also possible that the new system will use less office space, and so there will be benefits from selling or renting out the spare accommodation.

There might be *intangible benefits*, which it is impossible to give a money value to. These might include:

(a) greater customer satisfaction, arising from a more prompt service;

(b) improved staff morale from working with a better system;

(c) better decision-making resulting from better MIS.

Activity 3

Is it true that when a system is already computerised and a replacement computer system using improved technology is proposed, a feasibility study is pointless as it is already known to be feasible to computerise the system?

3.4   Cost-benefit analysis

There are three principal methods of evaluating a capital project. They generally come under the description of cost-benefit analysis.

(a) The *payback period* method of investment appraisal calculates the length of time a project will take to recoup the initial investment; in other words how long a project will take to pay for itself. The method is based on *cash flows*.

(b) The *accounting rate of return* method, also called *return on investment*, calculates the profits that will be earned by a project and expresses this as a percentage of the capital invested in the project. The higher the rate of return, the higher a project is ranked. This method is based on *accounting* results rather than cash flows.

(c) *Discounted cash flow* (DCF) is a method which may be sub-divided into two approaches.

   (i) *Net present value* (NPV), which considers all relevant cash flows associated with a project over the whole of its life and adjusts those occurring in future years to 'present value' by discounting at a rate called the 'cost of capital'. The net present value can be defined as follows.

   (ii) *Internal rate of return* (IRR), which involves comparing the rate of return expected from the project calculated on a discounted cash flow basis with the rate used as the cost of capital. Projects with an IRR higher than the cost of capital are worth undertaking.

4   SYSTEMS INVESTIGATION AND SYSTEMS ANALYSIS

4.1   Investigation

Techniques used in gathering information to investigate the present system include:

(a) interviews;

(b) questionnaires;

(c) observation and inspection of records.

The facts obtained from the investigation must be fully recorded.

Interviews

Interviews with members of staff can be the most effective method of fact finding. There are some guidelines for conducting a fact finding interview. Rather than following a standard routine, the interviewer must be able to adapt his approach to suit the individual interviewee and should be fully prepared for the interview. The interviewer should:

(a) inform employees *before* the interview that a systems investigation is taking place, and explain its purpose;

(b) ask questions at a level appropriate to the employee's position within the organisation;

(c) not be too formal, but encourage the interviewee to offer opinions and suggestions;

(d) not jump to conclusions or confuse opinions with facts;

(e) not propound any personal opinions in the interview;

(f) refrain from making 'off the record' comments during the course of the interview, for example about what he or she is going to recommend;

(g) conclude the interview by summarising the main points (so that the interviewee can confirm that the interviewer has understood what the interviewee has said).

Questionnaires

The use of questionnaires may be useful when a limited amount of information is required from a large number of individuals, or when the organisation is decentralised with many separate locations. Questionnaires may be used in advance of interviews to save the analyst's and employees' time.

It should be remembered that:

(a) employees ought to be informed before receiving questionnaires that a systems investigation is to take place, and its purpose should be explained;

(b) questions must be designed to obtain *exactly* the information necessary for the study;

(c) busy employees may consider it a waste of time to answer page after page of questions, and may be unwilling to do so; or they may put questionnaires in a 'pending' tray.

If a questionnaire is necessary, for example to establish the function of all employees within the organisation, the systems analyst may design a form that enables the individual to list his or her duties under various headings. The form should be designed with the specific organisation in mind.

Whenever possible, questionnaires should:

(a) not contain too many questions;

(b) be organised in a logical sequence;

(c) include an occasional question the answer to which corroborates the answers to previous questions;

(d) allow each question to be answered by 'yes' or 'no' or a tick;

(e) be tested independently before being used. The test answers should enable the systems analyst to establish the effectiveness of the questions and help determine the level of subsequent interviews and observations;

(f) take into account the sensitivity of individuals in respect of their job security, change of job definition etc.

Observation

Having gained some understanding of the methods and procedures used in the organisation, the systems analyst should be able to verify findings and clarify any problems areas by an observation of operations. Observation is a useful way of cross-checking with the facts obtained by interview or questionnaire. Different methods of recording facts ought to produce the same information, but it is not inconceivable that staff do their work in one way, while management believe that they do something different.

Activity 4

Criticise the following question addressed to a clerk in a department which might be computerised.

'Why do you think the present system is so inefficient and requires such gross overstaffing?'

4.2   Systems analysis

Systems analysis is a detailed look at a current system and what a new system will be required to do. It leads on to systems design, which is the development of a new system that will meet these requirements. Systems analysis is carried out by a systems analyst, who might be employed in the organisation's DP department or an external consultant.

The chief analyst, preferably the one who was also responsible for the feasibility study, will work with a team of individuals with differing backgrounds and experience (technical and business).

Systems analysis might be done in two stages, depending on the size of the project.

(a) The first stage is carried out during the feasibility study. The feasibility study team must go into some detail about the current system and the requirements for a new system, and this means having to do systems analysis work.

(b) If the feasibility study report recommends a new system, and the recommendation is accepted, the second stage in the systems analysis work might be an even closer analysis of the current system, which will then lead straight into systems design work.

These two stages in systems analysis would only differ in the amount of detail they go into, and so the length of time they might take. The two stages could be combined into one, and all the systems analysis work could be done during the feasibility study.

Activity 5

What might be the benefits of analysing an existing system in detail, rather than just listing in outline the tasks performed (such as 'record sales and produce invoices').

5   METHODOLOGIES AND TECHNIQUES FOR SYSTEMS ANALYSIS AND DESIGN

The systems development lifecycle approach to systems development was adopted by many organisations. It provided a model of how systems should be developed. The *success* of the cycle can be attributed to a number of factors. It imposed a disciplined approach to the development process, it encouraged communication between systems professionals and 'ordinary' users and it recognised the importance of analysis and design, previously much neglected. While it has some advantages, it had a number of drawbacks and in recent years a number of commercial methodologies, which approach the development process in a different way, have been developed.

Various methodologies are available to use in systems analysis and design. Most modern approaches to systems analysis and design:

(a) focus on the information needs and requirements of users as a justification for processing methods and techniques;

(b) work on a top-down philosophy from the general to the specific;

(c) leave physical implementation until last.

Definition

Methodologies are systems of methods for solving problems.

Methodologies like (structured systems analysis and design method) document the analysis and design process extensively. Each stage requires a number of documents to be provided, as a sign that it has been completed, and to ensure that the outputs from one stage are used as inputs to the next. Some methodologies may be too elaborate for some systems development, so users may adapt them to their own particular needs.

All methodologies use various techniques. Some techniques are helpful in creating the broad outline design of the system; others are used for the more detailed work of program or file analysis and design.

5.1 Data modelling

A data processing system is created to take input data, process it and produce output. The term 'data modelling' is sometimes used to describe the technique of looking at a system from a *data handling* perspective, and answering the following questions.

(a) What data is needed?

(b) Why is it needed?

(c) What is the data used for?

(d) Who uses the data?

(e) Where does the data originate and how?

The answers to these questions, once obtained, should then lead on to other, more detailed questions.

(a) When is the data needed, and how frequently?

(b) When does the source data originate?

(c) How should the data be processed?

(d) Where should the data be filed?

(e) How should the data be maintained and updated, and who should be responsible for this?

(f) Who should be allowed access to file data?

5.2 Data flow analysis

Data flow analysis is a broadly applicable design technique, which may be used for manual as well as computerised systems. The description of how data is handled does not in any way imply that a specific technology ought to be used, and so it is a method for understanding how a system works without forcing computerisation upon it.

When a systems analyst first looks at a system, to find out how the data is processed (or should be processed), all he or she wants to do is to sort out what data is used, who uses it, and where it is stored. One useful way of recording the ways in which data is processed, without bothering with the hardware used, is a *dataflow diagram* (DFD).

153

5.3 Dataflow diagrams

There are only *four* symbols used in dataflow diagrams. They should not be confused with any type of flowcharting symbols.

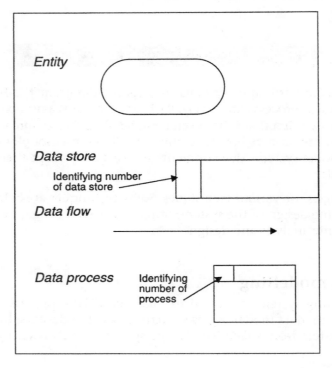

Figure 11.2 A dataflow diagram

Entity

An entity is a *source* or *destination* of data which is external to the system. It may be people or groups who provide data or input information or who receive data or output information.

Data store

Examples of data stores are transaction records, data files, reports and documents. A data store is a point which holds data, and receives a data flow. Data stores are not restricted as to their form, and might be held in a computer's CPU memory, or in the form of various magnetic media, or in the form of documents in a filing cabinet, or on microfiche.

Data flows

A data flow represents the movement or transfer of data from one point in the system to another. This may involve a document transfer or it may simply involve a notification that some event has occurred without any detailed information being passed. Multiple data flows may also exist. When a data flow occurs a copy of the data transferred may also be retained at the transmitting point. A data flow could be 'physically' anything, for example, a letter, a telephone call, a fax message, a link between computers, or a verbal statement.

Data process

Data processes are processing actions carried out from a data store, or which produce a data store. The processes could be manual, mechanised or automated/computerised. A data process will use or alter the data in some way. An example of a process which simply uses the data would be an output operation, where the data held by the system is unchanged and it is merely made available in a different form, for example, printed out. A process which alters the data would be a mathematical computation or a process such as sorting in which the arrangement of the data is altered. Systems vary widely in the amount of data processing they perform. Some systems are dominated by the amount of data movement they provide, while others are intensively concerned much more with transforming the data into a more useful form.

5.4   Levelled DFDs

The complexity of business systems means that it is impossible to represent the operations of any system by means of a single diagram. At the top level, an overview of the different systems in an organisation can be given, or alternatively the position of a single system in the organisation shown. This might be achieved by means of a *systems context diagram*. Next, a summary of the operation of a single system can be shown by means of a dataflow diagram. At this stage, a 'data process' symbol can be used to represent the workings of a whole department or of a series of related processes. This is in turn 'exploded' by means of a more detailed dataflow diagram, known as a level-one DFD. Further detail can be represented on a level-two DFD, until all individual processes, sources and sinks and files are shown.

Activity 6

The production department of a company requests some materials from stores on a form. The stores department files this form, after sending a note back saying that the materials requested are currently out of stock. The reply is filed by the production manager. Identify the data sources, data destinations, data flows and data stores involved.

Figures 11.3–11.5 show what a dataflow diagram records; each is prepared to record a certain level of detail. The example used here is a sales and warehousing system.

A level-0 DFD shows the inputs and outputs of the system and makes the system boundary clear. In the organisation shown, customers send in orders on an order form. The organisation despatches the goods and completes a two-part delivery note. The top copy goes to the customer and the bottom copy is sent to the accounts department for invoicing and accounting purposes. When suppliers send goods in, their despatch notes are retained.

A level-1 DFD details the data flows between the subsystems in the system. Here, the 'sales and warehousing system' process which was shown in a single box is analysed in more detail, and the dataflows between the separate departments within this function are shown. Customer orders are received by the sales department. The sales department checks with accounts that the order is within the customer's credit limit. If so, goods are requisitioned from the warehouse, from where they are passed to despatch. Two despatch notes are made out: one is sent to the customer and the other to the accounts department. Meanwhile goods have been received from suppliers; details of goods are enclosed on the supplier's delivery note, from which a GRN is made out and sent to the accounts department.

A separate level-2 DFD would then be prepared for each of the sales, despatch and warehouse subsystems. Figure 11.5 shows the data flows within the warehouse. Similar diagrams would be prepared for each of the other subsystems.

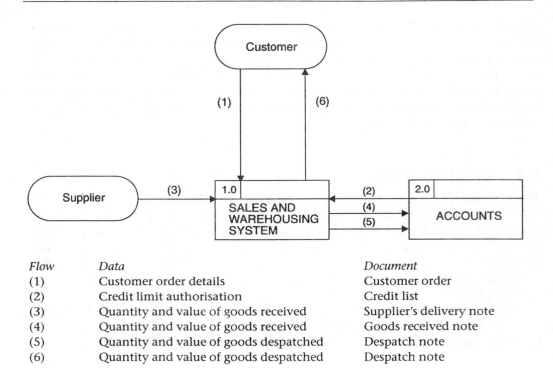

Flow	Data	Document
(1)	Customer order details	Customer order
(2)	Credit limit authorisation	Credit list
(3)	Quantity and value of goods received	Supplier's delivery note
(4)	Quantity and value of goods received	Goods received note
(5)	Quantity and value of goods despatched	Despatch note
(6)	Quantity and value of goods despatched	Despatch note

Figure 11.3 A level-0 dataflow diagram

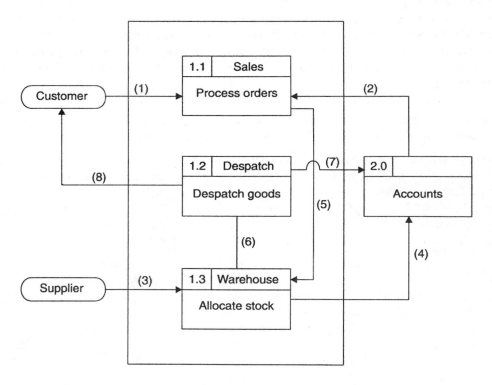

Flow	Data	Document
(1)	Customer order details	Customer order
(2)	Credit limit authorisation	Authorisation list
(3)	Quantity and value of goods received	Supplier's delivery note
(4)	Quantity and value of goods received	Goods received note
(5)	Customer order details	Requisition
(6)	Quantity of goods to be despatched	Despatch instruction
(7)	Quantity and value of goods despatched	Despatch note
(8)	Quantity and value of goods despatched	Despatch note

Figure 11.4 A level-1 dataflow diagram

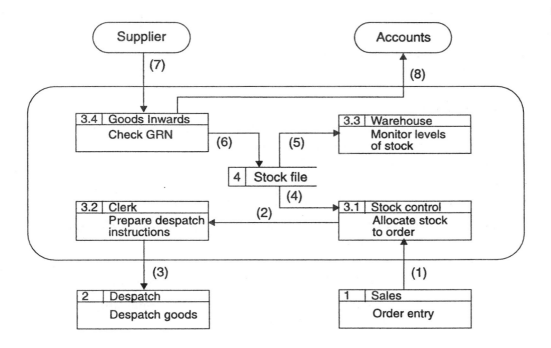

Flow	Data	Document
(1)	Customer order details	Requisition
(2)	Quantity and value of customer requirements	Order form
(3)	Quantity of goods to be despatched	Despatch instructions
(4)	Quantity of goods to be despatched	N/A
(5)	Stock levels	N/A
(6)	Quantity and value of goods received	N/A
(7)	Quantity and value of goods received	Supplier's delivery note
(8)	Quantity and value of goods received	Goods received note

Figure 11.5 A level-2 dataflow diagram

You may have noticed that flows 3, 4, 5 and 6 in the level-1 diagram are recognisable in the level-2 diagram as flows 7, 8, 1 and 3 respectively. This demonstrates the overall logic of levelled DFDs. To look at one of these further, in the level-1 DFD flow 3 shows quantity and value of goods received coming in on the supplier's delivery note. Flow 7 on the level-2 DFD shows the same thing, with the additional identification of the specific process within process 3 which is the destination of the flow. (You should note that the numbering of flows is not significant: it is used merely as a key.) You could compare the level-0 diagram with the level-1 diagram and track the same logical relationships in flows in and out of the subsystem under consideration.

Activity 7

A set of dataflow diagrams is to be prepared to show an organisation's entire system for paying its employees. Give some examples of sub-systems which would appear on a level-1 dataflow diagram and have their own level-2 dataflow diagrams.

5.5   Data analysis

Any set of data must be structured in such a way that users of the system can access and process data in the ways they want to. This is particularly true of databases, which require flexibility in the way in which information is handled.

The person creating the set of data must first carry out an analysis of all the data for processing and filing, because a full and accurate analysis of data in the system is crucial to the construction of complete and workable sets of data. Data analysis involves defining the items of data, not simply the flow of data.

Entity modelling

One approach to data analysis is *entity modelling* (also called *logical data analysis*). An entity is an item (such as a person, a job, a business, an activity, a product or a stores item) about which information is stored.

In single application systems (such as a sales ledger system, a payroll system or a purchase ledger system) a record will be created for an entity.

(a) In a sales ledger system, records will be created for customers. A customer is an entity, and all customers together are an *entity set*.

(b) Similarly, in a payroll system, records will be created about employees. An employee is an entity, and all employees together are an entity set.

We can identify *relationships* between attributes. Here are some simple examples. The diagrams are called *Bachmann diagrams*.

(a)

Figure 11.6 A one-one relationship

The relationship between the Bank of England and the governor is a *one-one* relationship because the Bank of England employs only one governor.

(b)

Figure 11.7 A one-many relationship

The university employs a large number of lecturers. The relationship is *one-many*.

(c)

Figure 11.8 A many-one relationship

Many students belong to one course. The relationship is *many-one*.

(d)

Figure 11.9 A many-many relationship

A large number of borrowers wish to reserve a large number of books. The relationship is *many-many*.

Activity 8

Of what types are the following relationships?

(a) Lecturer works for Edinburgh University.

(b) People work for employers.

(c) Programs are produced by Microsoft.

Figure 11.10 shows the relationships between some of the entities involved in running a business.

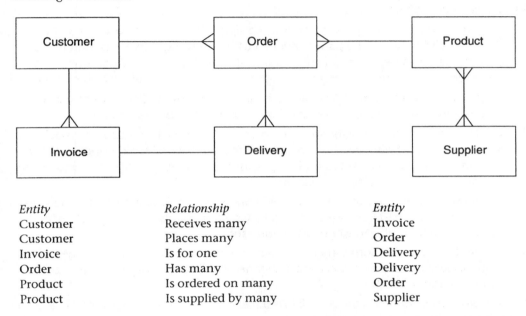

Entity	Relationship	Entity
Customer	Receives many	Invoice
Customer	Places many	Order
Invoice	Is for one	Delivery
Order	Has many	Delivery
Product	Is ordered on many	Order
Product	Is supplied by many	Supplier

Figure 11.10 Business entity relationships

Chapter roundup

- An information technology strategy is important because of the high costs involved, because of the difference information technology can make to an organisation's competitiveness and because of the impact which information technology can have on all levels of management.

- The systems development life cycle covers the recognition of a problem, the feasibility study, the investigation and analysis of the existing system, the design and implementation of a new system, the review and maintenance of the new system and the recognition of any new problems.

- A feasibility study is intended to ensure that the development of a new system is only undertaken if the benefits are likely to outweigh the costs.

- Existing systems may be investigated using interviews, questionnaires and observation.

- Systems analysis involves obtaining a detailed understanding of the existing system, using techniques such as dataflow diagrams and entity modelling.

Quick quiz

1   In what ways can information technology be used as a strategic weapon?
2   Which parties are likely to be interested in the use of information technology by a major organisation?
3   What are typical terms of reference of a feasibility study?
4   What benefits of the use of information technology are likely to be intangible?
5   What are the features of a good questionnaire?
6   What does SSADM stand for?
7   What might be shown in different levels of dataflow diagrams?
8   What types of relationship between entities can there be?

Answers to activities

1   A car hire company might introduce a computerised system to allocate cars to customers and pre-print the paperwork for customers to sign, thus ensuring that cars are available when required and are easy to collect and return. Customers would tend to use such a company in preference to other companies without such technology.

2   Programs are written to perform particular tasks. Only after the systems design stage has been completed is it clear exactly what tasks need to be performed.

3   No. The point of a feasibility study is to assess whether it is possible to achieve improvements cost-effectively. Such an assessment is needed for a proposed change from one computer system to another, just as much as for a proposed change from a manual system to a computer system.

4   The question is an insult to the department and would probably make the clerk fear for his job. After it had been asked, the clerk would probably not co-operate with the interviewer, and might give him false information.

5   It might be found that some small stages are unnecessary, or that some stages which might appear to be unnecessary are in fact needed because they provide important controls or input to other stages.

6   The production department is a data source and the stores department is a data destination for the data flow which is the request for materials. The stores department's file is a data store for the form. The stores department is a data source and the production department is a data destination for the data flow which is the notification that the materials are out of stock. The production manager's file is a data store for the note.

7   Collection of information on hours worked

    Collection of information on new employees and employees leaving

    Computation of gross pay, deductions and net pay

    Production of payslips

    Sending information to a bank to pay wages

    Paying tax and national insurance to the Inland Revenue

8   (a)   Many-one

    (b)   Many-many

    (c)   Many-one

Further question practice

Now try the following practice questions at the end of this text.

Multiple choice questions   **74 to 80**

Exam style question   **9**

Chapter 12

SYSTEMS DESIGN

Introduction

In this chapter we examine some specific issues relating to systems design. We are concerned here primarily with the interface between user and computer and you should read this material in the light of the earlier discussion of graphical user interfaces.

Your objectives

After completing this chapter you should:

(a) be aware of the distinction between outline design and detailed design;

(b) be aware of the main aspects of output design;

(c) know the main considerations affecting input design;

(d) know the main considerations affecting document design;

(e) be able to state the qualities of a good source document;

(f) be able to recognise well designed and badly designed keyboard/screen dialogues;

(g) know the main considerations affecting file design.

1   OUTLINE DESIGN AND DETAILED DESIGN

The first stage in systems design is to prepare an outline design showing the data flows. The methods used (such as dataflow diagrams) are the same as in systems analysis. The difference is that instead of finding out what happens in an existing system, the designer sets out what should happen in order to achieve the objectives of the new system.

The techniques used to prepare a detailed design for a computer system, once the outline system design has been prepared, are likely to vary between systems.

(a) Where a system uses application-specific files, the design of the system will involve deciding what data will be held on each file.

(b) When a system uses a database , the design of the system will focus on how the database should be structured.

In both cases, the designer must consider the form and contents of both inputs and outputs. In this chapter, we shall consider these detailed design issues. The design sequence might be:

(a) outputs (results), including documents, codes, screens and dialogues;

(b) inputs (data), including documents, codes, screens and dialogues;

(c) files;

(d) procedures (programs).

The writing of programs is not considered here, as it requires specialist knowledge of programming languages.

2   OUTPUT DESIGN

2.1   What output design covers

The specification of what output the user wants from a system dictates the requirements for both input and files in the system, since the data input or held on file must be sufficient to provide the output.

Output design will cover three separately identifiable types of results.

(a) *External results* will be sent out to people outside the user's organisation. These include invoices and purchase orders.

(b) *Internal results* will be distributed within the organisation. These include management reports, error reports and audit listings.

(c) *Internal system results* give information relating to the operation of the system itself, such as system operating statistics and control totals and reports.

The design of output will cover the following aspects.

(a) *Identification of output.* All output report documents and VDU screen displays must be clearly specified and uniquely identified.

(b) *Content and format.*

(c) *Frequency of production.* The frequency with which the output will be produced must be specified, including whether there might be cases of special urgency. Response times for keyboard interrogations should be specified. Reports might be routinely produced (every week, month or year) or produced only on demand.

(d) Where appropriate, the *conditions giving rise to the production of output* should be specified. That is, what needs to happen for a particular report to be produced?

(e) The *volume* of expected output must also be specified. When output volumes are very large, and a mainframe computer is being used, the systems analyst will probably opt for high-speed printer output. When output volumes are low, the systems analyst might choose to use a low-speed printer, perhaps situated at a location remote from the mainframe computer.

(f) The *sequence* in which output is produced must be specified.

(g) The *output medium* must be specified (for example, screen, paper or microform). Also the number of copies required must be considered. Output which will be used as input to another program will need a computer readable medium, such as a magnetic disk.

The choice of output medium will have regard to both whether a hard copy is required and the required quality.

2.2 Costs and benefits

The costs and benefits of output must be considered. The user might ask for information that would be too costly to produce in view of the benefits obtainable from it. Questions that the systems designer might consider in designing the output are as follows.

(a) Is the user asking for too much information?

(b) Can two or more required outputs be combined into a single multi-use output?

(c) Is the output required as frequently as specified, or can the frequency be reduced?

(d) Should output be produced automatically, or only on demand?

(e) Does the response time have to be short?

(f) Should the user be allowed some control over the format and sequence of output?

The answers to these questions cannot be decided by the systems analyst alone; they should also be discussed with the user.

Example

In a department store, there are 50 cash desks where customers pay for their goods. The department store has a point of sale computer system, with each cash desk terminal linked to a central computer. A stock master file includes details of selling prices and quantities held in stock for each item.

What would the possible contents of a printed output report be:

(a) for each customer;

(b) for management (on a daily basis)?

Solution

(a) The customer's output report is a receipt, which gives:

    (i)   the name of the store;

    (ii)   the store's VAT registration number;

    (iii) the date and time of the transaction;

    (iv) a list of items purchased, and their prices;

    (v)   the total price for all the customer's purchases;

    (vi) possibly, the method of payment;

    (vii) if payment is in cash, the amount of cash paid and the change given.

(b) The output for a daily management report might include:

    (i)   a list of the total quantity and value of sales for each stock item;

(ii)   total sales for the day, possibly analysed by department or cash desk;

(iii) a list of quantities of each item still held in stock;

(iv) a list of stock items for re-ordering and quantities already on order.

Activity 1

A factory includes 12 production lines, each making a different product. All materials, labour time, power used, good output and output rejected are recorded for each line on a computer system. Suggest contents for:

(a) a daily report for the production supervisor;

(b) a monthly report for the board of directors.

3   INPUT DESIGN

The design of input is important because in most computer systems, data is first of all collected in human-readable form and must be converted into computer input. People are thus very much involved in providing the data that the computer system will use, and in input design the systems analyst must balance the requirements of the system with the personal capabilities of its users.

3.1   Considerations

Considerations in input design include the following.

(a) Which input data will become 'standing' or 'static' master file data and which input will be regular transaction data? There should be no unnecessary re-input of data. For example, if master file data includes a customer's name, address and account number, it should only be necessary to input the account number with any transaction data. Transaction records should not contain the name and address.

(b) What volumes of input are expected? Large volumes are likely to lend themselves to a batch processing system rather than a demand processing system.

(c) What will the frequency of input be? Infrequent transaction data might suggest a demand processing system using keyboard terminals.

With batched input, we must consider:

(i)   how often transaction data must be input (daily, weekly or monthly);

(ii) how often input data must be used to keep the master file up to date with standing data, that is how often file maintenance should be carried out.

(d) In what sequence should batched data be input? For example, data for file maintenance ought to be input before transaction data, to ensure that the standing data on the master file is up to date before the transaction data is processed.

(e) Where will data be collected or captured for input? Where will it be converted into machine-readable form? In general, it is preferable to capture data (in machine-readable form) as soon as possible and to keep to a minimum the transcription of data from one document to another before input.

(f) What should the input medium be? Are inaccuracies costly or unacceptable, and so should there be verification of input? How extensive should checks be?

(g) What data should be input? and in what form?

3.2 Data preparation control

In addition to input design, the systems analyst should give some consideration to data preparation control. Depending on the system, data preparation control may be applied by data preparation staff at a computer centre. Alternatively, data might be keyed in by staff in the user department. Data preparation design work must try to ensure that:

(a) all the data to be input is received and fed into the system;

(b) all the data is processed through the system (apart from any erroneous data which is rejected, and which must also be accounted for).

Data preparation also includes any required *verification* of data.

Data preparation control in a batch processing system is achieved by means of batch control, that is collecting incoming documents into batches and attaching a batch control document (showing its serial number) to each batch. Batching offers several advantages.

(a) It helps in the allocation of work between data preparation staff; individual staff can be given specified batches of input to prepare, and their accuracy and speed can be monitored.

(b) Locating errors is simplified, because exception reports from the computer program notifying error conditions and rejected input can show which batch the incorrect entry belongs to.

(c) An incorrect batch can be removed individually, so that the remaining input can be processed without difficulty.

To help with batch control, the systems analyst should give some thought to:

(a) whether batches should be a constant size (all containing the same number of input records) or whether a batch control document record should identify the number (and perhaps the total value) of records in the batch;

(b) how data preparation management should be notified of what batches to expect. For example, can batches be received at regular intervals from the clerical staff preparing the original input forms, and can a list be provided of the batches sent?

Batch control assists with the control of input data. Control totals on batch control documents (for example the total value of all invoices in a batch) can be compared with control totals of records processed by the computer, so that a check can be carried out within a program that all the submitted data has been processed or can be accounted for by rejection reports.

Activity 2

Transactions data is collected on forms which are filled in by hand. Not all of the handwritten data is to be keyed into the computer system, and some of the data which is keyed in is not processed immediately.

(a) Suggest features of the forms which would make it easy for staff keying in data to identify the data which should be keyed in.

(b) Should the data not required immediately be keyed in straightaway or should it be keyed in later, when it is required for processing?

---

4 DOCUMENT DESIGN (FORM DESIGN)

4.1 Purpose

In designing a system, an analyst may have to design a large number of different forms or documents for input data and for output. Although document design is largely a matter of common sense and experience, you should not forget the purpose of the document, nor the points discussed below.

The purpose served by a document is to ensure the effective transmission of necessary information. A good document will allow the required information to be obtained, transmitted, interpreted, filed and retrieved at minimum total cost. The total cost includes not only the printing and paper costs but also the handling costs. The latter may be significantly increased by bad design.

4.2 Document design analysis form

Before attempting to design a document, the analyst must consider whether the document is really necessary, or whether there is another document, either existing or proposed, which serves or could be made to serve the same purpose. To help with analysing the documents, the analyst should prepare a document analysis form for each document in the existing system and for each document required in the new system.

The document analysis form for input documents is similar to a document description form and will include:

(a) the *identification*: the document title and number;

(b) the *purpose* of the document;

(c) the *origination* of documents, both the place and the means of origination;

(d) the *contents* of the document;

(e) the *sequence* of the data;

(f) the *volume* of use: maximum, minimum, average and seasonal fluctuations;

(g) the *frequency* of preparation, at present and in the foreseeable future;

(h) the *files* affected by the input, both transaction and master files.

Definition

A *document desciption form* is a form used to record facts about documents used in the existing system during systems investigation

The analyst must also consider the files used and should prepare a file analysis form to identify the purpose, content, layout and volume of records. The organisation and content of files may affect the format of the input document.

Activity 3

The production department of a company uses a standard requisition form to obtain goods from stores. Set out possible entries on a document analysis form in respect of such a requisition form.

In designing a form there are a number of decisions to be made. These can be split into five areas: content, lay-out, make-up, printing and paper.

Computer graphics packages now make form design a relatively simple task. A number of alternative designs can be prepared and tested.

4.3 Form content

Generally, the content of a form will be determined by the system to which it belongs. There are, however, some items which appear on most forms, including:

(a) a title;

(b) a serial number;

(c) a date;

(d) some narrative, in the form of instructions and subsidiary headings;

(e) units such as hours, £'s or tonnes;

(f) a signature (perhaps with authorisation);

(g) the destinations of copies (for example, copy 1 – accounts; 2 – production control).

The title of a form should be descriptive and easy to remember. The narrative, that is the headings or instructions relating to spaces where entries are required, must also be given careful consideration. The words used must be matched to the educational and technical level of both the originator and the interpreter.

4.4 Form layout

Points to consider include:

(a) the direction of the paper;

(b) the position of the title;

(c) the position of the identification code and the serial number (normally near a corner);

(d) the position of entry headings (near the spaces to which they relate);

(e) the entry sequence. Entries should always follow a logical sequence;

(f) the boxing of items, to make reading the form or filling it in easier.

The document may contain 'heading' information which is common to a number of repeated items ('variable' information). For example, on a sales invoice the customer name, address, account number and invoice number is heading information whereas the product details such as quantity, description, code number and price is variable information, with several products likely to be listed on a single invoice.

4.5 Make-up, printing and paper

Considerations in this area will include:

(a) make-up:

    (i) the size of the form (for ease of handling and filing; and to allow enough space for all the information);

    (ii) the colour (colour coding may be used for ease of identification);

(b) printing:

    (i) the number of copies required (multi-part sets may be needed);

    (ii) the filing requirements (the position of the identification code and the serial number);

    (iii) the typeface (for easy reading and to stress important data);

(c) the paper quality and thickness (how easily might a thin paper form be damaged, and how long will a form be kept?)

4.6 Qualities of a good form

A good form is one which is designed so that information can be easily:

(a) obtained: the layout of the form and instructions on how to fill it in should be clear to the user. As much information as possible should be pre-printed to avoid error and reduce the workload. The form must be easy to use. Turnround documents might be a possibility;

(b) transmitted: the form must allow for easy handling and transmission. For example, it may need to be sent by post, and should therefore fit into a standard size envelope;

(c) interpreted: the layout of information on the form must be in a clear, logical sequence so that it can be readily understood. A good title will help, and colour coding might also clarify its use. The use of different typefaces should be considered.

(d) filed: the size of filing cabinets or trays should be considered;

(e) retrieved: the problems of easy retrieval of a form from file should also be considered. In a hard copy file, the position of the serial number or some other key field of the record may be very important.

Activity 4

Why might different considerations apply to the design of forms purely for internal use and forms to be sent to users outside an organisation?

Printing forms costs money and waste (for example, by spending unnecessarily on form size, form quality or the number of copies in a set) should be avoided. Furthermore, data should only be gathered if the cost of doing so is justified by its value. Hidden costs may include the cost of writing the source documents, and the cost of data preparation and filing in a computer system.

In computer systems the entries on forms may have to be transcribed into a machine readable medium but the forms may have functions other than data collection for computer processing. For example, a sales invoice has to function as a sales invoice and so its contents may contain data which is not required for processing. The layout of the invoice must:

(a) indicate clearly which data is to be transcribed into a machine readable medium, for example by shading parts of the document, by entering the data in a particular section of the document or by using chemically coated or carbon backed documents for selective duplication;

(b) show the data in keying-in sequence from left to right and from top to bottom of the sheet.

5 SCREEN DESIGN, DIALOGUE DESIGN AND FILE DESIGN

Displays which contain a lot of data are often virtually useless since people cannot readily identify the important information. Whenever displays are being designed it is vital to consider their purpose and to present the information so that the users can quickly see and understand it.

5.1 Screen design

The VDU is used as both an input and an output device in many systems, and the systems designer has the job of designing the layout of the data on the screen. Relevant considerations are the same as those for the content and layout of forms.

5.2 Keyboard/screen dialogue

When the computer asks for information from the user, it should give a helpful prompt (such as 'please input sales total') rather than an uninformative '?'. The user should be able to ask for information from the computer in a natural way. This process can be helped by presenting the user with a menu of options, and inviting a choice between them.

Thus a library catalogue system might offer a list such as:

1 – Author search

2 – Title search

3 – Subject search

The user would then be invited to type 1, 2 or 3.

The dialogue should have a natural flow to it, clearly related to the user's understanding of the transactions being processed.

Activity 5

A company sells several products over the telephone, customers paying by credit card. At the start of a call, the salesperson initiates a computer program to take the customer's personal details and order, and in the course of the conversation the salesperson types this information into the computer, requesting information from the customer in response to prompts on a VDU. Suggest an appropriate sequence for the prompts, so that the customer will feel that the order is being taken in a natural way by a human being.

5.3 File design

A systems analyst must also design the transaction files, reference files and master files or the database used in a system.

In designing master files, considerations will include the following.

(a) Is random access of the file by the system or the user needed?

(b) Is a quick response time needed?

(c) What data should the files contain?

(d) How will the files be used for processing transaction data?

(e) What facilities should be available for file interrogation?

(f) How will the files be maintained?

(g) How large will the files be, and what capacity for file growth should be built in?

If there is a choice of file medium (essentially, a choice between tape and disk or between types of disk), the factors governing the decision are:

(a) the required speed of movement of data between the storage devices and the computer's memory;

(b) the way in which records should be ordered for access (for example, is sequential ordering appropriate?);

(c) the need to allow enough room on the file for both the current volume and expected expansion;

(d) the expected 'hit rate', that is the ratio of the number of transaction records in a typical updating run to the number of master file records.

The systems analyst must provide facilities to insert new records onto the file and to amend or delete existing records. Adequate space must be allowed in the file for newly-inserted records. There might also be a requirement to interrogate the file, which might involve random access from a remote terminal.

Activity 6

A company's accounting system is to be computerised. It is possible that eventually the number of products sold by the company will double, and the number of its customers will increase to three times the present number. All customers buy all products. The number of suppliers to the company is, however, expected to remain the same as at present. File sizes have already been calculated, based on the company's present level of activity but allowing for individual monetary and other amounts to have any reasonable number of digits. By how much would you multiply the calculated file sizes for each of the following files to determine the required computer file sizes, assuming that an extra 50% of the final anticipated level of activity is to be added as a safety margin?

(a) The sales (debtors) ledger, which requires an entry for each purchase of each product

(b) The purchases (creditors) ledger, which requires an entry for each order for each product

(c) The stock list

Chapter roundup

- The production of an outline systems design resembles the analysis of the existing system. In detailed systems design, outputs, inputs, files and programs must be designed.
- In the design of output, its content, format, frequency of production, volume, sequence of production and medium should all be considered.
- The designer of output should also consider whether all the output initially requested really ought to be produced.
- In the design of input, its volume, frequency, sequence and medium should all be considered, along with the method of data collection and conversion into machine-readable form, and what data actually needs to be input.
- Controls should be applied to the preparation of data.
- Proposed documents should be assessed for usefulness, and their contents and roles in the system should be analysed.
- There are certain standard contents which appear on most forms, and standard points to bear in mind in the layout of forms.
- A good form is one which makes it easy to record, file and retrieve information.

> ## Chapter roundup (*continued*)
>
> - A screen should be designed with the same care as a form. A keyboard/screen dialogue should use obvious English phrases, rather than codes which are hard to remember.
> - In the design of files, the first thing to consider is how the files will be used. Requirements for methods of access, speed of access and space for expansion are all relevant.

Quick quiz

1 What are the three types of output to consider in output design?

2 What questions could be asked if it is suspected that the output asked for is excessive?

3 How should the data held on a master file be used to avoid unnecessary re-input of data?

4 What items appear on most forms?

5 What considerations of make-up, printing and paper are relevant to form design?

6 List the factors which should be considered when designing master files.

Answers to activities

1 (a) Good output from each line

Rejected output from each line

Materials used on each line

Labour time used on each line, analysed into normal time and overtime

Good output per labour hour

   (b) Monthly output of each product

Total materials, power and labour costs

Cost per unit of each product, analysed into materials, power and labour

2 (a) Data to be keyed in should be surrounded by boxes, or data not to be keyed in should be written on shaded areas of the forms.

   (b) All data should be keyed in straightaway and stored in a storage device until required, so that each form need only be handled once by the keying in staff (in order to save time).

3 Title: Requisition form

Number: Req 1

Purpose: To obtain goods from stores for production

Origination: Production department, filled in by production supervisor

Contents and sequence: (i)   Date

                                (ii) Item required

                                (iii) Quantity required

                                (iv) Date required

                                (v)   Location to be delivered to

                                (vi) Special notes

Volume of use: Maximum 15 a day

                                Minimum 4 a day

	Average 10 a day
	Seasonal fluctuations – none
Frequency of preparation:	As volume of use; no changes foreseen
Transaction files affected:	Materials transfers
	Materials orders
Master files affected:	Production costs
	Purchases ledger

4   Forms for internal use need not look very smart, and they may use abbreviations which will be understood by all staff affected. Forms to be sent to users outside the organisation will probably need to be printed to a higher standard on higher quality paper, and they must not use abbreviations which are not generally used outside the organisation.

5   Name

Address

Products required (including quantities)

Credit card number

Credit card expiry date

6   (a) $2 \times 3 \times 1.5 = 9$

(b) $2 \times 1 \times 1.5 = 3$

(c) $2 \times 1.5 = 3$

Further question practice

Now try the following practice questions at the end of this text.

Multiple choice questions   **81 to 87**

Exam style question   **10**

Chapter 13

IMPLEMENTATION

Introduction

The main stages in the installation and implementation of a computer system once it has been designed are as follows.

(a) Installation of the hardware and software.

(b) Staff training.

(c) Testing.

(d) Master file creation (conversion of the files).

(e) Changeover.

The activities in this list do not necessarily happen in a set chronological order, and some can be done at the same time, for example staff training and system testing can be part of the same operation. The requirements for installation also vary from system to system.

Training is covered in the next chapter. The other activities are addressed below, following which we round off this chapter with an examination of the final stages of the systems development life cycle.

Your objectives

After completing this chapter, you should:

(a) know the main stages in installing and implementing a computer system;

(b) know how to install a PC system;

(c) know what special arrangements are necessary to install a mainframe computer;

(d) understand the importance of tests and the role of test data;

(e) be aware of the steps in file conversion and of the problems that can arise;

(f) know four methods of changeover, and the factors affecting the choice between them;

(g) be aware of the scope of a performance review;

(h) be aware of how to assess a system by considering its outputs;

(i) understand the role of system maintenance.

1 SYSTEMS INSTALLATION AND SYSTEMS IMPLEMENTATION

1.1 The installation team

The responsibility for successful system installation should rest with a team headed by a suitably senior manager, probably from the department which will use the new system. Membership of the team will vary from organisation to organisation, and according to the size and importance of the new system.

(a) In an organisation with its own data processing department, the team will include a systems analyst, or the data processing manager.

(b) In an organisation without a data processing department, the team should ideally include a person who already has some knowledge and personal experience of data processing systems.

(c) For a small office PC system using an off-the-shelf software package, the office manager will probably be given the job without other staff.

The tasks of this team are to co-ordinate the activities leading up to the installation and testing of the system and to make sure that these activities are carried out satisfactorily and on time.

The main stages in the installation and implementation of a computer system once it has been designed are:

(a) installing the hardware and software;

(b) testing;

(c) file conversion;

(d) changeover;

(e) post-implementation review;

(f) system maintenance.

Items (a) to (d) in this list do not necessarily happen in a set chronological order, and some of them can be done at the same time; for example, system testing and master file creation can be part of the same operation.

1.2 Installing PC hardware and software

With a PC system, the dealer may or may not agree to install the system for the customer. Installing the hardware should not be difficult, provided that the manufacturer's instruction manuals are read carefully.

The office accommodation for PCs and peripheral equipment will need some planning.

(a) PCs can be used in any office environment, but they generate some heat when they operate (just like any other machine) and it is therefore inadvisable to put them in small, hot rooms.

(b) Large desks may be advisable, to accommodate screens, keyboards and leave some free desk space for the users.

(c) There should be plenty of power sockets: enough to meet future needs as the system grows, not just immediate needs.

(d) If noisy printers (such as daisy wheel printers) are to be used, it may be advisable to locate these in a separate room, or at least fit them with printer hoods (covers), to cut down the noise for office workers.

(e) There should be a telephone close to the PC, for communicating with the dealer or other organisation which provides system support and advice when the user runs into difficulties.

The software may also need installing. To install the software, the computer user must follow the instructions in the user's manual.

There will be an initial software installation to load the operating system, such as MS-DOS. Thereafter, whenever the PC is switched on at the start of the day, the bootstrap program will automatically load the operating system.

Software packages can be loaded onto the hard disk. There is an initial registration process to register the package with the PC. When this has been done, the user is only licensed to use the package on that machine.

Once the PC is working, the user should learn how to make back-up copies of disks and should make working copies of the software disks supplied (keeping the originals as back-up copies). This will not be possible if disks are copy-protected (and the user's manual will say which disks are copy-protected and which are not) but it will protect at least some of the software from accidental erasure. Back-up copies of data files held on hard disk can be made on floppy disks. Back-up copies of an entire hard disk might be made on a tape streamer.

Insurance should be arranged against losses from fire or theft. It is also possible to obtain insurance against the accidental loss of data. If all the data on a hard disk were lost, for example, it could be a long job to re-enter all the lost data, but with insurance cover, the cost of the re-inputting would be paid by the insurance company.

Activity 1

What additional planning would be needed if a network of PCs, rather than a single PC, is to be installed?

1.3 The installation of a mainframe computer or minicomputer

A mainframe computer installation is a major operation which must be carefully planned. Minicomputers are also affected by some additional factors. Issues in planning the installation include the following.

(a) Site selection, whether in an existing or a new building. Factors in the choice of a site include the need for:

   (i)   adequate space for the computer and its peripherals, including room to allow servicing;

   (ii) room for expansion;

   (iii) easy access for computer equipment and supplies (it should not be necessary to knock holes in outside walls, as has happened, in order to bring equipment in);

   (iv) nearness to principal user departments;

   (v) strong flooring (so that the equipment does not fall to the floor below);

   (vi) space for a library, a stationery store, the data preparation department and programmers' offices.

(b) Site preparation, including the need for:

   (i)   air conditioning (temperature, humidity and dust);

   (ii) special electricity supplies;

(iii) raised floors (or false ceilings) to cover cables;

(iv) fire protection devices;

(v) furniture.

(c) Arrangements for standby equipment to ensure continuity of processing in the event of power or computer failure. Such equipment may include rechargeable storage batteries, standby generators and standby computers.

(d) Planning for delivery. Delivery can cause considerable disruption and it is often preferable for it to take place over a weekend.

Once all the required rooms have been completed, decorated and furnished, the equipment can be installed. This is the manufacturer's responsibility and his engineers will install it and carry out tests. Any further maintenance or repair of the equipment will normally be carried out by the manufacturer under a maintenance agreement.

In addition to the computer equipment, all the ancillary equipment (such as desks and trolleys) and the consumable stores (stationery, magnetic tapes, disks and so on) must be delivered and allocated to the appropriate work areas and stores.

2   TESTING

2.1   Scope

A system must be thoroughly tested before implementation, otherwise there is a danger that the new system will be implemented with faults that might prove costly. The scope of tests will vary with the size of the system.

(a) When a system is designed in-house there should be program tests for each individual program in the system. There will then be tests of the interfaces between individual programs, in overall system tests.

(b) The user department will want to carry out tests on the system, whether it is designed in-house or bought from a software house. The initial tests ought to be carried out by management personnel, who know the current operational system well and who also ideally know something about computers. The tests would be intended to sort out any major problems, using dummy (invented) data.

2.2   The personnel involved in testing

Various personnel will be involved in system tests.

(a) The project manager will have overall responsibility for the project, and must ensure that the tests are planned and executed properly, and that the system is fully documented.

(b) Systems analysts must check that the system achieves the objectives set for it, and does not contain any errors.

(c) Programmers must be on hand to cure any faults which program tests had not spotted.

(d) The computer operations manager will be in charge of data preparation work and operations in the computer room and will report any faults or weaknesses to the data processing manager and the chief systems analyst.

Test data should be constructed to test all conditions. Data including all the possible errors which the system ought to detect (such as wage payments to a non-existent employee) should be included. Unusual, but feasible, transactions should also be included in order to see how the system handles them. Examples could include several sales orders from the same customer in the same batch input, or two wage packets in the same week for the same employee.

As the data used in tests will not be wanted when the system is implemented, it does not matter whether data for the tests comes from current transactions or from historical data. Many managers prefer to use historical data, because it is then possible to check the output of the new system against the output that the current system actually produced.

2.3 Acceptance testing

Definition

Acceptance testing is the testing of a system by the user department, after the system has passed its system test

Tests are conducted by the user department's managers in order to:

(a) find software errors which exist but have not yet been detected;

(b) find out exactly what the demands of the new system are;

(c) find out whether any major changes in operating procedures will be necessary;

(d) test the system with large volumes of data;

(e) train staff in the new system and the new procedures.

These bulk tests on the system involve checks on:

(a) error correction procedures;

(b) the relationships between clerical and computer procedures;

(c) the timing of computer runs;

(d) the capacity of files;

(e) file handling, updating and amendment procedures;

(f) systems controls, including auditing requirements;

(g) procedures for data capture, preparation and input and the distribution of output.

Activity 2

What unusual or erroneous transactions might be included in the test data for a stock control system?

3 FILE CONVERSION

Definition

File conversion is the conversion of existing master file records and reference file records to a form suitable for the new system.

A system cannot become operational until master files for the new system have been created. File conversion is a major part of systems implementation. It can be expensive because it often means the conversion of existing manual file records into a medium usable by the computer. This may involve the transcription of records, or parts of them, onto specially designed forms before they are keyed in.

3.1 Checking

File conversion can be tedious and time consuming. Because of the volume of data that must be copied onto the new files, the problem of errors getting onto the master files is a serious one, in spite of data validation checks in the file conversion program. Once the file has been created extensive checking for accuracy is essential, otherwise considerable problems may arise when the new system becomes operational.

Where the file conversion is from manual records the manager or systems analyst in charge of planning the conversion must establish:

(a) the location of the data (is all the data for each record on one form or on several forms?);

(b) whether the existing forms are suitable for data capture;

(c) whether the data format and sequence are suitable for the computer system;

(d) whether the existing records are maintained centrally or not;

(e) whether each form is easily accessible;

(f) the volumes involved;

(g) whether the existing files are to be converted directly or amalgamated in some way.

Before starting to load data about actual customers, suppliers or employees, management should check whether the system must be registered under the Data Protection Act 1984.

3.2 The stages of file conversion

The stages in file conversion from manual files to computer files are normally as follows.

(a) Ensure that the original record files are accurate and up to date.

(b) Record the old file data on specially designed input documents. This will usually be done by the user department personnel (with additional temporary staff if required) following detailed instructions laid down by the systems analyst. These instructions will include the procedures for allocating new code numbers and for checking the accuracy and completeness of the data entered on the input documents (usually verification by another person and the calculation of control totals are used).

(c) Transcribe the completed input documents onto the computer media. This may be done by user department staff keying in the data from terminals or, in large systems, by data preparation staff at the computer centre.

(d) Use special programs to read the transcribed data and produce the required files in the appropriate form. These programs would include checks on the input data. The contents of the file must then be printed out and checked back in full to the data input forms (or to the original files if possible).

(e) Correct any errors that this checking reveals.

If there is an existing computer system, the difficulties of file conversion will usually be reduced. Existing computer files can be converted to new computer files by using a special conversion program.

Other problems of file conversion which must be considered and planned for by the systems analyst include the following.

(a) The possible need for additional staff, or the use of a computer bureau, to cope with the file conversion and prevent bottlenecks.

(b) The establishment of cut-off dates where files are being converted. Processing after a cut-off date is done on the new file.

(c) The decision as to whether files should be converted all at once, or whether the conversion should be file by file or record group by record group, with subsequent amalgamation.

Activity 3

What checks might be appropriate when existing computer files are converted using a specially written conversion program?

---

4 CHANGEOVER OPTIONS

Once the new system has been fully and satisfactorily tested the changeover can be made. This may be by direct changeover, parallel running, pilot operation or phased implementation.

4.1 Direct changeover

In this method, the old system is completely replaced by the new system in one move. This may be unavoidable where the two systems are substantially different, where the new system is a real-time system or where extra staff to oversee parallel running are unobtainable. While this method is comparatively cheap, it is risky (system or program corrections are difficult while the system has to remain operational) and management must have complete confidence in the new system. The new system should be introduced during slack periods and in large systems it may be introduced application by application, allowing several months between each stage to ensure that all problems are cleared up before the next stage becomes operational.

4.2 Parallel running

In this method the old and new systems are run in parallel for a period of time, both processing current data. Cross checks can then be made.

This method is fairly safe if there may be problems with the new system. However, if there are differences between the two systems cross-checking may be difficult or impossible. Furthermore, there is a delay in the actual implementation of the new system, a possible indication of lack of confidence in the new system and a need for more staff to cope with both systems running in parallel. This cautious approach, if adopted, should be properly planned, and the plan should include:

(a) a firm time limit on parallel running;

(b) details of how much data should be cross-checked;

(c) instructions on how errors are to be dealt with;

(d) instructions on how to cope with major problems in the new system.

4.3 Pilot operation

This is cheaper and easier to control than parallel running, and provides a greater degree of safety than does direct changeover. Only part of the data (say the sales in one region) is handled by the new system until it has been shown to work satisfactorily. If there is real concern about the new system, part of the data could be pilot run on the new system while still being processed on the old system – a combination of parallel running and pilot operation.

4.4 Phased implementation

In phased implementation, a complete logical part of the old system (for example, the invoice issuing system) is chosen and run as a unit on the new system. If this works well the remaining parts are then transferred. Gradually the whole system can be transferred in this piecemeal fashion. Again, planning should involve setting strict time limits for each phase and instructions on how problems are to be dealt with. It must be remembered that two systems have to be controlled and additional staff may be required.

When deciding upon which method, or combination of methods, should be used for the changeover, management should consider:

(a) how co-ordination of the changeover is to be achieved;

(b) how to ensure complete and accurate communication throughout the system during the changeover period;

(c) the method of controlling errors and the amount of system change or program modification that can be permitted;

(d) the people who are involved, how the change affects them and how they can be trained and get used to working the new system;

(e) the maintenance and operation methods of the new system;

(f) the method of monitoring and evaluating the results of the changeover.

The *duration* of any parallel running or pilot operation can vary quite substantially between systems, from days to months. However, with tailor-made software purchased from a software house, it may be important to complete the changeover quickly, because the software house's debugging warranty will normally expire three months after the date of purchase.

Definition

A *debugging warranty* is an agreement by a software house to correct program errors, known as bugs

Timing is important. The new system should be installed and become operational at a time that is convenient to the user, preferably when the workload is fairly light, and certainly not at a time of peak workload. An accounting system might be installed to coincide with the beginning of a new accounts year.

On the satisfactory conclusion of parallel running or pilot operation, the system will go fully operational, benefiting from the lessons learned during tests and the changeover period.

Activity 4

A company is computerising its sales system, using phased implementation. The system for debt collection is to be implemented first, followed by the system for issuing invoices. The debt collection system will automatically issue reminder letters based on the invoices issued but unpaid. Could there be problems if the invoice issuing system is amended during its implementation?

5 POST-IMPLEMENTATION REVIEW

The system should be reviewed periodically so that any unforeseen problems may be solved and to confirm that it is achieving and will continue to achieve the desired results. Indeed, in most systems there is a constant need to maintain and improve applications and to keep up to date with technological advances and changing user requirements.

The system should have been designed with clear, specified objectives, and justification in terms of a cost-benefit analysis or other performance criteria. Post-implementation review should establish whether the objectives have been met and, if not, why not and what should be done.

In appraising the operation of the new system immediately after the changeover, a comparison should be made between actual and predicted performance. This will include (amongst other items) consideration of throughput speed (the time between input and output), the use of computer storage, the numbers and types of errors and queries, and the cost of processing.

5.1 The scope of reviews

Reviews will vary in content from organisation to organisation, but the matters which will probably be looked at are as follows.

(a) The rate of growth of file sizes and the number of transactions processed by the system. Trends should be analysed and projected to assess whether there are likely to be problems with long processing times or inefficient file structures due to the volume of processing.

(b) The staffing needs of the system, and whether they are more or less than estimated.

(c) Any delays in processing and the consequences of any such delays.

(d) The efficiency of security procedures.

(e) The error rates for input data. High error rates may indicate inefficient preparation of input documents, an inappropriate method of data capture or poor design of input media.

(f) Whether any amendments to the system are needed.

(g) External factors. Unforeseen circumstances might have affected system performance.

(h) Whether output from the computer is being used to good purpose: how is it used? Is it timely? Does it go to the right people?

(i) The adequacy of the system documentation.

(j) The costs and benefits of the system.
   (i)   Have expected benefits been achieved or not?
   (ii) Are any unplanned benefits apparent?
   (iii) Are the costs of the system comparable with estimates?

(k) Users' comments on the system.

(l) Operational running costs, examined to discover any inefficient programs or processes. This examination may reveal excessive costs for certain items, even if costs in total may be acceptable.

A report on the review, making appropriate recommendations, should be prepared for submission to senior management.

The efficiency of a system can be assessed by looking at its outputs and inputs.

5.2 Outputs from a computer system

With regard to outputs, the efficiency of a computer system might be enhanced in any of the following ways.

(a) More outputs of some value could be produced with the same input, for example:
   (i)   if the system could produce more management information;

(ii)   if the system could make information available to more people who might need it.

(b) Outputs which have little or no value could be eliminated from the system. For example:

(i)   if reports are produced too frequently, they could be produced less often;

(ii)   if reports are distributed too widely, the distribution list could be shortened;

(iii) if reports are too bulky, they could be reduced in size.

(c) The timing and frequency of outputs might be improved. Information should be available in good time for the information user to be able to make good use of it. Reports that are issued late might lose their value. Computer systems could give managers immediate access to the information they require, using special software such as databases.

It might be found that outputs are not as satisfactory as they should be, perhaps because:

(a) *access* to information from the system is limited, and could be improved by the use of a database and/or a multi-user or network system;

(b) *output volume* is restricted because of the method of data processing used (for example, stand-alone PC systems might be slower and less efficient than multi-user systems) or the type of equipment used. A system's capabilities might be limited by:

(i)   the software's capabilities;

(ii)   the size of the computer's main store;

(iii) the capacity of the computer's backing storage;

(iv)   the number of printers linked to the computer;

(v)   the number of terminals.

A frequent complaint with many PC systems is that the operator may have to wait for certain outputs. For example, if an operator wants to call up a particular file, he or she might have to wait before the file becomes available. File enquiries can involve a lengthy wait too. Computer systems with better storage devices facilities can reduce this operator waiting time, and so be more efficient.

5.3   Inputs to a computer system

The efficiency of a computer system could be improved if the same volume and frequency of output could be achieved with fewer inputs or by inputting data more efficiently. For example, multi-user systems might be more efficient than stand-alone systems. Multi-user systems allow several operators to access the same files at the same time; this means that a person who is short of work can help another who has a heavy workload.

Management might also wish to consider whether the checks on input data are too extensive, or could be achieved at less cost.

(a) In traditional batch processing systems, it might be unnecessary to verify all input data.

(b) An alternative method of input might be chosen. For example, if an accounts system is switched to an integrated system (instead of separate systems for the sales ledger, purchase ledger and nominal ledger) a single transaction need be input only once, thus saving input time and effort and improving the accuracy and reliability of processing.

Activity 5

Why might a restructuring of a company's middle management, which does not affect the data processing department directly, make a review of the computer system appropriate?

6   SYSTEM MAINTENANCE

System maintenance involves:

(a) updating the system, to adapt it to developments in the user's methods of operation or to environmental changes as and when they occur (for example, new legislation). New processing requirements, changing volumes of processing and new methods of organisation and operation all make changes necessary. Systems must be amended to keep them up to date.

(b) correcting errors as and when they are found;

(c) documenting the system updates and corrections.

With large computer systems which are designed in-house a systems analyst and a programmer in the data processing department might be given the responsibility for system maintenance.

6.1   Software maintenance

With purchased software packages, the software supplier might agree with a customer to provide details of any new versions of the software package as they are produced, and might agree terms for providing new versions to replace old ones.

There is also likely to be an agreement between the supplier of software and the customer for the provision of a software support service. Software support involves providing experts in a system to give advice and help when a customer runs into difficulties. The help will initially be given by telephone. If a telephone call does not resolve the problem, the software expert will visit the customer's premises within a period of time agreed in the contract between the software supplier and the customer.

The key features of system maintenance ought to be flexibility and adaptability, so that:

(a) the system, perhaps with minor modifications, can cope with changes in the computer user's procedures or volume of business;

(b) the computer user can benefit from advances in computer hardware technology without having to switch to another system altogether.

If applications exceed the capabilities of computing resources all is not lost because it is possible to cope with increasing volumes and communication needs by enhancing the existing computer system, by:

(a) increasing its memory by adding memory modules;

(b) installing disks of greater capacity and higher speed;

(c) installing a more powerful processor;

(d) changing to faster printers;

(e) installing additional terminals or network facilities.

Types of maintenance

Maintenance may be classified into three types.

(a) *Corrective maintenance* means correcting errors as they arise.

(b) *Perfective maintenance* means making improvements, usually in response to user requests. Users may ask for more facilities, or for software to be made easier to use (more user-friendly).

(c) *Adaptive maintenance* means making changes to take account of changes in the environment. For example, changes in tax law might require changes in payroll programs.

6.2   Hardware maintenance

Computer hardware needs to be maintained. Maintenance services are provided:

(a) by the computer manufacturers themselves; or

(b) by third-party maintenance companies.

Maintenance of hardware can be obtained:

(a) on a contract basis. PC maintenance contracts are usually negotiated annually;

(b) on an *ad hoc* basis, calling in a maintenance company whenever a fault occurs.

Activity 6

Give examples of how changes in a computer system for the benefit of some users might adversely affect other users within the same organisation.

Chapter roundup

- When a new system is to be implemented, more needs to be done than physically installing the new hardware. The new system must be tested, files must be converted, the changeover must be carefully managed and the new system must be reviewed and maintained.

- Installing a PC system is fairly straightforward, but the instructions of the hardware manufacturer and the software suppliers must be followed carefully.

- Installing a mainframe computer requires careful planning and site preparation.

- Both individual programs and the whole system must be tested, using test data designed to reproduce all conditions which may arise in practice.

- File conversion is time consuming and prone to errors. Careful planning and thorough checking are therefore required.

- A new system may be implemented by direct changeover, parallel running, pilot operation or phased implementation.

- A post-implementation review should be wide-ranging, but should have clearly defined terms of reference.

- Inputs and outputs together define what a system actually does for its users, and should therefore be looked at closely in a review.

- System maintenance is needed so that the system can continue to meet the changing needs of its users.

Quick quiz

1 Which stages in the installation and implementation of a computer system could be carried out simultaneously?

2 In what ways should the layout of an office be considered when planning the installation of a PC system?

3 How do program tests differ from system tests?

4 What are acceptance tests?

5 What facts about manual files should be established before their conversion to computer files?

6 What are the normal stages in the conversion of manual files to computer files?

7 Distinguish pilot operation from phased implementation.

8 What matters might be considered in a post-implementation review?

9 What arrangements are normally available with software suppliers for system maintenance?

Answers to activities

1 The locations of all the PCs, the server and any shared peripherals (such as printers) must be planned. Cable runs between PCs must also be planned.

A decision is needed on which software is to be available on which machines. Special licences are needed to share software between all machines in a network.

2 Re-ordering an item which is already on order.

Ordering items not previously held.

Requesting non-existent items from stores.

Returning 20 units of an item to stores when only 15 were issued.

3 A sample of records on the new file should be compared with the corresponding records on the old file, to ensure that conversion was accurate. A sample of records on the old file should be compared with those on the new file, to ensure that all the old records did get converted.

4 Yes. The debt collection system will take data from files produced by the invoice issuing system. Any changes to the format of those files (for example, putting the date before the amount in the record for each invoice, when they had been the other way round), might make it impossible for the debt collection system to obtain the data it needs.

5 Managers need information in order to do their jobs. The information must be relevant to their areas of responsibility. If those areas change, the information which should be supplied will also change, and this may require some changes to the computer system.

6 Sales data might be presented by region to suit one manager, whereas another might prefer it to be presented by product.

Detailed production records might be required to help the purchasing manager to check on the amounts of materials issued, creating extra work for the production supervisor.

Further question practice

Now try the following practice questions at the end of this text.

Multiple choice questions **88 to 94**

Exam style question **11**

Chapter 14

TRAINING

Introduction

You should remember from the last chapter that one of the stages of systems implementation is training. Training covers everything from education of staff prior to development, for example to explain why the system is needed and to assure them that they will be consulted before major decisions are made, through to training in the use of the system so that users can work effectively once the system comes into operation.

Your objectives

After completing this chapter you should:

(a) understand the need for training at all levels in an organisation;

(b) be aware of the main methods of training available;

(c) understand the role of documentation in training;

(d) be aware of how people may react to the introduction of new systems;

(e) know some appropriate responses to adverse reactions to change;

(f) have an understanding of how a training strategy would be implemented within an HRM framework.

1 METHODS OF TRAINING

Staff training in the use of information technology is as important as the technology itself. Without effective operation at all levels computer systems can be an expensive waste of resources.

It is a major exercise to train possibly tens of thousands of employees. Here are some of the ways to meet these requirements.

(a) Traditional lectures given at training centres

(b) Computer-based training (CBT) involves on-screen practice on the system itself

(c) In-house video production, involving interactive videos

(d) Clear and comprehensive documentation and manuals for the system

Staff training policies should cover both technological skills needed and, if the job is to become more people-orientated, interpersonal skills.

Training is not simply an issue for clerical staff. As microcomputers are used more and more as management tools, training in information technology affects all levels in an organisation, from senior managers learning how to use an executive information system to accounts clerks learning how to record transactions.

1.1 Training senior managers

Managers who are knowledgeable about computers and related technologies make wiser decisions than less knowledgeable managers in the following areas.

(a) The allocation of resources to information systems

(b) Planning for information systems

(c) Establishing an appropriate corporate culture for technological development

(d) Appraising advice from information technology professionals

Senior management can be trained in a number of ways of varying degrees of formality:

(a) completely informal, such as:
   (i)   newspapers (most of the quality press run articles on computing);
   (ii) subordinates (getting subordinates to demonstrate a system);
   (iii) individual demonstrations of computer systems for senior executives;

(b) semiformal, such as:
   (i)   executive briefings;
   (ii) video demonstrations;
   (iii) short seminars, designed around an issue that is narrowly defined;

(c) formal sessions such as day courses, probably necessary if managers are to learn how to use a particular system.

1.2 Training middle managers

The type of training middle management receives is likely to be more structured and more tailored to the particular applications within their remit.

Middle management are responsible for the correct use of systems in an age of distributed processing and end-user computing. They are also responsible for implementing in detail the organisation's computer security policy. They therefore need to have some basic understanding of the actual systems they are responsible for.

Managers do not need to know in detail how computers work. They need to know how to define information requirements, how to integrate systems and what computing can do for them.

Activity 1

Senior and middle management need not learn programming languages such as COBOL. What computer skills should they acquire so that they can make good use of management information systems?

1.3 Training users

Users need a number of different types of computer and systems training.

(a) Basic literacy in data processing such as the concept of a file, updating, maintenance and so forth, is needed. This might help users to relate the workings of a manual system to its computer replacement. Also, some basic ideas on how to use a computer efficiently can be usefully taught.

(b) Users also need to learn how to use a particular application quickly, even if they do not go into the finer points of it. Such training may also give users an overall view of the system, its commands and procedures.

(c) Users might sometimes need a refresher course, especially if they do not use a particular application regularly.

(d) Users need training while operating the application (learning by doing).

(e) Users might need to be trained in the use of fourth generation languages.

Some of these facilities, for example, 'help' facilities, are provided by the computer system itself. The use of such facilities has the advantage of encouraging users to become acquainted with the technology they will be using, and to develop their skills at their own pace.

Definition

A 'help' facility is a set of operating instructions within a software package enabling users to call up on-screen information about a program while they are using it.

Training can also be provided by:

(a) reading the user manuals;

(b) disk-based tutorials provided by a software house;

(c) attending courses that the dealer or employer provides;

(d) attending courses on a leading software package (such as Excel) or an operating system (such as Windows 95) provided by a third party training establishment.

With large computer systems, extensive training of large numbers of staff will probably be necessary. Additional training measures may include:

(a) lectures on general or specific aspects of the system;

(b) discussion meetings, possibly following on from lectures, which allow the staff to ask questions and sort out problems;

(c) internal company magazines, to explain the new system in outline;

(d) handbooks, detailing the new documentation and procedures. Handbooks for different purposes will often be prepared by different persons, for example:

    (i)   systems specifications, prepared by systems analysts;

(ii)   software manuals, prepared by manufacturers or by software houses;

(iii) program specifications, prepared by senior programmers;

(iv) computer operating instructions, prepared by programmers or by the software supplier;

(v)   data preparation instructions, prepared by the operations department;

(vi) data control and library procedures, prepared by the operations department;

(vii) clerical procedure manuals, prepared by analysts and user departments.

(e) using tests on the new system to give staff direct experience before the system goes live.

Training will be the ultimate responsibility of the information director or of the personnel department in cooperation with users and computer professionals.

User documentation

At some stage before staff training takes place, the system must be fully documented for users. User documentation must tell users what they need to know in order to run programs.

User documentation is used to explain the system and to help to train staff. Additionally, it provides a point of reference should users have problems with the system in the future.

Explaining the system involves:

(a) specifying the inputs needed to the system, the format of input records, the content of each record field, the coding systems used and so on. If the system uses keyboard input, the user documentation should also set out the VDU screen designs for input, the nature of any menus or other screen prompts, the nature of any interactive processing and so on;

(b) explaining the nature of the processing methods, for example on-line input and file enquiry;

(c) specifying the nature of the system's files and what they contain;

(d) explaining the system's outputs, for example reports and documents, including the meaning of any exception reports where input data has been rejected as invalid or queried;

(e) giving instructions about what to do in the event of a system failure;

(f) establishing the clerical procedures or other ancillary procedures needed.

Activity 2

Some computer systems incorporate documentation which the user can access during processing, by entering a 'help' command. However, only one screenful of information can be displayed at once, and different users may need different kinds of advice. How might menus be used so that users can quickly access the information they need?

2 THE HUMAN FACTORS IN SYSTEMS DEVELOPMENT AND IMPLEMENTATION

2.1 Technological change and the working environment

Technological changes have extensive effects on the world of work.

(a) Semi-skilled jobs will be taken over by robots and computers. There will be fewer jobs or more part-time jobs, and so less need for supervision.

(b) There may be degrading of old skills, or an end to the need for old skills. New skills will be needed, and:

    (i) there will be more pressure on managers to provide training or re-training for staff;

    (ii) management development will be more important, to keep managers up to date, and to motivate them as advancement gets harder.

(c) As equipment becomes simpler to use, there could be opportunities for greater flexibility in manning, with one worker able to carry out more varied tasks. In manufacturing, there may be more continuous shift work working (24 hours a day), to keep expensive assets in constant use.

(d) Since more jobs will be part-time, there will be less need for full-time employees. More work will be contracted out, and full-time jobs will be lost. Managers will have to deal with external contractors instead of issuing directions to their own staff.

(e) Better communications systems, portable computers and so on reduce the need for people to work together in an office. There will be more working at home. Several managers can then share the same small office, and come into work only occasionally.

(f) Working at home is likely to speed up moves towards contracting out, and some managers might become self-employed consultants with a main client (the former employer) and a number of smaller clients who are picked up as individuals gradually markets their services more widely.

(g) Improved information systems should help managers to plan and control work more effectively.

(h) Better information systems open up opportunities for:

    (i) more centralisation of decision making by top management;

    (ii) reducing the number of middle managers.

2.2 Areas of concern

Job security and status

Employees might think that a new system will put them out of a job, because the computer will perform routines that are currently done manually.

Even when there is no threat of losing jobs, a new system might make some staff, experienced in the existing system, feel that all their experience will be worthless when the new system goes live, so that they will lose status within the office.

Resistance to a new system might stem from a fear that it will result in a loss of status for the *department* concerned. For example, the management of the department concerned might believe that a computer system will give control over information gathering and dissemination to another group in the organisation. Dysfunctional behaviour might include:

(a) interdepartmental squabbling about access to information;

(b) a tendency to disregard the new sources of information, and to stick to old methods of collecting information instead.

Career prospects

Managers and staff might think that a new system will damage their career prospects by reducing the opportunities for promotion. When the effect of a system is to reduce the requirement for staff in middle management and supervisory grades, this could well be true. On the other hand, today's successful manager should be able to adapt to information technology, and developing a career means being flexible, accepting change rather than resisting it.

Social change in the office

New systems might disrupt established social systems in offices. Individuals who are used to working together might be separated into different groups, and individuals used to working on their own might be expected to join groups. Office staff used to moving around and mixing with other people in the course of their work might be faced with the prospect of having to work in isolation at keyboards, unable to move around the office as much. Where possible, new systems should be designed so that the social fabric of the workplace is left undamaged. Group attitudes to change should then be positive rather than negative.

Bewilderment

It is easy for individuals to be bewildered by change. The systems analyst must explain the new system fully, clearing up doubts and inviting and answering questions, from a very early stage in systems investigation onwards through the design stages to eventual implementation.

Fear of depersonalisation

Staff may be afraid that the computer will take over and they will be reduced to being operators chained to the machine, losing the ability to introduce the human touch to the work they do. This is not wholly unrealistic.

Dysfunctional behaviour might follow from antagonism of operating staff towards data processing specialists who are employed to design and introduce a computer system. It might include:

(a) an unwillingness to explain the details of the current system, or to suggest weaknesses in it that the new system might eradicate. Since data processing staff need information from and participation by the operating staff to develop an efficient system, any such antagonism would impair the system design;

(b) a reluctance to be taught the new system;

(c) a reluctance to help in introducing the new system.

A new system will reveal weaknesses in the previous system, and so another fear of computerisation is that it will show up exactly how inefficient previous methods of information gathering and information use had been. If individuals feel that they are put under pressure by the revelation of any such deficiencies, they might try to find fault with the new system too. When fault-finding is not constructive, that is not aimed at improving the system, it will be dysfunctional in its consequences.

In extreme cases, dysfunctional behaviour might take a more drastic form. Individuals might show a marked reluctance to learn how to handle the new equipment, they might be deliberately slow keying in data, or they might even damage the equipment in minor acts of vandalism.

Activity 3

How might staff working on PCs at home linked to a central computer be monitored to ensure that their productivity does not fall?

2.3   Overcoming the human problems

To overcome the human problems with systems design and implementation, management and systems analysts must recognise them, and do what they can to resolve them.

(a) Employees should be kept fully informed about plans to install new systems, how matters are progressing and how new systems will affect what people do.

(b) It should be explained to staff why change is for the better.

(c) User department employees should be encouraged to participate fully in the design of a new system, when the system is a tailor-made one. Participation should be genuine.

   (i)   Their suggestions about problems with the existing system should be fully discussed.

   (ii) The systems analyst's ideas for a new system should be discussed with them.

   (iii) Their suggestions for features in the new system should be welcomed.

(d) Staff should be informed that they will be spared boring, mundane work because of the possibility of automating such work and will therefore be able to take on more interesting, demanding and challenging work.

(e) Employees should be told that they will be able to learn new skills which will make them more attractive candidates either for internal promotion or on the external labour market. For example, experience with databases or spreadsheet models could greatly enhance an office worker's experience.

(f) A training programme for staff should be planned in advance of the new systems being introduced. If there are to be job losses, or a redeployment of staff, these should be arranged in full consultation with the people concerned.

(g) Careful attention should be given to:

   (i)   the design of work organisation;

   (ii) the development or preservation of 'social work groups';

   (iii) the relationship between jobs and responsibilities in a new system.

(h) Change should be planned and managed. Reductions in jobs should be foreseen, and redundancies should be avoidable if plans are made well in advance (for example, staff could be moved to other jobs in the organisation). Training (and retraining) of staff should be organised.

(i) A member of staff should be appointed as the office expert on the system, to whom other members of staff can go to ask for help or advice. When the software is bought as an off-the-shelf package, this office expert should be the person who contacts the software supplier about any problems with the system.

(j) *Management and a new system.* When a system is designed in-house, the systems analyst should:

   (i)   produce changes gradually, giving time for personnel to accept the changes;

   (ii) build up a good personal relationship with the people he or she has to work with;

   (iii) persuade management to give sound guarantees for the future;

   (iv) work towards getting employees to accept change as a matter of course;

   (v)   be willing to listen to and act on criticisms of the system under design.

(k) The system should not be introduced in a rush. Users of the system should be given time to become familiar with it. Implementation by means of parallel running might be advisable.

(l) Confidence between the systems analyst and operational staff should be built up over time.

(m) The systems analyst should have the full and clearly expressed support of senior management.

This checklist has concentrated on staff. However, in the long term it is also likely that middle management will be affected by computerisation.

3 TRAINING WITHIN A HUMAN RESOURCE MANAGEMENT FRAMEWORK

Definition

Human resource management is a strategic and coherent approach to the management of people

3.1 HRM features

Human resource management (HRM) is a top-management driven activity yet places strong emphasis on the key role of line management. Typical HRM features include the following.

(a) Employees are considered to be valued assets.

(b) Corporate strategy should work towards integrating employees with corporate objectives, particularly in developing and reinforcing the desired corporate culture.

(c) Emphasis is placed on employee commitment, rather than on employee compliance.

(d) Line management play a key role in the management of their staff.

(e) Team work is emphasised.

(f) Rewards are differentiated.

3.2 Stages of training

In line with the structured approach favoured by HRM, training of staff would be undertaken through a set of clearly defined stages.

Stage one: the identification and analysis of training needs

This stage is further broken down into the following steps.

(a) Job breakdown, in which the job is broken down into its constituent parts for instructional purposes.

(b) Manual skills analysis, which focuses on the physical requirements of the required task, involving detailed records of, say, hand and eye movements.

(c) Task analysis, in which the tasks are analysed with regard to levels of importance and of difficulty.

(d) Faults analysis, where typical faults in the performance of the task are identified.

Stage two: the definition of training objectives

Measurable goals are defined in terms of the improvements or changes expected.

Stage three: the preparation of training plans

As well as a detailed description of the training plans, this should contain a cost-benefit analysis and an account of the planned record keeping of training, against the measurable goals defined in Stage two.

Stage four: the measurement and analysis of results, including evaluation

Stage five : the feedback of the results of the evaluations

Activity 4

What concerns might middle management have about the effects of computerisation?

Chapter roundup

- Staff training, in both technological skills and interpersonal skills, is essential to the success of new computerised systems.
- Managers who will not be engaged in the daily operation of the system still need to be trained, so that they may make wise planning, resource allocation and control decisions.
- Users need detailed training in the operation of a system. They also need to be provided with good quality user documentation, so that they can find out what to do in any situation which might arise.
- Staff may well react adversely to the introduction of a new system, because methods of working and the social structure of the organisation may change, and because staff may be concerned about job security.
- To overcome such problems, staff should be kept fully informed and consideration of the human factor should be built into the development and implementation process.

Quick quiz

1 What methods are available to train senior managers?

2 What types of training are needed by users?

3 What methods are available to train users?

4 How is the working environment likely to be changed by the introduction of new technology?

5 What are the main fears which office workers might have when new technology is introduced?

6 What steps can be taken to overcome resistance to technological change?

7 Name the three core concepts of an HRM strategy.

Answers to activities

1 How to extract data from files
   How to formulate queries to get data from databases
   How to use spreadsheets and financial modelling packages
   How to combine text, figures and graphs to produce reports

2   When the 'help' command is used, an initial screen relevant to the type of processing being carried out at the time could be given. This would give some basic information, and would end with a menu including options such as:

(a) exit from help and resume processing;

(b) details of commands which can be used at the current stage of processing;

(c) how to obtain printed output of the results of processing so far;

(d) information on other topics (to be specified by the user).

3   The central computer could record the times when a PC is switched on and the number of transactions processed (or number of words typed) each day. However, companies considering such monitoring should be aware that it may lead to low staff morale and even to legal action for repetitive strain injury brought on by pressure of work.

4   They might be concerned that top management might no longer need middle management as gatherers and processors of information, because a computerised MIS could do that job just as well. The number of staff might fall, reducing the requirement for middle management.

Further question practice

Now try the following practice questions at the end of this text.

Multiple choice questions   **95 to 101**

Exam style question   **12**

Chapter 15

SECURITY AND CONTROLS

Introduction

This is a fairly long chapter, but it does cover a range of very important topics for anyone working with information technology.

Data, software and hardware are valuable resources and must be kept secure from being wrongly changed or being destroyed accidentally or deliberately. Data must also be secured against wrongful disclosure. Organisations which lose computerised data, perhaps because of a hardware fault or a telecommunications fault, can suffer financial loss. They might, for example, lose records of amounts of money owing to them for purchases.

Data about a company's operations which might be of interest to the company's competitors should not be allowed to fall into their hands. Confidential data which is being word processed might be vulnerable to unauthorised access.

Additionally, the Data Protection Act 1984 incorporates a principle that computerised personal data be kept secure against wrongful disclosure. Finally, If computerised data is not protected properly, there will also be scope for computer fraud.

Your objectives

After completing this chapter you should:

(a) understand the need for security and controls;

(b) be aware of the main risks to data;

(c) know the main personnel controls;

(d) know the main physical security and access controls;

(e) understand the need for protection against hacking and viruses;

(f) know the elements of good office practice in relation to computer systems;

(g) be aware of the main back-up procedures and the need for standby facilities;

(h) understand the need for systems development controls

(i) understand the purposes of data processing standards;

(j) know the uses and contents of system documentation;

(k) understand the need for application controls;

(n) know how data capture, data transcription and data transmission may be controlled;

(m) know what validation checks may be applied;

(n) know what output, file and database controls may be applied;

(o) be aware of some hardware controls.

1   THE NEED FOR SECURITY AND CONTROLS

1.1   The problems associated with computers

Data processing by computer creates extra problems for control because of its special characteristics, which are that:

(a) large volumes of data are concentrated into files that are physically very small;

(b) large quantities of data are processed without human intervention, and so without humans knowing what is going on. This places great reliance on the accuracy of programs and of data on file;

(c) it is easy to lose data on file. Equipment can malfunction, data files can become corrupt and store meaningless data, data can get lost when files are copied, and data files are susceptible to loss through theft, flood or fire;

(d) unauthorised people can gain access to data on files, and read confidential data or tamper with the data. This is a particular problem with on-line systems because access to a computer program and master file can be from any remote terminal. It is even possible for 'hackers' to use their home computers to gain access to the files and programs of other systems;

(e) information on a computer file can be changed without leaving any physical trace of the change.

It does not help matters that computers lack judgement, and errors in data processing by computer can go undetected when this would not be the case with manual data processing. For example, a payroll system might produce a salary cheque for an employee of £0.00 or for £1 million, and would not know that it had done something wrong. This sort of problem can be overcome by building range checks and reasonableness checks into a program as a data validation routine.

A further problem is that programmers are experts, and with careful planning, dishonest programmers can tamper with programs to their own benefit. A case has been recorded, for example, of a programmer who arranged for all fractions of a penny in salaries to be paid into a bank account which the programmer opened and from which he took the money. Several thousand payments mounted up over time into substantial sums of money.

Accidental error can cause problems too. What is to stop a computer operator from using a disk containing master file data to take output from a different program? If this were done, the data on the master file could be wiped out. This is such an important source of potential error that controls to prevent this from happening should be built into any computer system.

Computer systems controls must be maintained regardless of the size of application or method of processing (batch or real time). If certain controls are difficult to establish in a microcomputer system (for example, division of responsibilities), more emphasis must be placed on other controls.

Activity 1

To what extent is a sole trader with no employees, keeping accounting records on her own PC, at risk from the dangers to data and systems mentioned above?

1.2 The risks to data

The dangers associated with information storage on a magnetic medium include the following.

(a) *Physical security*. Tapes or disks can be stolen, mislaid or damaged or destroyed by fire, flood or vandalism.

(b) *Environmental security*. Tapes and disks are susceptible to magnetic fields, dust and extremes of temperature and humidity. Although in modern PCs the problems of environmental control have been reduced, they are still quite important.

(c) *Loss of confidentiality*. Information stored in magnetic files may be accessed by unauthorised persons. This is a particular problem in larger systems with remote terminals, or in time sharing or computer bureau applications.

(d) *Processing the wrong file*. Since data is in magnetic form, and not visible, the wrong file could be read, or a file could be overwritten when its data is still needed.

(e) *Hardware or program corruption*. Hardware or software faults may damage or destroy the data on files.

Controls which can be implemented to counter the risks described above fall into two categories. General controls ensure that the computer environment is secure. They fall into two groups:

(a) administrative controls, which are designed to support the smooth continuing operation of systems;

(b) system development controls, which are designed to ensure that any new system does not present new risks to the environment.

Application controls are built into operations, and ensure that processed data is accurate and complete.

2 ADMINISTRATIVE CONTROLS

Some controls can be applied at relatively small cost, simply by introducing sensible administrative and organisational measures. Administrative controls are controls over data and data security that are achieved by administrative measures. They should be applied in the *data processing department*, or computer centre, where an organisation is large enough to have one, and in other offices. With PC systems, administrative controls will include controls over handling the computer hardware, software and files.

Administrative controls should include:

(a) controls over personnel;

(b) the segregation of duties;

(c) physical security;

(d) access controls;

(e) protection against hacking and viruses;

(f) good office practice;

(g) back-up and standby facilities.

2.1 Personnel

Controls related to personnel, which were developed before the advent of computers, include:

(a) job rotation, so that employees change jobs at random intervals, thus making it uncertain that an individual will be able to set up a breach of security in the time available;

(b) enforced vacations;

(c) access to information granted not on the basis of rank in the management hierarchy or precedent, but on a need-to-know basis.

Some employees, such as the systems analyst and the computer security officer, are always in a position of trust. However, a well-designed security system puts as few people as possible in this powerful position.

Activity 2

Why is it a useful control to force staff to take their holiday entitlements?

2.2 The segregation of duties

Work should be divided between systems analysts, programmers and operating staff, and operations jobs themselves should be divided between data control, data preparation and computer room operations. The functions of an organisation structure, as far as control is concerned, are:

(a) to assign responsibility for certain tasks to specific jobs and individuals. A person in a given job is responsible for ensuring that certain controls are applied. Some jobs are specifically control jobs. These are the jobs of the data control clerks and, to a large extent, of the file librarian;

(b) to prevent fraud. It is easier for someone who can input data, write programs and operate the computer alone to commit fraud. By dividing up the work, it is made harder to commit fraud or tamper with data, except in collusion with others.

Duties may be segregated by ensuring that no member of staff works on more than one of:

(a) data capture and entry;

(b) computer operations;

(c) systems analysis and programming.

In addition, within the computer operations section, the computer operators should ideally not be responsible for data control, nor should they be responsible for looking after the computer file library.

An organisation chart and procedure manuals which set out clearly who does what, and what practices are forbidden, should be prepared.

In the case of PC systems these organisational controls often do not apply. The person who operates the computer also inputs data, and may even write his or her own programs for it. In these cases, however, it is essential that the data being processed is not such as to have a bearing on the assets of the business. For example, if a PC were to be used for a sales ledger system or a payroll system, the person responsible for data input and operating the PC should neither design the system nor write its programs, and there must also be suitable internal and external audit checks of the system.

Data processing staff should be properly trained in security and control measures and the need for them.

Activity 3

Give an example of a fraud which might be committed by a dishonest employee responsible both for entering data and for dealing with exception reports, but which would be prevented if the exception reports went directly to a manager for review.

2.3   Physical security

Physical security comprises two sorts of controls:

(a) protection against disasters such as fire and flood;

(b) protection against intruders gaining physical access to the system.

The physical environment has a major effect on information system security, and so planning it properly is an important part of an adequate security plan.

Fire is the most serious hazard to computer systems. The destruction of data can be even more costly than the destruction of hardware. A proper fire safety plan is an essential feature of security procedures, in order to prevent fires, detect fires and put out fires. Fire safety includes:

(a) site preparation (appropriate building materials and fire doors);

(b) detection (smoke detectors);

(c) extinguishers (such as sprinklers);

(d) training for staff in observing fire safety procedures.

Methods of controlling human access include:

(a) personnel (security guards);

(b) mechanical devices (such as keys, whose issue is recorded);

(c) electronic identification devices (such as card-swipe systems, where cards are passed through readers).

It may not be cost effective or convenient to have the same type of access controls in the whole building all of the time. Instead, the various security requirements of different departments should be estimated, and appropriate boundaries drawn. Some areas will be very restricted, whereas others will be relatively open.

Physical installation security

Measures to ensure physical security in the computer room are as follows.

(a) Computer rooms should be kept locked when not in use. Only authorised personnel should have keys. Locks to computer rooms should be secure.

(b) Computer files should be kept locked in a safe place, such as a fireproof safe.

(c) The physical conditions in which the hardware and files are kept should be suitable, that is not too hot, damp or dusty. Unscreened electric motors should not be used in or near the file library, because they might corrupt data on magnetic file media.

(d) Measures should be taken to minimise the risks of fire. Waste paper should not be allowed to pile up. Computer rooms should have smoke alarms and be fully equipped with fire extinguishers.

Activity 4

What are the relative advantages and disadvantages of security guards and electronic identification devices?

2.4 Access controls

Access controls which can be built into a system's software are:

(a) passwords;

(b) encryption and authentication.

Definition

Access controls are controls designed to prevent unauthorised access to data files or programs.

Passwords

Passwords can be applied to data files, program files and parts of a program. The computer does not allow a user access to the relevant facilities until he or she has typed in the appropriate password.

(a) One password may be required to read a file and another to write new data.

(b) The terminal user can be restricted to the use of certain files and programs. For example, in a banking system, low grades of staff are only allowed access to certain routine programs.

Virtually all mainframe or distributed processing systems use passwords. In order to access a system the user needs first to enter a string of characters as a password. If the entered password matches one issued to an authorised user the system permits access, otherwise the system excludes the user and may record the attempted unauthorised access. Keeping track of these attempts can alert managers to repeated efforts to break into the system, and so the culprits might be caught.

Many password systems come with standard pre-set passwords. It is essential that these be changed if the system is to be at all secure, since such common passwords may become widely known to people in the industry.

Passwords ought to be effective in keeping out unauthorised users, but they are by no means foolproof. Experience has shown that unauthorised access can be obtained.

(a) By experimenting with possible passwords, an unauthorised person can gain access to a program or file by guessing the correct password. This is not as difficult as it may seem when too many computer users specify obvious passwords (such as their spouses' names).

(b) Someone who is authorised to access a data or program file may tell an unauthorised person what the password is, perhaps through carelessness.

Data communications controls: encryption and authentication

When data is transmitted over a communications link or within a network, there are three security dangers:

(a) a hardware fault;

(b) unauthorised access by an eavesdropper;

(c) direct intervention by someone who sends false messages down a line, claiming to be someone else, so that the recipient of the message will think that it has come from an authorised source.

Encryption is the only secure way to prevent eavesdropping (since eavesdroppers can get round password controls, by tapping the line or by experimenting with various likely passwords). Encryption involves scrambling the data at one end of the line, transmitting the scrambled data and unscrambling it at the receiver's end of the line.

Business Basics: Information technology

Authentication is a technique to make sure that a message has come from an authorised sender. Authentication involves adding an extra field to a record, with the contents of this field derived from the remainder of the record by applying a formula that has previously been agreed between the senders and recipients of data.

Activity 5

If passwords are issued to operators by a manager, there will probably be a list of passwords on paper, which could fall into the wrong hands. How could a system be arranged so that each operator has a password which has never been written down?

2.5   Protection against hacking and viruses

As it becomes common for computers to communicate over long distances, the risks of corruption or theft of data or even whole programs becomes much greater. Two interconnected security issues are hacking and viruses.

Hacking

Hackers are normally skilled programmers, and have been known to find out passwords with ease. The fact that billions of bits of information can be transmitted in bulk over the public telephone network has made it hard to trace individual hackers, who can therefore make repeated attempts to invade systems. Hackers have in the past mainly been concerned to copy information, but a recent trend has been their desire to corrupt it.

Definition

A *hacker* is a person who attempts to invade the privacy of a computer system.

Viruses

Computer viruses are currently the cause of much concern. A virus is a piece of software which infects programs and data and which replicates itself. There are a number of types of virus.

A *trojan* is a program that while visibly performing one function secretly carries out another. For example, a program could be running a computer game, while simultaneously destroying a data file or another program.

A *logic bomb* is a piece of code triggered by certain events. A program will behave normally until a certain event occurs, for example disk utilisation reaches a certain percentage. A logic bomb, by responding to such conditions, maximises damage. For example, it will be triggered when a disk is nearly full, or when a large number of users are using the system.

A *time bomb* is similar to a logic bomb, except that it is triggered at a certain date. Companies have experienced virus attacks on April Fool's Day and on Friday 13th. These were released by time bombs.

A *trap door* is not itself a virus, but it is an undocumented entry point into a computer system. It is not to be found in design specifications but may be put in by software developers to enable them to bypass access controls while working on a new piece of software. Because it is not documented, it may be forgotten and used at a later date to insert a virus.

Viruses can spread via data disks, but have been known to copy themselves over whole networks. The most serious type of virus is one which infects an operating system as this governs the whole running of a computer system.

How can organisations protect themselves against viruses?

(a) *Vaccine* programs exist which can deal with some viruses, but if the virus lives in the bootstrap program, the virus can work before the vaccine is loaded.

(b) Organisations must guard against the introduction of unauthorised software to their systems. Many viruses have been spread on pirated versions of popular computer games.

(c) Organisations should as a matter of routine ensure that any disk received from outside with data on it is virus-free before the disk is used.

(d) Any flaws in a widely used program should be rectified as soon as they come to light.

(e) There should be a clear demarcation between the storage of *data files* and *program files* on disk.

(f) Overall, organisations need to establish procedures and reviews to minimise the chance of infection. Virus protection controls should become part of the internal control system of an organisation, as with controls to prevent fraud.

Activity 6

Viruses may be planted by disgruntled employees. What implications does this have for procedures when an employee is subject to disciplinary procedures, is dismissed or is made redundant?

2.6   Good office practice

There are several points of good practice which may seem minor, but which can together make a major contribution to the integrity of a system.

Data is often shared between users. There should be a designated data owner for each file, responsible for:

(a) keeping the data accurate and up to date;

(b) deciding who should have access to the data;

(c) developing security procedures in conjunction with the data security manager.

If computer printout is likely to include confidential data, it should be shredded before being thrown away.

Disks should not be left lying around an office. They can get lost or stolen. More likely, they can get damaged by spilling tea or coffee over them, or by allowing the disks to gather dust which can make them unreadable.

The computer's environment (humidity, temperature and dust) should be properly controlled. This is not so important for PCs as for mainframes, and hard disks are protected from dust. Even so, the computer's environment and the environment of the files should not be excessively hot. Temperature changes can cause disk failure, even with PCs.

Files should be backed up regularly. Procedures should not be allowed to slacken, with office staff not bothering to create back-up files because it takes them too much time.

Maintenance and support

All computers are covered by some kind of warranty from the manufacturer when they are bought new. Warranty periods range in length, typically up to one year. But what should the computer user do after the warranty period has expired?

(a) The user can decide to do nothing until the computer has a breakdown or other fault, and can then ask a third party computer repair company to come in and do the repair work. The drawbacks to this approach are that:

(i) repair companies give priority treatment to contract customers. The waiting time for a non-contract customer might be very long;

(ii) one-off repair charges will be very high.

(b) Instead, the user can arrange a maintenance contract with the manufacturer or a third party repair company. The cost of these contracts will be quite high (perhaps 10% to 20% of the hardware cost each year).

(c) A third option is breakdown insurance, which provides cover for breakdowns and certain consequential losses. Insurance provides cover against expense, but the computer user is left with the operational problem of how to get the repair work done within a reasonable time.

Computers are supplied with a diagnostic disk, which can be used to check for certain hardware faults such as a faulty microchip or a faulty disk drive. These faults can then be detected before any data is corrupted or lost.

Not all the data handling problems of a computer user are attributable to hardware or program faults. Quite often, computer users come across a problem that they do not know how to deal with. A telephone support service might be provided by the software or hardware supplier to help in these circumstances. Computer users can call for advice from an expert. Telephone support might also be provided to user departments by an information centre within the organisation.

Another important control measure, with PC systems in particular, is the appointment of a system expert in the office. This is a person who should be made responsible for learning as much technical detail about the office computer system as possible, so that the problems of other users of the system can first of all be referred to the office expert.

Activity 7

What problems could arise if it is not clear who is the data owner for a file?

2.7 Back-up and standby facilities

A major aspect of system security is to ensure provision of the required services continuously without deterioration in performance. For many applications this will require that some duplication in the system be tolerated or even encouraged. For example, data may be made more secure by using back-up files to archive data. It would then be fairly easy to recover from data loss or system faults.

Administrative controls should be introduced:

(a) to enable file data to be recreated when a file is lost or corrupted;

(b) to provide stand-by hardware facilities whenever a hardware item breaks down.

Recreating file data when a file is lost or corrupted

One of the worst things that could happen in data processing by computer is the loss of all the data on a master file or the loss of a program. Files might be physically lost, for example the librarian might misplace a file, or a file might be stolen, but it is also possible for a file to become corrupted when it is amended and so come to include false data. A file might also be physically damaged and become unreadable.

Controls are therefore needed to enable a data or program file to be recreated if the original is lost or corrupted.

To recreate a master file, it is possible to go back to earlier generations of the master file and transactions files, do the data processing all over again and create a new version of the up-to-date master file.

The grandfather, father, son technique

The reconstruction of files may be achieved by use of the grandfather, father, son technique of keeping as many generations of master files, transaction files and reference files as is considered necessary. It is common to keep three generations (grandfather, father and son) of master files, and sufficient transaction files to recreate the father from the grandfather. If the most recent ('son') file out of a run is found to contain corrupted data, a corrected master file can be recreated by going back to the previous master file (the 'father') and the associated transaction file, and repeating the run. However, this technique cannot be used if the only copy of a file is overwritten during processing.

Dumping disk files

Disk files are often overwritten during updating, and so the grandfather, father, son technique cannot be applied. Instead, a copy of the disk file is periodically 'dumped' onto a back-up file, usually a tape.

A typical procedure in a PC system is to make a copy, on to floppy disks, of each file on the hard disk every time the file is amended. Alternatively, the entire contents of the hard disk can be dumped onto a tape streamer as a matter of routine at the end of each day.

It might not be necessary to back up every disk which holds transaction data, or even some standing data. For example, word processing data is not necessarily of such importance as to warrant back-up copies. However:

(a) all program disks should have back-up copies. Some program disks which are bought from software manufacturers are copy-protected and cannot be backed up, but in these cases, the manufacturer is normally willing to provide a back-up copy to the customer as part of the package;

(b) all master files should be backed up after each updating run.

Backing up data on floppy disks can be done on a PC with two floppy disk drives by inserting the disk to be copied into one disk drive and a blank disk into the other, and using a DISKCOPY or COPY command to copy the data onto the blank disk.

Backing up a hard disk on to floppy disks can be more tedious, because a hard disk holds much more data than a floppy disk. Backing up a hard disk on to a tape streamer is quicker.

Back-up copies should be stored in a different place from the original files.

Stand-by hardware facilities

Hardware duplication will permit a system to function despite a hardware breakdown. The provision of back-up computers is costly, particularly where these systems have no other function. Many organisations will use several smaller computer systems and find that a significant level of protection against system faults can be provided by shifting operations to one of the systems still functioning. Where an organisation has only a single system to rely upon this ready recourse to a back-up facility is unavailable. In these instances one response would be to negotiate a maintenance contract which provides for back-up facilities. Alternatively, many computer bureaux will also provide access to back-up facilities though this will usually be rather expensive.

Activity 8

Give some examples of businesses or activities where delays caused by the non-availability of computer facilities could be disastrous.

3   SYSTEM DEVELOPMENT CONTROLS

When a computer system is developed from scratch, either in-house or by a software house, there should be controls over the system design, development and testing. Because of the time spent on systems development, the cost of it and the complexity and volume of work involved, it is essential to lay down high standards of control.

3.1   Objectives

The main objectives of system development controls are as follows.

(a) To ensure that new computer systems are developed only if they appear to be beneficial. System justification should be on the grounds of favourable cost-benefit analyses or other performance criteria.

(b) To ensure that each system under development has clear, specified objectives.

(c) To control the scheduling of development work. This can be achieved through techniques such as critical path analysis.

(d) To ensure that suitable operational and administrative controls are built into the system design when it is being developed. The adequacy of operational controls in the system will depend on the ability of the systems analyst to write suitable controls into the system during the design process.

(e) To ensure that users acquire an understanding of the new system. The handover of the computer system from the software and hardware experts to non-technical staff must be done in such a way that the computer users are able to learn as much about their system as they need to know. Training of staff will be necessary, but there should also be full, clear and non-technical documentation of the system (for off-the-shelf packages as well as for tailor-made software) in a user's manual.

(f) To ensure that the system is properly tested, provides a suitable degree of control and also achieves its objectives. Program testing, system testing and the user department's acceptance tests are all important ingredients in development controls, to ensure that the programs are free of bugs (errors) and that the system works and meets its objectives.

(g) To establish a basis for management review of the system.

(h) To ensure that systems and programs are maintained when the system becomes operational.

(i) To ensure that proper and complete documentation of the system is created and maintained.

Many of these controls will be provided by the systems development methodology adopted.

3.2   Control over amendments

Control over amendments to the system design is needed. Once development has started, it is all too easy for the systems analysts or user department managers to think of new features to add to the system, or improvements that can be made, with the result that amendments get written into the system as the design work progresses. Some amendments might be desirable; others might not be worthwhile.

Controls should be exercised over amendments, so that if any amendments are proposed which were not included in the system specification, they must be authorised at a suitable managerial level. The authorisation and details of the amendment should be included in the amendments section of the system specification.

Activity 9

A sales system is being developed. The original specification makes no reference to discounts. An amendment to allow discounts for quantity, based on purchases in the previous six months, is proposed. What implications for the system as a whole would need to be considered before the amendment was approved?

3.3 Controls over file conversion

The conversion of master files is one of the big problems of systems implementation and proper procedures and controls must be laid down to ensure that there are no unauthorised conversions and that the correct records are accurately and completely transferred onto magnetic files. The procedures may include:

(a) full planning of the file conversion, including staff to be used, records to be converted (possibly via data preparation forms), controls to be set up and the date of conversion;

(b) the establishment of a control group to follow up errors which may occur during the conversion;

(c) printing out master files after conversion and manually checking them back to the original records (or data preparation forms);

(d) the reconciliation of accounting records to those kept under the old system;

(e) division of responsibilities among the conversion staff (additional staff may have to be brought in to help with the conversion);

(f) testing of the new master files using the test data and the control and documentation of any changes necessary.

Activity 10

A company is converting from one computer system to another, and has some very large files to convert. It would be impractical to check full printouts of the old and new files against each other. In what other ways might the conversion process be checked for accuracy?

3.4 Data processing standards

Definition

Data processing standards are standards for the development, procedures and documentation of computer systems.

The purpose of standards is to minimise the likelihood of errors and misunderstandings in both the development and the operation of computer systems. More specifically, standards are helpful in the following ways.

The documentation of a computer system

Documentation is needed for systems and program specifications, and also for operator instructions. The existence of standards for documentation:

(a) establishes the need to document a system;

(b) provides a standard format for documenting the system, which helps to ensure that nothing is left out of the specification;

(c) gives the people operating a system somewhere to look up and learn the system's operating requirements.

Management control

Standards should provide guidelines for managers to plan and control system development and then system operations.

(a) Standards should suggest how management meetings should be scheduled during systems development, and how projects should be costed.

(b) There should be performance standards, so that actual performance can be measured against what should be expected.

(c) There should be standard job specifications, indicating who is responsible for each part of the system.

Communication of information about the system

Standard documentation provides a means whereby information about a system can be communicated, for example between programmers and systems analysts, and between system developers and the users and operators of the system.

Continuity after staff changes and an aid to training

People leave their jobs from time to time, or are absent for one reason or another. Unless a system is well-documented in a standard way, or has been designed according to standard procedures, it may be difficult for a person's stand-in or replacement to pick up the job where his or her predecessor left off.

Standards help people to learn a system. They are particularly helpful for staff moving from one job to another because they will have some familiarity with the format of documentation standards. For example, a computer operator moving from a job in A Ltd to a new job in the computer centre of B Ltd will be able to learn the new job partly by referring to B Ltd's standards for computer operations. These standards will be similar in format to the ones used in A Ltd, and so the operator will know how and where to look up information.

An aid to system analysis and systems design work

Having standards helps the systems analyst in design work, in the following ways.

(a) Standards help to ensure that no aspect of system design is overlooked.

(b) Standards can help to steer a systems analyst's mind in the best direction. For example they can suggest controls to be built into the system.

(c) Standard documentation provides evidence that systems development controls have been carried out and that the system incorporates sufficient procedural and processing controls.

Activity 11

What are the relative advantages and disadvantages of an organisation's writing its own data processing standards and its using externally published standards?

3.5 Documentation

Documentation for a system includes user manuals, hardware and operating software manuals, system specifications and program documentation. Documentation is a feature of most systems analysis and design methodologies.

Data processing standards should ensure that all staff involved in the use of a computer system have proper instructions and that these have been fully documented. This means that there must be:

(a) operating instructions for each computer installation;

(b) operating instructions for each program;

(c) file library instructions, specifying how files should be labelled, safeguarded, issued and if necessary reconstructed;

(d) data conversion instructions for the data preparation staff;

(e) data control instructions for the control section;

(f) user department instructions.

The system specification

The system specification is a complete description of the whole system and must be kept up to date as parts of the system are changed or added to. Many of the problems in computer installations arise because of inadequate documentation and controls must be set up to ensure that updating procedures are always carried out.

Program specifications

Program specifications (excluding listings of the programs themselves) are drawn up by the systems analyst. A copy of a program specification is given to the programmer responsible for writing the program, and the programmer then uses the specification as the basis for writing and testing the required program. When the program has been written and tested, one copy of the final specification will form part of the overall systems specification, and a second copy will be retained by the programmer to form part of the programmer's own documentation for the program.

Definition

A *program specification* (also known as program documentation) is a description of a program using charts, full listings of the program and details of test data and results.

Activity 12

Why might an organisation restrict access to detailed program specifications, rather than make them available to all staff?

Computer operations manuals

A computer operations manual provides full documentation of the procedures necessary to run the system. Among the matters to be covered by this documentation are:

(a) systems set-up procedures, including details for each application of the necessary file handling and stationery requirements;

(b) security procedures. Particular stress should be placed on the need to check that proper authorisation has been given for processing operations and the need to restrict use of the system to authorised operators;

(c) reconstruction procedures. Precise instructions should be given for matters such as file dumping and also the recovery procedures to be adopted in the event of a systems failure;

(d) system messages. A listing of all messages likely to appear on operators' consoles should be given together with an indication of the responses which they should evoke;

(e) operating system manuals. These are manuals that describe an operating system.

User manuals

User manuals or user documentation explain to users how to run a system, but do not give unnecessary technical details such as program listings. Matters to be dealt with include:

(a) acceptance testing: responsibilities for the preparation of test data and subsequently checking the test results;

(b) input: responsibilities and procedures for the preparation of input including requirements for the establishment of batch control totals and for authorisation;

(c) error reports: full explanations of the nature and form of error reports (such as reports of items rejected by computer checks) and instructions as to the necessary action to be taken;

(d) master file amendment procedures: full explanations of the authorisation and documentation required for master file amendments;

(e) output: what is produced, what form it takes and what should be done with it.

System changes manuals

Amendments to the original systems specification will almost inevitably occur, in addition to the computerisation of additional activities. The objective of a system changes manual is to ensure that such changes are just as strictly controlled as the original systems development and introduction.

Activity 13

A computer operator using a batch processing system sees the message 'Batch control total discrepancy' on his screen, but does not know what to do about it. In which manual should he look for advice?

4 APPLICATION CONTROLS

Errors in data processing can easily occur. Application controls are intended to detect errors and ensure that they are corrected before processing proceeds further.

Input data can get lost, or it might contain errors. Human error is the greatest weakness in computer systems. The extensiveness of the input controls will depend on the method of processing input data (for example, keyboard input or OCR document input) and the cost of making an input error. If the consequences of input errors would be costly, the system should include more extensive input controls than if the cost of input errors were insignificant.

Errors may occur at various stages of data processing.

4.1 Data capture

Mistakes include:

(a) writing an incorrect figure, such as £1243 instead of £1234; swapping figures around by mistake is referred to as a transposition error;

(b) spelling mistakes, such as getting a customer's name wrong;

(c) measuring mistakes, such as a timekeeper misreading the time and writing down an incorrect time for a job;

(d) classifying mistakes, such as a cost accountant recording a direct labour cost as an overhead item, or an expenditure in administration as a production cost.

Errors in data capture are difficult to spot once they have been made, because they are often errors on the source document. They can be reduced by checking. One person's work might provide a check on the accuracy of another's. For example, the recording of suppliers' invoices could be checked by getting another person to add up the total amount of invoices received that day, from the invoices themselves. This total could then be checked against the total for invoices recorded.

Another way of dealing with errors in data capture is to reduce the likelihood of errors arising in the first place, by including as much pre-printed information on the data recording documents as possible, and by giving clear instructions about how the documents should be filled in.

The use of turnround documents and OCR, MICR, bar coding or, in some applications, plastic cards with magnetic stripes containing some of the input data reduces the need for manually-prepared input data, and so reduces data capture errors.

4.2 Transcription

Transcription errors occur when data is copied from one form to another. For example, a person might jot down some data on a piece of scrap paper, and then copy it incorrectly onto a formal document later on.

Data preparation errors occur when the original captured data has to be transcribed into a form that the computer can read, such as a magnetic tape or magnetic disk. Errors arise because the original data can be copied wrongly into the machine-readable form. These errors are sometimes referred to as data conversion errors.

If input data must be prepared manually, controls can be applied to minimise the number of errors.

(a) Staff who prepare data for input should be well trained and properly supervised.

(b) Data input documents should be in a format which helps the person preparing the data to fill them in properly.

(c) When data is input by keyboard, the screen should be formatted so as to help the keyboard operator to input the correct data. User-friendly software packages might provide on-screen prompts and formatted screens for input data.

If data must be converted from one form to another for input, for example from a paper document onto disk, the data could be keyed in twice to check for copying errors. However, this is expensive.

The staff who prepare the data should be encouraged to look for errors.

(a) If input is done by keyboard, the input data will be shown on the VDU screen and a visual check on the data can be made.

The input record will often have a key field identification code. For example, a sales ledger file will consist of customer records, with each customer having a code number for identification. When a transaction record is keyed in, the customer code would be part of the input data and the program might search for the customer record on the sales ledger file, and display it on the VDU screen. The input operator could then check visually that the correct customer record is being processed.

(b) If input is done in batches, the program might produce a listing of the input data which could be checked for accuracy. Printed listings of input data also provide an *audit trail* in computerised accounting systems, so that internal and external auditors can follow transactions through the system later.

4.3 Data transmission

Errors in transmitting data involve the loss or corruption of data which is sent to the computer, by post, courier or telecommunications link from a remote terminal.

When data is input from a terminal, the terminal user should be able to check that the data has been input fully and accurately by obtaining a printout back from the computer of all accepted data.

When input data is batched and physically despatched to a computer centre for processing, batch control checks can be applied to ensure that all the data that has been despatched is safely received at the computer centre. These checks involve:

(a) the user department giving each batch a unique identification number;

(b) the identification numbers of all batches being written on to a batch control document, by the user department supervisor. This document will be sent to the computer centre, with a copy being retained by the user;

(c) the data control clerks in the computer centre checking that the batches that are received tally with the batch numbers on the batch control document.

4.4 Processing

Errors might occur or come to light during data processing, for three broad reasons.

(a) It may become apparent during processing, when it would not necessarily have been apparent at the data capture stage, that there is something wrong with the transaction data. An attempt should be made to locate these errors as soon as possible, to prevent the computer from acting on invalid data. A data validation (or data vet) program is used to check the input data for errors that can be spotted by computer logic.

(b) It may become apparent during processing that there is something wrong with the master file data, or that it is impossible to match a transaction record properly with a master file record. Examples would be:

(i) trying to record an invoice sent to customer number 234, when no such customer account has been opened;

(ii) trying to delete employee number 678 from the payroll, when there is no such employee in the payroll records;

(iii) trying to open a new account for supplier number 372 when there is already an account for that supplier.

These are referred to as updating errors because they come to light when the master file is updated.

(c) There may be a programming error, that is a flaw in the logic of the computer program.

Activity 14

Why is a programming error likely to be more serious than an updating error?

It is preferable to identify errors as they occur, rather than to leave dealing with them until later on in processing, because processing incorrect data would be time-consuming and wasteful, and it might also result in further errors caused by the original error.

Activity 15

Invoices received from a company's suppliers are batched, and are then given to the company's computer staff together with batch control slips showing control totals. What mistake could the batching staff make, which would definitely not be detected by the system of control totals?

4.5 Validation checks

Some checks on the validity of input data can be written into the system's programs. These data validation checks (or data vet checks) might be performed by a separate data validation program in a batch processing system. Alternatively, any program can incorporate validation checks on input data, for example on data keyed in from a terminal into an on-line system.

Data validation

The data validation program, or a program which incorporates data validation routines, will be the first program in each batch processing application.

Definition

A *data validation program* is a program which attempts to find errors in the input record or batch, to prevent them being processed any further.

The checks that can be made are logical checks which prevent some of the worst types of error from getting through to be processed. Data validation does not provide a comprehensive error check, however, and some errors on source documents are likely to go undetected. This emphasises the need for control over source document creation.

The main types of data validation check are outlined below. Note that the same type of check can be made on different fields of a record, and that not all types of check need appear in a data validation program. However, a single program might carry out dozens of validation checks on different records and fields.

(a) *Range checks* are designed to ensure that the data in a certain field lies within predetermined limits. For example, in a wages application, the program may contain instructions to reject any clock card with 'hours worked' outside the range from 20 to 80 hours, and to print out a special report (for checking) on any clock card with hours worked outside the range from 35 to 60 hours.

(b) *Limit checks*, sometimes called credibility or reasonableness checks, are very similar to range checks, but check that data is not below or above a certain value. In the previous example, the check on 'hours worked' might be that the value in the record field does not exceed 80. With a range check, there is an upper bound and a lower bound, whereas with a limit check, there is either an upper bound or a lower bound, but not both.

(c) *Existence checks* are checks on record fields to ensure that the data is valid for that field. For example:

   (i)   check that the record type is 1, 2 or 3;

   (ii) check that the stock code exists by looking up the stock code number of the record in a reference file.

(d) *Format checks* (picture checks) check that the record has the required data fields and that each data field has data in the correct format. For example:

   (i)   check that the format is all numeric   9999   (here, four figures);

   (ii)   check that the format is all alphabetic   AAAAA (here, five letters);

   (iii)   check that the format is alphanumeric   A999   (here, one letter followed by three figures).

(e) *Consistency checks* check that data in one field is consistent with data in another field. For example, in a payroll system, there might be a check that if the employee is a Grade C worker, he or she belongs to Department 5, 6 or 9.

(f) *Sequence checks* check that records and batches are processed in the correct sequence.

(g) *Completeness checks*

   (i)   A check can be made to ensure that all records have been processed. For example, if a weekly processing run must include one record for each of the five working days of the week, a completeness check can ensure that there are five input records.

   (ii)   Completeness checks on individual fields would check that an item of data has not been omitted from an input record.

(h) *Check digits* are numbers (or perhaps letters) added to a code to give it some special mathematical property, which can be checked by the computer.

(i) *Batch total checks.* In a batch processing system, the number and/or the total value of the records processed by the computer from each batch, including rejected records, should reconcile with the control total(s) in the batch control slip, which will also have been input to the program.

When a validation check identifies an error, there are a number of possible outcomes.

(a) The record concerned will probably be rejected and processed no further with perhaps a message on screen. *Rejection reports* may be printed out at some stage during processing.

(b) The record concerned may not be rejected, but an *exception report* might still be output or the operator advised in some way on screen. This may happen, for example, where a range or limit check is not satisfied. Just because a record is not within pre-set limits, it does not automatically mean that it is incorrect. If it is valid, then not processing it would be a waste of time. However, administrative controls must ensure that all exception reports are followed up.

(c) If an error is revealed by batch controls, the whole batch must be rejected and checked.

Activity 16

A computer program processes the monthly expenses claims of travelling sales staff. Give three examples of validation checks which might be carried out on the claims.

4.6 Output controls

There should be controls over output from computer processing.

(a) In a batch processing system, where data is batched and sent off to a computer centre, there should be a check to make sure that the batches that were sent off have been processed and returned.

(b) All input records that have been rejected by data validation checks and master file update checks must be looked at to find out the reasons. Corrected data should then be prepared for re-input. Some errors might need immediate correction, such as those on input records which have been rejected by data validation checks in a payroll program for preparing salary payments to staff.

(c) Output should be correctly distributed, and a log should be kept of the distributions that have been made. In a computer centre, this is the responsibility of the data control staff. In an office, someone has to be responsible for dealing with output from the printer.

(d) Output onto magnetic files should be properly labelled and stored.

4.7   File controls

Controls can be applied to ensure that:

(a) the correct files are used for processing;

(b) data is not lost or corrupted;

(c) if data is lost or corrupted, then it can be recreated;

(d) unauthorised access to data is prevented.

In a large computer centre, the administrative responsibility for the physical security of files belongs to the file librarian. With smaller computer systems, such as office PCs, responsibility for the correct labelling of disks and their physical security should be assigned to a member of staff.

Software controls over files

A number of controls can be written into program software. These include file identification checks, checkpoints and recovery procedures and control totals.

File identification checks

The computer will check that the correct file has been loaded for processing before it will begin its processing operations. It can do this by checking the file header data written on the file in magnetic form, and compare this data with data about the file that it has been instructed to process. If the computer has been instructed to process master file A, it will first of all check that master file A has indeed been loaded for processing, and that the correct generation of the file has been loaded.

Checkpoints and recovery procedures

A checkpoint or restart program is a utility that intervenes at certain points (checkpoints) during the running of a program, and dumps the entire contents of memory onto a storage device.

Should anything turn out to be wrong with the running of the application program, the application program can be taken back to the checkpoint before the error occurred, and restarted with conditions exactly as they were before.

Control totals

A control total could be:

(a) the number of records on a file;

(b) the total of the values of a particular field in all the records on a file, for example the total of debts outstanding in all the customer records on a sales ledger file;

(c) the number of records in a batch (a batch control total);

(d) a hash total. This is a total that has no meaning, except as a control check; for example, the total of customer account numbers.

Control total checks are written into programs to ensure that:

(a) no records have been lost;

(b) no records have been duplicated;

(c) input files have been read fully;

(d) all output records have been written to output files.

Control totals are established in two different ways, for example, by adding up the account numbers after the most recent run, and by taking the total after the previous run and adjusting it for new accounts and for accounts closed. Any difference between the totals can then be investigated.

Activity 17

Why is it often worth having checkpoints part way through a processing run, rather than simply restarting a run from the beginning whenever something goes wrong?

4.8   Database controls

Databases present a particular problem for computer security. Databases can often be accessed by large numbers of people, and so there is a high risk of alteration, unauthorised disclosure or fraud.

It is possible to construct complicated password systems, and the DBMS can be programmed to give limited views of its contents to particular users. However, there are problems in ensuring that individuals do not circumvent the controls by means of inference. For example, an employee database might forbid you to ask whether John is an employee in category A. However, if you know there are only three employee categories, A, B, and C, and there is no prohibition on asking about categories B and C, you can work out the members of category A by elimination. Inference controls may make this difficult by limiting the number of queries, or by controlling the overlap between questions.

Chapter roundup

- Data needs to be protected from processing errors, system failures, unauthorised access and physical damage to the storage media.

- Administrative controls apply to the data processing environment. They include controls over personnel (such as segregation of duties), physical security measures, access controls (such as passwords), measures against hacking and viruses, rules for office practice and the provision of back-up and standby facilities.

- System development controls apply to the development of new systems or the amendment of existing systems. They are intended to ensure that systems are developed which meet the needs of the organisation and which do not cost more than they are worth.

- As part of the design process for a new system, controls will be built into the system. This addition of controls itself needs to be controlled, so that the controls built in are appropriate to the uses to be made of the system.

- Programs must be tested, and the conversion of files must be carefully controlled.

- Formal procedures are needed to control amendments to an existing system.

Chapter roundup (*continued*)

- Data processing standards are intended to ensure adequate documentation and management control, to ensure continuity after staff changes and to facilitate the design of systems.

- The documentation for a system should include a system specification, program specifications, a computer operations manual, a user manual and a system changes manual.

- Application controls are incorporated within applications, in order to ensure complete and accurate processing of data. Controls are first applied to data capture, transcription, conversion and transmission. Data validation checks can then be applied, to ensure that the data input is reasonable both on the basis of inherently likely values and in the light of data already held on master files.

- The distribution of output, including error and exception reports, needs to be controlled, to ensure that all output is correctly acted upon. File controls are needed to ensure that the correct files are used for processing, and that files are retained for appropriate periods.

- Databases need to be controlled, to prevent unauthorised access or alteration.

Quick quiz

1 What are the objectives of data controls?

2 What are the two main classes of controls, and the two sub-classes of the first class?

3 What are the main personnel controls apart from the segregation of duties?

4 What are the main physical security measures which can be taken?

5 What access controls can be applied to data transmission?

6 Give some examples of types of computer virus.

7 What arrangements for maintenance of an office computer system can be made after the warranty period has expired?

8 Why is it important to create back-up copies of files?

9 How can the cost of developing new systems be controlled?

10 What criteria should be applied to the incorporation of controls in a new system?

11 How may data processing standards help continuity after staff changes?

12 What are the contents of a program specification?

13 What should be dealt with in a user manual?

14 Give some examples of errors which may occur or come to light during data processing.

15 How may the transcription and conversion of data be controlled?

16 Give one example of each of a limit check, a format check and a completeness check.

17 How does a computer check that it has been supplied with the correct files for processing?

18 What is a control total?

Answers to activities

1 Fraud and unauthorised access are unlikely to be serious risks, but the accidental loss or corruption of data are significant risks, especially because it is easy to forget about precautions if there is no-one else to insist that they are taken.

2 If a member of staff is perpetrating a fraud, this is more likely to come to light if he or she is not there all the time to cover up the evidence as it arises.

3 An employee in the purchasing department might arrange for payments to a supplier to exceed the amounts owing, and in fact divert the excess to a personal bank account. Such payments would show up on exception reports, which if they went to the employee in question could then be destroyed.

4 Security guards can get to know the staff and can act on their own initiative if intruders are spotted. On the other hand, they are expensive and they may become lax about security procedures.

Electronic identification devices are cheap to run and always apply controls to the same standard. On the other hand, they cannot show initiative, and a device which reads a card cannot tell if a card has been stolen and is being used by an intruder.

5 Initial passwords could be issued on paper, but operators would be required to change them immediately to passwords of their own choosing. Each new password would be known only to the operator and the computer, and would never have been written down.

6 Employees who might have grievances should not have any access to computer systems. It may be necessary to make them serve out any period of notice at home.

7 Different people could update the file in an unplanned way, and could undo each others' work.

The file might not get updated at all, because each user would assume that updating was someone else's responsibility.

8 Share and currency dealing businesses; computer-controlled manufacturing involving dangerous processes; air traffic control.

9 The need to keep six-month running totals of purchases by each customer; these would often span the company's accounting year-end, so detailed data would have to be preserved after the year-end.

The need to create a system for fixing discount rates and the quantities which will trigger discounts. Are these to be standard, or may they vary between customers? If the latter, who is to approve the rates and who is to input them? How is fraud to be prevented? (An operator might give a discount to a customer improperly, in return for a bribe.)

10 Samples from the old and new files could be printed out and checked against each other. The old and new files could be copied onto disks and the copies checked against each other by a separate computer program.

11 An organisation's own standards will be tailored to its own needs, and will be well-understood by its employees. However, good standards take a lot of time and resources to write.

Externally produced standards are cheaper to obtain, but they may not fit the organisation's needs so well. However, they may raise important quality control issues which would simply not have occurred to people within the organisation. Similarly, the use of externally produced standards prevents members of the organisation from building existing slackness into the standards.

12 Someone who knows exactly how a program works might be tempted to amend it without authorisation, either because they think they know how to improve it or in order to perpetrate a fraud.

13 The user manual.

14 A programming error may affect every transaction processed by the program, whereas an updating error may only affect one master file record.

15 An invoice could be lost before the batches were prepared.

16 Range check: is each claim between £100 and £900 in total?

Existence check: does each person making a claim exist?

Completeness check: have all the sales staff submitted claims?

17 A run might take up a lot of computer time, and it may therefore be worth saving the results of processing up to the last checkpoint before things go wrong. Also, working forwards slowly from that checkpoint may make it easier to find out what the problem is.

Further question practice

Now try the following practice questions at the end of this text.

Multiple choice questions   **102 to 108**

Exam style question   **13**

Chapter 16

COMPUTERS AND THE LAW

Introduction

In recent years, there has been a growing popular fear that information about individuals which was stored on computer files and processed by computer could be misused. In particular, it was felt that individuals could easily be harmed by the existence of computerised data about them which was inaccurate or misleading and which could be transferred to unauthorised third parties at high speed and little cost.

There was also a clear possibility that, unless the UK passed legislation adopting the principles of the Council of Europe Convention for the Protection of Individuals with regard to Automatic Processing of Personal Data, access to information about individuals which is stored on overseas computers might be restricted for UK firms. This would inevitably have put the UK at a trading disadvantage against firms in other countries where such legislation had been passed already.

The Data Protection Act 1984 was passed to address these particular concerns in the area of data processing.

Your objectives

After completing this chapter you should:

(a) understand the background to the Data Protection Act 1984;

(b) understand the terms 'personal data', 'data user', 'computer bureau' and 'data subject';

(c) know the main provisions of the Act;

(d) know the Data Protection Principles;

(e) know the main exemptions from the Act;

(f) be aware of the offences which may be committed under the Act;

(g) know how an organisation should act to ensure compliance with the Act;

(h) be aware of how copyright law applies to computer software;

(i) know the main provisions of the Computer Misuse Act 1990;

(j) be aware of some other legal matters which arise in the context of computer systems.

1 THE DATA PROTECTION ACT 1984

The Act is an attempt to afford some measure of protection to individuals. The terms of the Act cover data about individuals, not corporate bodies, and data which is processed mechanically, that is 'equipment operated automatically in response to the instructions given for that purpose', not data processed manually.

The Data Protection Registrar has suggested where the dividing line comes between equipment covered by the Act and equipment not affected by the Act. Modern telephones, which store some telephone numbers for automatic redialling, do not come under the Act, nor does telex or facsimile equipment which transmits data but does not process it. However, equipment other than computers is covered if it processes data automatically.

1.1 Definitions of terms in the Act

In order to understand the Act it is necessary to know some of the technical terms used in it.

Personal data

Personal data is information about living individuals, including expressions of opinion about them. Data about other organisations is not personal data, unless it contains data about individuals who belong to those other organisations.

(a) Personal data includes facts or opinions about a living individual, but does not include data about the data user's intentions towards the individual.

(b) The individual must be identifiable from the data. If the data does not contain a name, but contains a code number (for example, an employment number or an account number) from which the data user can identify the individual, it is personal data.

Data users

Data users are organisations or individuals who control the contents of files of personal data and the use of personal data which is processed automatically. Since the Act was passed the definition of 'data user' has been subject to much uncertainty and discussion, and some guidance has therefore been given by the office of the Data Protection Registrar. For example:

(a) do subsidiary companies in a group have to register as data users, as well as the holding company? Usually they do;

(b) are employees of an organisation data users? No, because they are only exercising control on behalf of their employers;

(c) educational institutions will usually be regarded as the data users of any personal data held on their computer files but there may be special circumstances, for example, teachers or students using the computer for extra-curricular activities, when the institution is acting as a bureau and the individual teacher or student becomes the data user.

Computer bureaux

These are organisations (or individuals) which process personal data for data users, or allow data users to process personal data on their equipment. An organisation or an individual may be classified as a computer bureau under the Act even though not actually in business as a computer bureau.

Data subjects

These are individuals who are the subjects of personal data.

Activity 1

Which of the following statements would be personal data?

(a) John Smith will probably earn £25,000 next year.

(b) X Ltd is insolvent.

(c) I intend to sell my car to John Smith.

1.2 The main provisions of the Act

The Act can be summarised as follows.

(a) With certain exceptions, all data users and all computer bureaux must register with the Data Protection Registrar. To hold personal data without being registered as a data user, or to operate as a computer bureau without being registered as such, is an offence under the Act.

(b) Data subjects have certain legal rights.

(c) Data users and computer bureaux must adhere to the Data Protection Principles.

(d) The Act establishes certain civil legal proceedings and a number of offences.

(e) The Data Protection Registrar:

    (i)   maintains a register of data users and computer bureaux;

    (ii)   disseminates information on the Act and its operation;

    (iii) promotes the observance of the Data Protection Principles;

    (iv) considers complaints about contraventions of the Principles or of the Act's provisions.

Registration under the Act

The Data Protection Registrar keeps a register of all data users and computer bureaux.

Each entry in the register contains the following information.

(a) The name and address of the data user or the computer bureau

(b) A description of the personal data held by the data user and the uses made of the data

(c) The source or sources of the data

(d) Details of any other person or persons to whom the data might be disclosed

Only a data user with an entry in the Register may hold personal data. Even if the data user is registered, he or she must only hold data and use data for the purposes which are registered.

A data user must apply to be registered. The Registrar may refuse an application for the following reasons.

(a) The Registrar thinks that the data user has not given sufficient information when making the application.

(b) The Registrar believes that the data user might not adhere to the Data Protection Principles.

The Act requires a data user both to limit the use of personal data to the uses which are registered and also to abide by the Data Protection Principles. A Registrar who thinks that the Principles are being breached by a registered data user may issue an enforcement notice which orders the data user to take steps to remedy the breach. It is an offence to ignore an enforcement notice. In extreme cases, the Registrar might have the data user struck off the Register.

There is a right of appeal to a Data Protection Tribunal if a data user believes that he or she has been unfairly and unreasonably refused registration, or has been unfairly served with an enforcement notice or unfairly struck off the register.

The rights of data subjects

The Act establishes the following rights for data subjects.

(a) Data subjects may seek compensation through the courts for damage and any associated distress caused by:

   (i)   the loss, destruction or unauthorised disclosure of data about himself or herself;

   (ii) inaccurate data about himself or herself.

(b) Data subjects may apply to the courts for inaccurate data to be put right or even removed from the data user's files altogether. Such applications may also be made to the Registrar.

(c) Data subjects may obtain access to personal data of which they are is the subjects. (This is known as the subject access provision.)

(d) Data subjects can sue data users (or bureaux) for any damage or distress caused to them by personal data about them which is incorrect or misleading as to matter of fact (rather than opinion).

Activity 2

What sorts of damage might a data subject suffer from incorrect or misleading data?

The Data Protection Principles

There are certain Data Protection Principles which registered data users must comply with. These are as follows.

Personal data held by data users:

(1) The information to be contained in personal data shall be obtained, and personal data shall be processed, fairly and lawfully. Processing means amending, adding to, deleting or re-arranging the data, or extracting the information that forms the data.

(2) Personal data shall be held only for one or more specified (registered) and lawful purposes.

(3) Personal data held for any purpose or purposes shall not be used or disclosed in any manner incompatible with that purpose or those purposes.

(4) Personal data held for any purpose or purposes shall be adequate, relevant and not excessive in relation to that purpose or those purposes.

(5) Personal data shall be accurate and, where necessary, kept up to date. 'Accurate' means correct and not misleading as to any matter of fact. An opinion cannot be challenged on the grounds of inaccuracy.

(6) Personal data held for any purpose or purposes shall not be kept for longer than is necessary for that purpose or those purposes.

(7) An individual shall be entitled:

   (a)   at reasonable intervals, and without undue delay or expense:

      (i)   to be informed by any data user whether he or she holds personal data of which that individual is the subject; and

      (ii) to access to any such data held by a data user; and

   (b)   where appropriate, to have such data corrected or erased.

Personal data held by data users or in respect of which services are provided by persons carrying on computer bureaux:

(8) Appropriate security measures shall be taken against unauthorised access to, or alteration, disclosure or destruction of, personal data and against accidental loss or destruction of personal data. The prime responsibility for creating and putting into practice a security policy rests with the data user.

The disclosure of personal data

The Act does not prevent a data user from disclosing personal information about an individual, if the user wishes to do so, and if:

(a) the person to whom the disclosure is made is described in the disclosures section of the data user's entry on the Register; or

(b) disclosure is required or permitted by one of the exemptions to the non-disclosure provisions.

This means that a data subject does not have an unrestricted right to object to the disclosure of personal data about himself or herself.

Exemptions

There are some exemptions from the Act or parts of it.

Unconditional exemptions from the Act as a whole cover:

(a) personal data which must be exempt so as to safeguard national security;

(b) personal data which the data user is required to make public by law;

(c) personal data held by an individual and concerned only with the management of that individual's personal, family or household affairs or held for recreational purposes.

Conditional exemptions from the Act as a whole cover:

(a) personal data held as payroll and pensions data or for keeping the accounts of the data user. The exemption is conditional because if payroll details or accounts details are used for any purpose in addition to paying wages or pensions and keeping simple books of account, no exemption is available; the data user must register the fact that he or she uses payroll or accounts details both for a purpose that would normally be exempt and for the purpose or purposes which cause the exemption to be lost. For example, if a sales ledger file is used to assess the creditworthiness of customers, the exemption is lost;

(b) data held by unincorporated members' clubs and relating only to club members. The condition is that data subjects have been asked whether they object to these uses of data and they have not objected. Disclosure of such data may only be made with the data subjects' consent.

(c) data held only for the distribution of articles or information to the data subjects (for example, for mailshot advertising) and consisting only of their names and addresses, or other particulars necessary for the distribution. The condition is as for (b), with the same requirement of consent for disclosure.

Exemption from subjects' right of access to data on them is available for:

(a) personal data held for the prevention or detection of crime, the apprehension or prosecution of offenders or the assessment or collection of any tax or duty;

(b) data for which legal professional privilege could be claimed. This would apply to a solicitor and the solicitor's client;

(c) data held solely for statistical or research purposes.

Exemptions from the non-disclosure provisions cover:

(a) disclosures to safeguard national security;

(b) personal data which is disclosed for the prevention or detection of crime, the apprehension or prosecution of offenders or the assessment or collection of any tax or duty, where not to disclose the data would prejudice one of those purposes;

(c) disclosures to, at the request of or with the consent of the data subject;

(d) disclosures to the employees or agents of a data user or a computer bureau so that they can perform their functions as such;

(e) disclosures which are urgently needed to prevent injury or damage to the health of anyone;

(f) disclosures required by law or by a court order;

(g) disclosures for the purpose of obtaining legal advice or in the course of legal proceedings.

Apart from the main exemptions detailed above, there is also a word processing exemption. Operations performed only for the purpose of preparing the text of documents are not covered by the Act.

Activity 3

A car dealer keeps data on potential customers for marketing purposes. The data includes details of each potential customer's current car. Which data protection principles might be breached if:

(a) the data is updated only once every two years?

(b) the dealer makes the data available to a journalist investigating customer dissatisfaction with a particular make of car?

1.3   The practical implications of the Act

It is important to be aware of some of the implications of the Act.

(a) It is an offence for a company to transfer personal data to an overseas branch office, unless that office is in a country which has been named in the data user's register entry. Even then, the Registrar can issue a transfer prohibition notice to prevent any such overseas data transfers being made, for example, if the recipient branch might not apply the Data Protection Principles. Such notices will usually be issued where it is believed that the data will be directly or indirectly transferred to a country which is not a signatory to the European Convention.

(b) When personal data is *printed out* from a computer file, the data on paper is not 'data' within the meaning of the Act, but it is 'information extracted from the data'. As such, it remains subject to the non-disclosure provisions of the Act. Appropriate security measures should therefore be taken to protect such printouts. But if a data user receives a subject access request, the data user need only supply a copy of the data currently on file. Any information on a printout, which is no longer held on file as data, does not have to be disclosed.

Offences under the Act

The following offences are created by the Act.

(a) Data users are liable to prosecution if:

   (i)   they hold personal data without being registered, or without having applied for registration;

   (ii)   they knowingly or recklessly use, obtain, disclose, transfer or hold data otherwise than as described in their registered entry;

     (iii)   they knowingly or recklessly supply the Registrar with false or misleading information on an application for registration or a change of particulars;

     (iv)   they fail to comply with an enforcement notice;

     (v)   they fail to comply with a transfer prohibition notice.

(b) A computer bureau is liable for prosecution if:

     (i)   it knowingly or recklessly operates as a computer bureau in respect of personal data without being registered as such;

     (ii)   it knowingly or recklessly supplies the Registrar with false or misleading information for registration or a change of particulars;

     (iii)   it fails to comply with an enforcement notice.

Activity 4

The managing director of a data user obtains a printout of personal data and then leaves the printout unattended in the company's public reception area for the sales director to collect. Before the sales director does so, a member of the public comes in and reads the printout. No members of the public had appointments to visit the company on that day. Has an offence been committed under the Data Protection Act?

Ensuring compliance with the Act

To ensure compliance with the Act, the following steps are recommended.

(a) The organisation should appoint a data protection co-ordinator. The co-ordinator's job is to arrange the organisation's registration and to ensure continued compliance with the Act's provisions after registration.

(b) In order to ensure complete and accurate registration and also continued compliance with the Act after registration, all relevant staff must be made fully aware of the implications of the Act.

(c) The registered entry should be amended whenever there is a change to the personal data that is being held and used.

(d) The co-ordinator should set up systems which will allow him or her:

     (i)   to monitor compliance with the Principles;

     (ii)   to meet subject access requests;

     (iii)   to be made aware of any changes in the organisation which may require amendment to the registered entry.

(e) Whenever a new computer system is planned, or a new software package purchased, consideration should be given to whether a registration of the system under the Act is necessary. This should be a formal step in system design and development, so that it is never overlooked.

3   COPYRIGHT

3.1   The Copyright, Designs and Patents Act 1988

Copyright in the UK is governed by the Copyright, Designs and Patents Act 1988. For the purposes of the Act, a computer program is a literary work, and copyright is infringed if it is 'stored or adapted' (this does not include storage in memory) without permission.

The problem for companies which produce software is that computer users can copy software from a program disk to a blank disk, much like recording music from a purchased cassette to a blank cassette. The Act gives the protection of copyright law to software writers, and to all software written before the Act as well as to software written subsequently.

(a) It is illegal to copy a program, for example from one floppy disk onto another disk, without permission from the copyright owner.

(b) This means that it is illegal for a firm to buy a program, copy it, and then sell the copy to another user. (However, enforcing legislation against piracy might be difficult, especially in those parts of the world where software piracy is common.)

(c) The legislation also affects computer users who want to use the same software themselves, but on several different computers. Generally speaking, each copy of the program must be authorised, unless there is some prior agreement. Software suppliers advise customers to make back-up copies of their programs, for security reasons, and if making a copy is authorised in this way, the law will not be infringed. Often, use of a program is limited to specified computers, or to all computers on a specified site, by the software supplier.

Users of software should institute appropriate procedures to prevent breaches of the law. These procedures should include the following.

(a) Draw up a set of rules for copying software, so that the organisation is not in breach of copyright through the ignorance of management and staff. For example, the organisation could require that every copy of a software package be authorised by the organisation's legal department. They would ensure that the copying did not breach the contract with the supplier.

(b) Ensure that employees are made aware of the organisation's rules in this regard.

(c) Make illegal copying a disciplinary offence.

(d) Maintain a record of copies made of software packages, identifying the computer hard disks where they are stored. The organisation can do an audit of its computers to ensure that there has been no copying in breach of the law or the agreement.

3.2   Federation Against Software Theft

Software suppliers in the UK have formed the UK Federation Against Software Theft (FAST), which is prepared to bring legal action against organisations breaking copyright law. Moreover, if a breach is found, not only does the organisation have to pay damages and legal costs, but also the licensor might terminate the agreement to use the software. Imagine the chaos caused in many finance departments if the right to use Lotus 123 suddenly disappeared. It might also be hard to obtain licences from other software suppliers if the legal action results in a bad reputation. An alternative to the embarrassment of legal action is to submit to an audit conducted by FAST.

3.3   Reverse engineering

One of the greatest sources of competition in the PC market has been the growth of clones, or cheap imitations of products currently available. To a large extent, this has been achieved by a process of so-called reverse engineering.

Definition

Reverse engineering is the dismantling of a product to see how it is made, and so learning how to make a similar product.

The European Union has considered legislation which would greatly restrict the scope of reverse engineering.

(a) A user lobbying organisation, Computer Users in Europe, is against restrictions on reverse engineering, on the grounds that it will limit the number of add-on programs.

(b) The manufacturers stand to benefit as their control over software development will be maintained.

Such legislation would affect users if the competitive nature of the computer market is not maintained.

Activity 5

What sort of illegal copying of software within an organisation would not be detected by an audit of the organisation's computers and disks?

---

4 THE COMPUTER MISUSE ACT 1990

The Computer Misuse Act 1990 was enacted to respond to the growing threat of hacking to computer systems and data. There was some dispute as to whether hacking was a crime. For example, if you had illegally read data, this was not theft, as the original data was not stolen.

4.1 Offences under the Act

The Act has created three new offences.

(a) *Unauthorised access.* An offence is committed by a hacker, who, knowing that he or she is unauthorised, tries to gain access to another computer system. It is the attempt which is the crime: the hacker's success or failure is irrelevant.

(b) *Unauthorised access with intent to commit another offence* results in harsher penalties than (a) above. It might be a suitable charge if a hacker had been caught in the early stages of a fraud.

(c) *Unauthorised modification of data or programs.* Amongst other acts, the deliberate introduction of computer viruses into a system is an offence. However, the simple addition of data is not an offence, just its corruption or destruction. Guilt is based on the intention to impair the operation of a computer or program, or to prevent or hinder access to data.

4.2 Penalties under the Act

The maximum penalty for each offence is as follows.

(a) Unauthorised access: imprisonment for up to six months and/or a fine of up to £2,000

(b) Unauthorised access with intent to commit another offence: imprisonment for up to five years and/or an unlimited fine

(c) Unauthorised modification: imprisonment for up to five years and/or an unlimited fine

Individuals or companies may take out private criminal prosecutions. Prosecuting someone for a breach of the Computer Misuse Act need not be left to the Crown Prosecution Service.

5 OTHER LEGAL MATTERS

So far in this chapter we have dealt with data protection, copyright and computer misuse. There are other areas of an organisation's use of computers where the law can intervene, or where attention to the legal aspects of a decision can be beneficial to the organisation.

If an organisation is buying a computer system, or having one designed and installed by an outside supplier or consultancy, then the contract should specify performance targets and penalties for breaching them.

A faulty computer program which produces incorrect VAT or tax returns may result in legal action by HM Customs & Excise or the Inland Revenue. The faulty program may not be sufficient excuse to avoid penalties. An organisation might ask the software supplier to indemnify it against any penalties caused by errors in the software.

Employers can be prosecuted under the Health and Safety at Work Act 1974. Also, sufferers from repetitive strain injury or other illnesses related to the use of computer terminals, might be able to sue their employers for negligence. The design and use of VDUs is the subject of a European Union directive, which came into force (for new equipment) at the end of 1992. Equipment purchased before that date must be brought up to standard by the end of 1996.

Activity 6

How might an organisation's computer operations be adversely affected by the unauthorised addition of data, without any corruption of existing data?

Chapter roundup

- The Data Protection Act 1984 was passed to safeguard the privacy of living individuals (data subjects).
- Personal data comprises both facts and opinions about data subjects. The Act applies to both data users and computer bureaux.
- Data users and computer bureaux must register under the Act, and must notify any changes to their registrations.
- Data subjects may see the data held about them, and may challenge factual inaccuracies.
- Data users should comply with the eight data protection principles.
- There are some exemptions to the Act as a whole (both unconditional and conditional exemptions), to subjects' right of access to data and to the non-disclosure provisions.
- There are several offences under the Act.
- Organisations should institute procedures to ensure compliance with the Act.
- Computer software is covered by copyright legislation. A buyer of software is normally authorised to make only specified use of the software, which may be restricted to certain computers or to all computers on a certain site.

Chapter roundup (*continued*)

- Under the Computer Misuse Act 1990, unauthorised access to a computer system and the unauthorised modification of data are offences.

- A contract for the supply of a computer system should clearly specify what is to be supplied, and any liability of the supplier for consequential losses should the system not perform as it is meant to.

- The health and safety risks to employees from computer systems should be borne in mind.

Quick quiz

1   Give some examples of electronic equipment not covered by the Data Protection Act 1984

2   Are employees of a company which is a data user themselves data users?

3   What information is included in a data user's registration?

4   What rights do data subjects have?

5   State the data protection principles.

6   What unconditional exemptions to the Data Protection Act 1984 as a whole are available?

7   What offences are created by the Data Protection Act 1984?

8   What procedures should be established by an organisation to avoid breaches of copyright in software bought and used by it?

9   What are the three offences under the Computer Misuse Act 1990?

10 Give an example of consequential loss which may be suffered by a user of a computer system which does not perform as it should do.

Answers to activities

1   (a) Personal data: an expression of opinion about a living individual.

    (b) Not personal data: about a company.

    (c) Not personal data: an expression of intention.

2   The data subject might be pursued for a debt he does not owe, falsely recorded as having previously defaulted on debts (and therefore be unable to obtain credit) or falsely recorded as having been convicted of a crime (and therefore be unable to get a job).

3   (a) Principle (5), because the data is not kept up to date.

    (b) Principle (3), because the disclosure may be nothing to do with the data user's registered purposes.

4   Yes: the data was disclosed through the managing director's recklessness, because there is always a risk that someone will come into a company's public reception area.

5   Copying onto disks which employees then take home.

6   Files could be filled up, and processing slowed down, by the addition of, for example, fictitious customers to the sales ledger (even if they all had nil account balances so that no monetary amounts were affected).

Further question practice

Now try the following practice questions at the end of this text.

Multiple choice questions   **109 to 115**

GLOSSARY

4GLs Fourth generation computer languages

Access Microsoft's database management system

ACL automated cartridge libraries

ALT The ALT (alternate command) key signifies a command action

ALU Arithmetic and logic unit, part of the CPU

Application specific files Files whose structure and use are specific to a given application, as opposed to a database

ASCII American standard code for information interchange, a standardised 'alphabet' code for PCs and Minicomputers

Assembly language A symbolic representation of the machine code

Asynchronous transmission Data is sent one character at a time bracketed by start and stop signals

BACS Bankers automated clearing system

Bandwidth The range of frequencies that a channel can carry, this is proportional to the rate of information transfer

Bar coding A standardised system of lines and gaps, which allows goods to be marked and tracked quickly

BASIC Beginners all symbolic instruction code developed by Dartmouth College used to teach elementary programming

BCD Binary coded decimal, a form of numeric coding which allows 2 numeric digits to be 'packed' into a single byte

Binary number A number system with base 2 having two stages: 0 – off and 1 – on

Bit Binary digit

Buffering Storing data in a temporary store to reduce the overhead of input/output transfers

Bus A signal route common to the system

Byte A group of 8 binary digits

C A terse/concise programming language developed by Bell Labs used for general/ systems programming

C++ An object oriented version of C

CAD Computer aided design

CD-ROM A compact disk recording digital data, read by means of a laser

Chips Thin semiconductor material (usually silicon) with embedded electronic circuits

CIM Computer Integrated Manufacture

Circuit switching The connection along a channel is maintained for the duration of the conversion blocking its use even during idle period

Clones Computers using the same design architecture as the IBM PC

COBOL Common business orientated language developed by US Department of Defence

COM Computer output on microfilm

Compiler A program which does a once-and-for-all translation of a program

Control information A comparison between actual results and plan

CPU Central processing unit

CTRL The Control key signifies a command action

Cursor A visible indicator of the data entry focus

Cursor control keys The 'arrow' keys and Home, End, Page Up, Page Down keys

Daisy wheel printer An impact printer which has the available font on a wheel which rotates in front of the striking hammer

DAT Digital audio tape

Data field An item of data relating to a record

Data independence The ability of programs to access data via logical data structures without needing to know the details of the physical data structures, eg an operator can extract data from an Access file without having to know how that file is structured

Data input The act of entering data into the system

Data processing The use of automation (ie computers) to process raw data (input) to create meaningful information (output)

Data record A logically definable unit of information

Data redundancy Wasteful and unnecessary duplication of data

Data striping A method of storing data in parallel across a series of disks in such a manner that the loss of a disk can be compensated for by performing calculations on the remaining disk

Database A structured system

DBA Database administrator

DBMS Database management system

DIP Digital image processing or document image processing

Direct access A method of access in which the key field is used to calculate directly the position of a record, usually by means of a hash function

Distributed database A database in which the data is spread across a number of systems in the network

Dot matrix printer A printer which constructs the character image from an array of metal pins

DSS Decision support system

DTP Desktop publishing

Dumb terminal A terminal with no inherent processing capability of its own

EBCDIC Extended binary coded decimal interchange code, a standardised 'alphabet' code for IBM mainframes

EDI Electronic data interchange

EFTPOS Electronic fund transfer at point of sale

EIS Executive information system

E-mail Electronic mail

Emulation The use of specialised hardware to make a computer appear to behave as another model

EPOS Electronic point of sale

Esc The Escape key; it is generally used to end an action

233

Exception reporting A system which focuses attention on items that are significantly different

Feedback The return of part of the output of a system as input, in order to control the system's behaviour

File server A computer dedicated to holding a network's file system

Firmware Software which has become fixed in place by, for example, being burned into ROM

Floppy disk Direct access storage device which uses a magnetic recording medium coated onto a disk of mylar film.

Modern 'floppy disks' actually a have a rigid plastic cover.

Forecasting packages Packages which enable a user to prepare forecasts from historical data

FORTRAN Formula translation language developed by IBM commonly used for scientific applications

Full duplex Data can travel in both directions simultaneously

Function keys The F1-F10 (F12) along the top or on the right of the keyboard. These keys are programmable. F1 has been standardised as a 'help' key

Gigabyte Gb 1,024 megabytes

Graphics Pictorial images

Graphics card An additional circuit board placed in the PC to enable graphic display

GUI Graphical user interface

Half duplex Data can travel in both directions (but only one way at any given time)

Hard disk Direct access storage device which uses a magnetic recording medium coated onto a rigid disk. The rigidity allows a greater spin speed, hence faster access/read times

Hardware The real physical part of the system, the computer, peripheral devices etc

HDA Hard disk assembly

Hierarchical database A form of database where each level of data is dependent on the layer above. Similar in form to a tree

HTML Hypertext mark up language

Http Hypertext transfer protocol

Icon An image used to represent an abstract idea or process

Information technology The use of automation (ie computers) to process raw data (input) to create meaningful information (output)

Ingres A large system DBMS

Input Data which enters the system from outside

Internet An international scope WAN of interlinked computer networks sharing data via the TCP/IP protocols

Interpreter A program which translates the program on the fly

Intranet The application of Internet technology to a limited local network to allow the co-operative sharing of data within an organisation

ISAM Indexed sequential access method - records are stored sequentially but access is obtained by way of an index to locate individual records

Just in time A method of controlling stock flow to minimise inventory overheads

Justified Both right and left borders of the text are straight

Key fields The field which contains the data capable of uniquely identifying a record

Kilobyte (Kb) 1,024 bytes (210)

LAN Local area network

Laser printer A page printer which uses a xerographic method of fusing carbon particles onto paper

LISP List processing language used for artificial intelligence programming and expert systems

Logical data structures An abstract view of how the data is structured

Machine code A literal numeric representation of the machine state which represents the computer program

Macro language (macro assembler) A text processing tool which allows commonly repeated assembly language code to be itself represented symbolically

Macro language (spreadsheet) A means of recording commonly repeated actions and 'playing' them back to automate tasks

Magnetic stripe cards A plastic card with an embedded magnetic strip capable of storing small amounts of data

Magnetic tape Mylar tape embedded with magnetic recording material

Magneto-optical A system using a combination of laser and magnetic recording methods to store and access data

Mainframes A standard model computer system, large in size, power and speed. Capable of supporting many users at once, eg IBM, Amdahl, ICL

Master file A file containing the model the changes are to be applied to

Megabyte Mb 1,024 kilobytes

Memory The circuity used to store data within the processor while the computer is operating

MHz MegaHertz, one million cycles per second

MICR Magnetic ink character recognition

Microcomputer A computer which is based on a single chip microprocessor CPU

Microfiche A form of microfilm which stores the images on pages of sheets rather than on rolls

Minicomputer Originally used to describe a computer cheaper and less well equipped than a mainframe

Minitel A French viewdata system widely used due to their replacing telephone directories

MIPS Mega (1 million) instructions per second

MIS Management information system

Modelling packages Packages which enable a user to develop a model for financial forecasting

Model A modulator-demodulator which converts a digital signal into an audio signal capable of transmission on a telephone line

Mouse A palm-sized input device, which moves across the desk on a rubber coated ball, sending signals along a 'tail' like a cable enabling the user to co-ordinate the position of a screen pointer

MRP Materials requirements planning

MS-DOS Microsoft disk operating system

Multimedia The combination of text, sound and images into an integrated information system

Multiplexor A device which allows a single channel to be shared by several devices

Network database Each records acts as a node which may be linked to other nodes in the database. Think of a bowl of spaghetti

Numeric keypad The calculator style array of numbers to the right of the main keyboard

O/S2 (includes **WARP** and **Merlin**) IBM's 32 bit operating system for PCs

Object oriented programming (OOP) A programming paradigm which focuses on representing data and the methods of manipulating it as abstract entities called objects

Object program The machine readable form of a computer program, the output from a program translator

OCR Optical character recognition

OMR Optical mark reading

Open systems 'Open systems' represent a trend of movement away from proprietary operating systems towards those whose capabilities have been set by the international standards bodies

Operating information Information needed to do the work

Operational information Information used in the 'front line' to make day-to-day decisions

Oracle A large system DBMS

Origination of data The business transaction which gives rise to data

Output Information the system generates

PABX Private automatic branch exchange

Packet switching The network is shared by packets each travelling their own route

Parallel transmission Groups of bits are sent simultaneously through separate channels

PASCAL (not an acronym!) Developed by N Wirth, used to teach structured programming

PC Personal computer

Peripherals Devices on the edge/boundary of the system, typically responsible for input/output

Physical data structures How the data is actually stored

Planning information Information needed to create plans

Plotters Devices which draw images onto paper with coloured pens

Portable A computer small enough to be carried around

POSIX Opening systems standard for UNIX

Procedural programming A programming paradigm which focuses on how the task is to be carried out, breaking the task down into discrete sub-tasks called procedures

Processing Actions carried out by the system

Processor The part of the computer which co-ordinates its actions

PROLOG *Pro*positional *logic* language used for artificial intelligence programming and expert systems

Proportional spacing Each letter occupies a space related to its width

Pull-down menu A means of selecting a task form a list of those available

RAD Rapid application development

RAID Redundant array of inexpensive disks

RAM Random access memory (read/write)

Random access Read records in any order

Reference file A file containing data which is infrequently changed

Relational database All records are stored in tables. Links between tables depend on the value of key fields. Think of well ordered ranks and columns. Remember the discipline required to keep it that way

Return/enter key This key signals the end of a line of text, or commits an action

Risk analysis packages These packages use probability distributions to deal with larger numbers of variables

ROM Read only memory

Scanner A devise for digitising images to allow them to be stored in a computer

SCSI Small computer systems interface a data bus standard popular on UNIX machines and PCs

Sequential access Read records in the order they are stored

Serial transmission Bits are sent one after another along the same channel

Simplex Data travels one way only

Simulation The use of software to make a computer behave as another model

Software The intangible part of the system, which comprises the instructions to perform given tasks, ie the programs

Source program The human readable form of a computer program, the input to a translation program

Spreadsheet Generic term for table style modelling software

Spreadsheet cell A discrete data component of a spreadsheet

Spreadsheet column A set of vertically grouped cells

Spreadsheet formula An instruction to provide the result of a calculation based on neighbouring cells

Spreadsheet label Literal text

Spreadsheet row A set of horizontally grouped cells

Spreadsheet value Static numerical value

SQL Structured query language (pronounced as either 'ess kew ell' or 'sequel') an ANSI standard data manipulation language for RDBMSs

SSADM Structured system analysis and design methodology

Storage A place where the current state of the system is recorded

Strategic information Information used by senior managers to plan the objectives of an organisation

Sub-system A clearly distinguishable unit, function or operation, related to other subsystems within the overall system

Supercomputers Specialised systems used to process vast amounts of data very quickly, eg Cray

SYBASE A large system DBMS

Synchronous transmission Data is sent and received at a constant rate controlled by clock signals

System A clearly distinguishable unit, function or operation

Tactical information Information used by middle management to obtain short-term objectives

TCP/IP Transmission control protocol/Internet protocol

Telecommuting Communicating with the work place via electronic links rather than actually going there

Teleconferencing A centralised e-mail system allowing pooling of messages and ideas

Teletext Digital information carried in the lines between television pictures

Thermal printers Printers which use a heating element to transfer an image into the paper either by directly burning a heat sensitive coating or by melting ink onto the paper

Trackball A form of inverted mouse

Transaction file A file containing changes to be made

Transcription of data Converting data into a machine readable form

UNIX A multi-user multi-tasking operating system used on many mainframes and minicomputers. Easily ported to new environments as it is largely written in a high level language ('C')

URL/(URI) Uniform resource locator (identifier)

VANS Value added networks

VDU Visual display unit

Videoconferencing A system of using live video links to bring people to a virtual meeting it might otherwise be too costly to arrange

Videophones Phones capable of carrying video images as well as voice

Virus A piece of software which infects programs and data and which replicates itself

Voice mail A system of digitally recording messages in a voice mailbox

WAN Wide area network

WIMP interface Windows icons menu pointer or Windows icons, mouse, pull-down-menus

Winchester disks Sealed hard units, so named after the town in which they were invented

Windows A generic term for the practice of dividing the screen into areas to distinguish tasks. A brand name relating to the Microsoft's operating system products

Windows NT Microsoft's 32 bit operating system for PCs

Word processing An application for storing and manipulating text

World wide web A co-operative network of hypertext resources

WORM Write once read many, a recordable form of CD-ROM

WYSIWYG What you see is what you get

MULTIPLE CHOICE QUESTIONS

Chapter 1

1 Computer components can be divided between hardware and software. Which of the following is *not* hardware?

A Printer

B CPU

C Word for Windows

D Keyboard

A B C D

2 Hardware can be divided into input, output and processing devices. Which of the following is an input device?

A Screen

B Keyboard

C Printer

D CPU

A B C D

3 Input, output and storage devices are often referred to as peripherals. Which of the following is *not* a peripheral?

A Modem

B Mouse

C Scanner

D DOS

A B C D

4 Computers can be described by type. What type of computer would you use to play games on?

A Mainframe

B PC

C Supercomputer

D Electronic Organiser

A B C D

5 A PC has three major components. Which of the following is *not* a PC component?

A Input devices

B CPU

C VDU

D Printer

A B C D

6 The processor is divided into three areas. Which of the following is *not* part of the processor?

A Operating system

B Control Unit

C ALU

D Memory

A B C D

7 Memory is measured in bytes. How many bytes is 16 MB?

A 1,024

B 8,388,608

C 16,777,216

D 17,179,869,184

A B C D

Chapter 2

8 Computer data is frequently stored on disk. Which of the following has the greatest storage capacity?

A CD ROM

B Floppy disk

C Hard disk

D RAID

A B C D

9 Floppy disks have a variety of uses. Which of these uses is *not* recommended?

A Storage

B Backup

C Coaster

D Transportation

A B C D

10 Backing up important data is essential. Which of the following would you not back up?

A A client database

B The company report

C Multiple copies of a standard letter

D A memo

A B C D

11 Data can be stored on a variety of mediums. Which of the following is *not* a storage medium?

A Mouse

B CD-ROM

C Magnetic tape

D WORM

A B C D

12 A record can contain a number of fields. Which of the following is not suitable as a field for a customer record?

A Title

B 0171 342 5768

C Lastname

D Postcode

A B C D

13 Fields are usually identified as being of particular types. Which of the following would be a numeric field?

A Date of birth

B Price

C Phone No

D Catalogue number

A B C D

14 Data can be accessed in a variety of ways. Which of the following is *not* a suitable method of accessing data?

A Sort

B Sequential

C Serial

D Random

A B C D

15 Which of the following statements is true?

A Computer output on microform is human-sensible

B An inkjet printer is an impact printer

C Daisy wheel printers print a character at a time

D A pixel is the technical term for the 'dot' in ' dot-matrix printer'

A B C D

16 Fast tapes used to create back-up files quickly are known as

A tape writers

B tape spoolers

C tape streamers

D tape copiers

A B C D

17 Which of the following is *not* an advantage of magnetic disk over magnetic tape?

A Direct access

B Updating by file overlay

C Integration of systems applications

D Less chance of data corruption

A B C D

Chapter 3

18 Computer keyboards have additional keys to those displayed on the normal typewriter QWERTY layout. Which of the following is also present on the typewriter keyboard?

A CTRL

B RETURN

C ALT

D ESC

A B C D

19 Using a mouse has a number of advantages over using the keyboard. Which of the following tasks is *not* assisted by mouse use?

A Drawing

B Choosing menu items

C Keying in text

D Moving around the screen

A B C D

20 Which of the following is *not* true? Dot matrix printers

A produce 'letter quality' output

B can print graphics

C are impact printers

D are character printers

A B C D

21 User-friendly systems can include a number of features. Which of the following is *not* user-friendly?

A GUI

B WIMP

C Icons

D DOS

A B C D

22 Document reading methods enable the computer to read data direct. Which of the follows is *not* a document reading method?

A OCR

B OMR

C WYSIWYG

D MICR

A B C D

23 A thermal printer is an example of

A a line printer

B a page printer

C an impact printer

D an electrosensitive printer

A B C D

24   Which of the following is *not* true? A laser printer

A   can print graphics

B   can print in a variety of different fonts

C   can use continuous stationery

D   contains a microprocessor

A B C D

Chapter 4

25   Which of the following statements is *incorrect*?

A   Computers do not require special equipment to communicate with each other over the public telecommunications network

B   Computers can communicate with each other by satellite

C   Computers can communicate with each other using optical fibre technology

D   Users of one computer system can access data stored by another system

A B C D

26   Protocol is

A   the way in which data is translated into a form compatible to a different computer system from the one which processed it originally

B   a means by which access by networked microcomputers to commonly held files is governed

C   an agreed set of operational procedures governing the format of data being transferred and the signals initiating, controlling and terminating the transfer

D   the process by which the interface between two computer systems is efficiently managed

A B C D

27   A multi-user system is

A   a system linking together several computers with their own processors

B   a system, based around one processor, that serves more than one user with apparent simultaneity

C   a data processing system of uniform stand-alone microcomputers, using standard software

D   an organisation that does data processing work for other organisations

A B C D

28 A mainframe computer using EBCDIC (extended binary coded decimal interchange code) would communicate with a microcomputer using ASCII (American standard code for information interchange) via

A an emulator

B a protocol converter

C an ethernet cable

D a simulator

A B C D

29 Emulation is

A the execution by one computer of a program written for another computer, with the use of special hardware and software to mimic the operation of the computer for which the program was originally designed

B the imitation, or modelling, of the behaviour of an existing or proposed system

C the translation of a program designed for one type of computer into a form suitable for another type of computer

D the cloning by one computer manufacturer of the hardware and computer architecture of the equipment of another manufacturer

A B C D

30 Which of the following statements is *incorrect*? A local area network (LAN)

A relies on a PABX line to link it together

B consists of a number of independent computers which require network software to function as a network

C is incapable of extensive geographical dispersion

D is likely to contain a central server computer

A B C D

31 A configuration where a number of processors are *combined* to do one particular task is known as

A distributed data processing

B a network

C a multi-user system

D a multiprocessing configuration

A B C D

Chapter 5

32 Which of the following statements is *incorrect*?

A All software has to be loaded into RAM memory

B Any item of software must be translated into binary code

C Software can be written using other software

D Utility programs are applications software

A B C D

33 The software which links the hardware resources in a data processing operation to applications software is known as

A utility software

B firmware

C an operating system

D an interpreter program

A B C D

34 Which of the following is *not* a typical function of an operating system?

A booting

B translating a program from one language to another

C formatting a floppy disk

D deleting files under user command

A B C D

35 Which of the following statements is correct?

A A computer can only use one operating system

B Part of an operating system must reside in ROM

C All operating systems are machine-specific

D Operating systems are expert systems

A B C D

36 Which of the following statements is *incorrect*?

A A programming language is software

B Programs that translate programming languages are software

C Machine code is a programming language

D Machine code is machine-specific

A B C D

37 Which of the following statements is correct?

A Programs written in low-level languages use the computer less efficiently than those written in high-level languages

B It is easier to test programs and correct errors in a program that has been written in machine code

C A program written in a low-level language takes longer to execute than a program written in a high-level language

D A statement in high-level language does not indicate how the program will appear in machine code

A B C D

38 When a compiler program translates a program that has been written in a high-level language, it also

A corrects errors in the program's logic

B checks for errors in the program's logic

C corrects errors in syntax

D checks for errors in syntax

A B C D

Chapter 6

39 You work for a small charity which uses a microcomputer and dot matrix printer with word processing software and you want to set up a desktop publishing operation. Which of the following statements is correct?

A The charity has all the hardware and software it needs to set up a desk top publishing operation

B The charity needs additionally a laser printer and a graphics package

C The charity needs additionally special desktop publishing software only

D The charity needs additional desktop publishing software and a laser printer

A B C D

40 Which one of the following features distinguishes desktop publishing from word processing?

A Production of printed pages with a variety of 'fonts' (eg 'bold', 'italic' etc)

B Easy manipulation of text layout, and combination of text and graphics

C Output can be used as input to a phototypesetter

D Output to high resolution laser printers

A B C D

41 Which of the following is *not* an example of a word processing software package?

A Word

B WordPro

C Access

D Display Write

A B C D

Data for questions 42–45

You have acquired a spreadsheet package, Excel. You want to use it to devise a monthly schedule of your firm's income and expenditure over the past three months, in a format as shown below. The schedule is to be updated every month. (At the end of July, for example, the months shown will be July, June and May.) You decide that columns should represent months, with one to contain 'year-to-date' totals and each row should represent an item of income or expenditure, with a final profit figure at the bottom of each column, as in the illustration below. You also want to list the amount owing to your firm by its clients at the end of each month.

	A	B	C	D	E
1	Item	Total 3	June	May	April
2		months			
3		£	£	£	£
4	Fees		21500	22000	22500
5					
6					
7	Salaries		13500	12500	12500
8	Postage		200	200	200
9	Telephone		200	200	200
10	Stationery		200	200	200
11	Rent		1500	1500	1500
12	Accountancy		300	200	
13	Bank charges		–	400	
14	Rates		600	600	600
15	Other		1000	1200	
16					
17	Net profit		4000	5000	6000
18					
19	Owed by clients		7170	10995	9000
20					
21					
22					
23					

---

42 What should you enter in cell B4 when you construct the model, to make *best* use of the spreadsheet's facilities?

A 66000

B 21500 + 22000 + 22500

C =SUM(C4:E4)

D (C:E)*4

A B C D

43 Which of the following would *not* be entered in the total column, on the row entitled 'Net profit'?

A =B4–SUM(B7:B15)

B =SUM(C17:E17)

C B4–B7–B8–B9–B10–B11–B12–B13–B14–B15

D =-SUM(B7:B15)+B4

A B C D

44 You now wish to make your model more sophisticated, to include various items of a statistical nature. (1) The percentage change in revenue month by month is required. (2) The outstanding debt at the end of each month to be expressed as a proportion of the average daily revenue per month (assume each month has 30 days). Which of the alternatives below best expresses how you would input these requirements to your spreadsheet?

A (1): =(C4–D4)/D4 formatted as a percentage

(2): =C19/(C4/30)

B (1): =C4–D4/D4 formatted as a percentage

(2): =C19/C4/30

C (1): =C4–D4/D4 formatted as a percentage

(2): =C19/C4/30

D (1): =C4–D4/D4 formatted as a percentage

(2): =C19/(C4/30)

A B C D

45 You wish to retain your file for further use. Which of the following set of keystrokes should you enter?

A /FILE LIST {file name}

B /SAVE {file name}

C /FILE/SAVE AS {file name}

D /FILE {file name} SAVE

A B C D

Chapter 7

46 Questionnaires might be used by a systems analyst to gather information about an existing system for a feasibility study. Which of the following statements about questionnaires is correct? Questionnaires *without interviews* are best suited for fact-finding whenever

A a large amount of data has to be gathered from a large number of people

B a large amount of data has to be gathered from a small number of people

C a limited amount of data has to be gathered from a large number of people

D a limited amount of data has to be gathered from a small number of people

A B C D

47 In any feasibility study the costs of a system must be estimated. Some system costs recur regularly. Others are one-off costs. One-off costs can be divided into 'capital' items and 'non-capital' items. The difference is that non-capital costs are charged in full against profit in the year the costs are incurred, whereas the 'capital' costs are spread over a number of years of the project.

Which of the following is treated as a 'capital' item?

A   Hardware maintenance

B   Rewiring and other installation costs

C   Staff training

D   Staff recruitment fees

A B C D

48 Burke and Hare Spares Ltd have asked you to design the documentation for a computer system to maintain and update a stock master file. Five source documents for the system are

(1) materials issued to factory notes

(2) materials returns from factory notes

(3) goods received from suppliers notes

(4) goods returned to suppliers notes

(5) order placed with supplier notes

A sixth essential source document will be

A   suppliers' invoices

B   suppliers' confirmation of order notes

C   list of standard reorder quantity for each stock item

D   materials requisition notes

A B C D

49 Famiadriat plc are about to install a computer system, using off-the-shelf modular application software for a network of microcomputers sharing access to common files, which include

File

1   Customer file

2   Supplier file

3   Stock file

4   Orders file

5   Payroll file

6   Sales commission file

Which files will be accessed to process a customer order?

A Files 1, 2, 3, 4, 5, 6

B Files 1, 3 4, 5, 6

C Files 1, 3, 4, 6

D Files 1 and 4

A B C D

50 You are designing for Bodgett Builders a microcomputer-based sales ledger system, which records invoices sent to customers and payments from them. The system is required to keep a record of each individual sale to any customer, until it is matched by a payment received. This method of maintaining the sales ledger is known as

A an open item system

B a brought forward balance system

C an aged balance system

D a simple balance system

A B C D

51 An organisation with several branches changes over the computer system in one branch first to see if the system works well. This type of systems changeover is known as

A staged implementation

B direct changeover

C phased implementation

D pilot operation

A B C D

52 A situation where data is run on both old and new systems for a specified time is an example of

A indirect changeover

B parallel running

C restricted data running

D pilot operation

A B C D

Chapter 8

53 A system is often subject to control. Control depends on information, and one type of information provided is *feedback*. Feedback, in systems terminology, is

A   information derived from sources external to the system, indicating whether the system is achieving its goals

B   comments and ideas for improving a system obtained from users of the system

C   output information generated by the system itself, and returned to the system as input

D   external information relating to the system used as input for control purposes

A B C D

54 An open loop system is

A   a system where control is not an integral part of the system

B   a system open to the environment

C   a system where control is built into the system

D   a subsystem controlling other systems

A B C D

55 Feedback is described as being either positive or negative. When you receive positive feedback

A   you know that everything is going according to plan

B   you are encouraged to carry on deviation from the plan

C   you realise you must bring yourself back in line with the plan

D   you know that no alterations are needed to the plan

A B C D

56 Ingsoc plc is a large, widely diversified organisation with a number of systems for handling, processing and displaying information. Mr O'Brien is taking you round the Miniluv department, of which he is the manager.

The first room you are shown, room 100, is the centre of a system which updates payroll files every month. This payroll system is an example of

A   a transaction processing system

B   a decision support system

C   a database management system

D   an expert system

A B C D

57 Which of the following is most appropriately described as control information?

> A A report comparing actual monthly sales figures with budget
>
> B A report prepared by the marketing department detailing long-term social trends
>
> C A print-out detailing the day's cash receipts and payments
>
> D A price list

A B C D

58 You have been given two weeks off work from 14 September, and you have asked your travel agent for details of flights to and from Shangri-La. It is now 12 September. Through your letter box falls a heavy package with airline timetables from all eastward-flying airlines. This has been sent by a travel agent, who has attached the following note. "You should find what you want somewhere in here, but I'd definitely try Himalay-air for flights first. You'll probably need to make a few connections though." You look through the timetables, find no mention of Himalay-air, but find that Compare will fly you to Shangri-La.

In what way does the information received from the travel agent display what is commonly felt to be the qualities of *good* information?

> A It was relevant
>
> B It was accurate
>
> C It was timely
>
> D It was clear

A B C D

59 Exception reporting within business is

> A the reporting of exceptional events, outside the normal course of events
>
> B the analysis of those items where performance differs significantly from standard or budget
>
> C where reports on routine matters are prepared on an 'ad hoc' basis
>
> D the scrutiny of all data as a matter of course, save in exceptional circumstances

A B C D

Chapter 9

60 The term database is used in a variety of ways. Which of these statements is *not* a description of a database?

A A database consists of data that is structured in such a way that it is independent of any particular application

B A database exists to duplicate identical data across several related files, thus avoiding inconsistency of data used in different applications

C A database may be a file where any of the data fields can be used as a key field to specify queries

D A database is, in concept, a file where programs are written around the database, rather than a file structured around the needs of specific software

A B C D

61 *Data independence* means that

A a variety of application programs can process the same data, as the logical and physical arrangement of records are independent of each other

B only one application can use a database at one time

C all applications are independent of each other

D data in the database pertaining to one application is separate from data pertaining to other applications

A B C D

62 Which of the following would be the most suitable field to identify as a key field?

A Lastname

B Company

C NI No

D Phone No

A B C D

63 Which of the following statements relating to data in a database is correct?

A Logical relations between records are reflected in the way in which they are stored physically

B Two or more logical records which use the same data do not require the physical duplication of the data on file

C Data retrieval in different formats requires the data to be physically restructured

D A stored report format restructures the data when it is called up

A B C D

64 A data structure where data items on lower levels can only be reached through one data item on a higher level is known as

- A relational data structure
- B a network structure
- C a ring structure
- D a tree structure

A B C D

65 A network data structure

- A is a hierarchy
- B relates data on a one-to-many basis
- C relates many items of data with many other items of data
- D is a relational database

A B C D

66 A database administrator is

- A a civil servant, employed under the Data Protection Act, to ensure that public databases do not abuse confidential information about members of the public
- B a person in an organisation delegated with the task of controlling, maintaining and enhancing the database for user benefit
- C another term for database management system
- D an item of software residing in the data base management system, which provides the links between database files

A B C D

Chapter 10

67 Which would be the fastest way to transmit a document from London to New York?

- A Post
- B Fax
- C E-mail
- D Telex

A B C D

68 Which of the following is *not* a viewdata system?

- A Minitel
- B Ceefax
- C VEM
- D Prestel

A B C D

69   A form of electronic filing is called

A   PABX

B   Telex

C   DIP

D   EDI

A B C D

70   What will *not* be reduced by telecommuting?

A   Office rent

B   Phone bills

C   Travel time

D   Conference time

A B C D

71   Timesharing occurs when

A   a data transmission link is shared between users

B   the CPU uses a common set of programs to process user-specific files at the same time

C   the CPU processes a common set of files according to individual user programs in one shared operation

D   jobs relating either to central or user-specific programs and files are executed at the same time by the CPU, which allocates its time between them

A B C D

72   Polling occurs when

A   data sent down a packet switching network is reassembled on its arrival at its destination

B   a terminal contacts the computer to which it is attached to send data for output to other terminals

C   a computer contacts another computer to access data or to send data

D   a computer regularly contacts a terminal to see where the terminal has data to send or whether the terminal is due to receive some data

A B C D

73

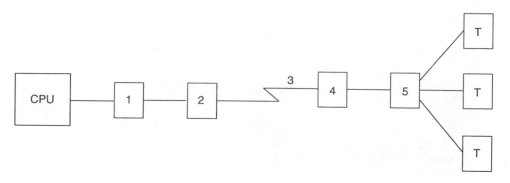

Which of these items represents a modem?

A   Item 1 only

B   Item 2 only

C   Items 2 and 4 only

D   Items 1 and 5 only

A B C D

Chapter 11

74   Which of the following is *not* likely to be in the terms of reference of a feasibility study?

A   Problem definition

B   Establishment of key performance factors for any new system

C   Cost benefit analysis of proposed new system (or alternative systems)

D   Data flow analysis

A B C D

75   Which of the following is a financial evaluation that is used to assess whether a systems project should be chosen, and which takes the time value of money into account as well as the full expected costs and benefits of the project?

A   Payback

B   Accounting return on capital employed

C   CVP analysis

D   DCF analysis

A B C D

76   A feasibility study involves the identification of *system requirements*. Which of the following would *not* be part of this process?

A   Deciding what processing speeds are needed

B   Deciding what standard of output is expected

C   Deciding the numbers and qualifications of staff who will be required by the new system

D   Discerning the information needs of senior management

A B C D

77   Which of the following will *not* be included in a feasibility report?

A   Alternative systems considered

B   Clear recommendation of preferred system option

C   Implementation timescale

D   Detailed design of proposed system

A B C D

78 A disadvantage of purchasing off-the-shelf software, rather than having software custom-built from scratch, is

A system testing and implementation take longer

B software errors will be more frequent

C input errors will be more common

D the software may either carry out fewer or more functions than the user actually needs

A B C D

79 A mail-order organisation which was having difficulties recruiting clerical staff has recently computerised many of its systems using OCR as an input medium. Additionally, the sales order and stock systems have been integrated. Which of the following would be classified as an *intangible* benefit of computerisation?

A Savings in staff costs

B Better decision-making, due to more and/or better information

C Processing of orders more quickly resulting in fewer items being kept in a central warehouse

D Reduction in staff time spent correcting input errors

A B C D

80 Structured analysis

A is the definition of data structures

B means the design of a system so that additional modules can be added to it

C is a staged approach of systems design that goes from the general to the particular, leaving physical implementation issues to the end

D is a technique of computer programming

A B C D

Chapter 12

81 The list below shows some of the activities necessary for software development and operation in a computer system project.

Activity

1 Requirements analysis

2 System design

3 Program testing

4 Implementation

5 Detailed specification

6 Maintenance

7 Program writing

8 System testing

Which is the normal sequence in which these activities are carried out?

A 1, 2, 5, 7, 3, 8, 4, 6

B 1, 5, 2, 7, 3, 8, 4, 6

C 1, 5, 2, 8, 7, 3, 4, 6

D 1, 2, 5, 8, 7, 3, 4, 6

A B C D

Data for questions 82 and 83

Below is a diagram of document flows between a company and its customers, and between the various departments of the company.

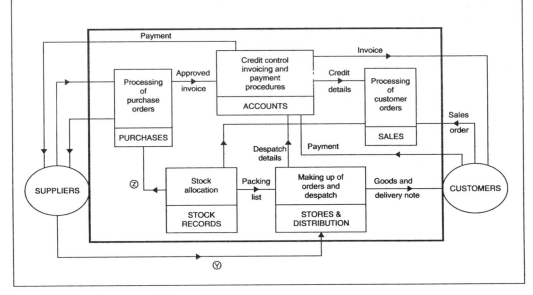

82 Document Y represents

A delivery notes

B invoices for goods received

C purchase orders

D goods received notes

A B C D

83 Document Z represents

A goods received notes

B reorder details

C invoices

D despatch notes

A B C D

84   You are reviewing the current system of Overbooked Airlines Ltd. You obtain an example of all the documents that are currently used in the system. Which of the following would not be relevant information for a *document description form*?

A   The sequence number given to the document after filing

B   The number of copies of each document

C   The number of data items on the document

D   The size of the data items

A B C D

85   A document description form is used in systems analysis and design for the following purposes, with one exception. Which is this exception?

A   To describe the contents of input/output forms in the current system

B   To help with the design of input/output forms in a new system

C   To describe the use of the form

D   To design the layout of a form

A B C D

86   You are employed as a systems analyst by Superhacker plc. You are required to design output for a VDU screen. Which of the following items might you include in the design of a screen *format*?

Items

1   Form design for keyboard input

2   'Windows'

3   On-screen prompts (eg menus)

4   Icons

5   Cursor positions

6   Content of error messages

A   Items 1, 2, 3 only

B   Items 1, 2, 3, 4 only

C   Items 1, 2, 3, 4, 5 only

D   Items 1, 2, 3, 4, 5, 6

A B C D

87 You decide that some of the output in a system you are designing will have to be on VDU and some of the processing will be *interactive*. Data entry is likely to be quite complicated and you are planning to use a system of commands for input of keyboard instructions. Which of the following statements is correct?

A A command system of VDU input involves a rigid screen format which commands the user to enter items in a particular order

B A command system formats the screen so that it is easy for users to enter data correctly

C A command system has a hierarchy of menu commands which the user can invoke

D A command system of VDU input allows the user to enter commands directly

A B C D

Chapter 13

88 The frequency with which standing data on a *master file* is inserted, amended and deleted is referred to as

A hit rate

B volatility

C purge rate

D file enquiry access rate

A B C D

89 File updating is

A the adding, amending or deletion of standing data

B the processing of details held on a transaction file to a master file

C the interrogation of a file for information

D the copying of a file on to a new storage medium

A B C D

90 File conversion

A is a technical issue relating to how data is transferred from one magnetic medium to another

B is the process by which logical file designs are implemented physically

C only occurs when the system goes live

D is the process by which data from old files are transferred to files used by the new system

A B C D

91 System maintenance is a stage in the system development life cycle. To which of the following items does maintenance refer?

Item

1 Correction of software errors

2 Alteration of programs to meet changes in user requirements

3 Alteration of programs to meet changes in external factors, such as changes in legislation and regulations

4 Changes in programs caused by user decisions to alter hardware and operating system configurations

A Item 1 only

B Items 1 and 2 only

C Items 1, 2 and 3 only

D Items 1, 2, 3, 4

A B C D

92 If a system has to cope with larger volumes of data than it was originally expected to handle, which of the following consequences would be expected?

Consequence

1 Increase in run-times over the run-times originally planned, and slower response times

2 Increase in input errors at data validation

3 Greater number of software errors

4 Higher incidence of hardware malfunction

A Consequences 1 and 2 only

B Consequences 1 and 3 only

C Consequences 2 and 4 only

D Consequences 3 and 4 only

A B C D

93 Acceptance testing is when

A the new system is checked on delivery

B the systems design is agreed

C the system is tested by the user department

D the bill is paid

A B C D

94 Parallel running is when

A all the data in the new system flows smoothly

B old and new systems are run in parallel for a time

C the new system is up and running

D the old system is replaced by the new one in one move

A B C D

Chapter 14

95   Which of the following would *not* be a suitable method of training a large number of staff?

A   CBT

B   Interactive videos

C   Self-study manuals

D   Use of training centres

A B C D

96   Skills once taught need to be maintained, especially if they are infrequently used. What might be the preferred method of those listed below?

A   Seminars

B   Training software

C   Quality circles

D   Refresher courses

A B C D

97   Procedural handbooks are becoming more important, and are produced by different people. Which of the following would *not* typically produce such a handbook?

A   Company secretary

B   Systems analysts

C   Software houses

D   Operations department

A B C D

98   Which of the following is a reason why employees might resist the opportunity of improving their skills through training?

A   Job enhancement

B   Fear of depersonalisation

C   Job promotion

D   Payment by results

A B C D

99   Which of the following is *not* a method for introducing new training requirements?

A   Staged implementation

B   Rapid implementation

C   Explanation

D   Participation

A B C D

100 HRM has both centralising and decentralising features. Which of the following is a decentralising feature?

A Top management driven activity

B Focus on corporate culture

C Key role for line management

D Cost benefit analysis

A B C D

101 Which of the following stages of an HRM training strategy would come first?

A Faults analysis

B Training plans

C Feedback

D Analysis of training needs

A B C D

Chapter 15

102 A little while ago, your organisation's magnetic tape system developed a hardware fault and destroyed a master file which was being updated during a processing run. The file had to be reconstructed from scratch. Which of the following is the best description of the reconstruction technique associated with a tape-based system?

A A file copying system

B The generation cycle

C A file dumping system

D Reference files

A B C D

103 You want to implement controls to provide backup facilities for your organisation's real-time disk-based systems. Which one of the following would you *not* implement for this purpose?

A Regular and frequent dumping of disk files on to magnetic tape

B Separate copies of program files kept on a different site

C Grandfather-father-son technique

D Maintenance of backup hardware to take over in case of system breakdown

A B C D

104 Two terms which relate to the use of codes to ensure controls over data transmission are encryption and authentication. Which of the following statements is correct?

   A Authentication ensures that the message goes to an authorised recipient by use of a commonly determined algorithm and encryption ensures that the message has come from an authorised source

   B Authentication is carried out to ensure that a message has been encrypted successfully

   C Authentication is the reassembly and decoding of an encrypted message

   D Encryption involves scrambling in cipher a message to prevent eavesdropping by third parties, and an authentication code is a check appended to a message to ensure that the message has not been tampered with

A B C D

Data for questions 105 and 106

Data valuation is an important software control over data. Five types of validation check are listed below.

Type

1   Check digit check

2   Range or limit check

3   Compatibility check

4   Format check

5   Code validity check

Data validation checks are to be incorporated into a new computerised stock control, order processing and invoicing system.

---

105 Which type of check would be most appropriate to check for errors where an input record specifies that a product is to be despatched form a warehouse which does not stock the item?

   A Type 1

   B Type 2

   C Type 3

   D Type 4

A B C D

106 Which type of check would be most appropriate for checking transcription errors resulting in the input of an incorrect stock code?

   A Type 1

   B Type 2

   C Type 3

   D Type 5

A B C D

107 A *checkpoint program*

A requires the use of several passwords, as the user passes through a number of 'checkpoints' in the program

B is used to check the accuracy of a processing operation by checking its calculations at randomly selected points in the program

C is a program that 'dumps' the entire contents of main storage on to backing store at certain specified points in the running of an application program

D is a programming tool which checks the accuracy of the conversion of a program from source code into object code

A B C D

108 Three of the features of your organisation's data processing are listed below.

Feature

1 A record is kept of adjustments that are made after verification to incorrectly keyed-in input data

2 Batch control totals are manually computed on a list containing each transaction in the batch. The computer only displays the control total of each batch processed

3 A sales ledger print-out displays the date and identifying number of each transaction that updates it

Audit trail is provided by

A feature 1 only

B features 1 and 2 only

C features 2 and 3 only

D feature 3 only

A B C D

Chapter 16

109 Which of the following statements is true? The Data Protection Act 1984 covers

A data about corporate bodies and individuals

B manual and computer records relating to individuals

C only mechanically processed data relating to individuals

D only data relating to individuals processed by computer

A B C D

110 In relation to the Data Protection Act 1984, data held on a company's computer payroll relating to employees is

A not covered by the Act

B unconditionally exempt from the provisions of the Act

C conditionally exempt from the provisions of the Act

D always covered by the Act

A B C D

111 The Data Protection Act 1984 gives certain types of data unconditional exemption from the provisions of the Act. Which of the following has *not* been granted such an exemption? Personal data

A needed to safeguard 'national security'

B which the user has a legal obligation to make public

C held by an individual solely for the management of personal, family or household affairs, or held for recreational purposes

D held by unincorporated members clubs relating only to club members

A B C D

112 The Data Protection Act 1984 grants *data subjects* certain rights. Which of the following statements is *incorrect*? A data subject

A may obtain access to personal data of which he or she is the subject

B may apply to the courts to have inaccurate personal data rectified or erased from the user's files

C can sue a data user for any damage or distress caused by data misleading as to a matter of opinion

D can seek compensation through the courts for damage or distress caused by personal data that is factually inaccurate

A B C D

113 A *data protection officer* is

A one of the Data Protection Registrar's deputies

B appointed by an organisation to ensure that it complies with the Data Protection Act 1984

C an official whose job it is to ensure that the organisation's networks are safe from unauthorised access

D an official in charge of an organisation's data archive

A B C D

114 Which of the following is responsible for the implementation of the Data Protection Act?

A   Comptroller & Auditor General

B   Audit Commission

C   Data Protection Registrar

D   Department of Trade & Industry

A B C D

115 Which of the following statements relating to the Data Protection Act 1984 is *incorrect*? Data is exempt from access by the data subject if it is

A   held for more than six years without challenge by the data subject

B   held for the prevention or detection of crime

C   held strictly for statistical or research purposes

D   data to which legal professional privilege could be claimed

A B C D

EXAM STYLE QUESTIONS

Chapter 1

1 FEASIBILITY STUDY

A company which acquired its first computer five years ago is now experiencing considerable trade expansion and the increased usage has created heavy demands upon the computer systems.

The board, which is now considering whether the computer should be replaced, probably during the next two years, has asked you, the deputy financial controller, to chair of the feasibility study group, of which there are to be two other members.

Indicate the matters to which you will give particular attention both before and during the feasibility study, including the formation of the group.

Guidance notes

1   A feasibility study team should include representatives with technical knowledge and operational experience.

2   Start by considering what your actions in relation to the existing system should be, before going on to consider alternative possibilities.

3   One way of demonstrating that you know what areas should be addressed would be by means of a list of the contents of a feasibility study report.

Chapter 2

2 WHIN RIGG   *45 mins*

Whin Rigg is a firm of shipping agents which uses PCs for various aspects of the business including maintenance of ledgers, control of goods in transit and management accounting. Staff at head office are experiencing serious delays in response times. When making enquiries you ascertain the disk housekeeping is poor and that the hard disks on several PCs are over 90% full. It is clear that other backing storage devices, besides floppy disks and the hard disks themselves, must be required very soon. In addition, the client ledger (sales ledger) is due for replacement, as it is six years old and only just handling current volumes.

Answer two questions from the following.

(a) Explain why it is necessary to divide computer storage into main storage and backing storage.

(b) Draw up a table showing the different types of computer memories, both primary and secondary, indicating how each type stores information and including details of other features such as speed, cost and capacity.

(c) What are the steps involved in creating a new client master file?

(d) In view of the range of existing problems, it has been decided to undertake a full systems investigation. Describe, and discuss the relative merits of, four techniques of collecting relevant data about both the current and the required system.

Chapter 4

3 CLAIFE HEIGHTS   *45 mins*

The local authority at Claife Heights is embarking upon a major new computerisation project. The key requirements are for a management information system which is accessible from any local centre and a higher level of office automation in administrative departments.

Senior personnel at the local authority are concerned about the costs of the system and have still to be persuaded that the benefits of widespread computerisation are worthwhile. They are also worried that the system will quickly become out of date, ie that it will only be able to cope with the circumstances and environment which exist at the time it is designed, and that as soon as the authority makes changes to its own operations or structure, the system will need replacing.

Answer two questions from the following.

(a) What do you think are the likely benefits arising from the introduction of office automation?

(b) Describe how adaptability, flexibility and responsiveness would be incorporated in the design of the management information system for senior managers.

(c) What role will feedback play in the development of the MIS?

(d) Explain, with reference to the need to provide open access from various locations, the advantages and disadvantages of local area networks, wide area networks and a mini/ mainframe multi-user environment.

Chapter 5

4 GRAPHICS   *22 mins*

The senior management of a company have been advised that presentations made at conferences could be improved by using computer-based graphics. However, there is some confusion amongst the management between a computer aided design package and a graphical presentation package. Explain, in general terms, the differences between these two types of software and how a presentation package could improve the delivery of a subject area.

Chapter 6

5 THORNTHWAITE CRAG   *45 mins*

Thornthwaite Crag is a company which lets out holiday cottages and caravans on behalf of their owners. The company has used a proprietary word processing system for some years but has always had difficulty employing temporary staff who are familiar with the system. It has been decided to buy two IBM-compatible PCs running a popular WP package and, at the same time, to bring brochure production and advertising in-house.

Answer two questions from the following.

(a) Discuss the factors which would affect your choice of file organisation and access methods for a mailing list to be used for direct mail shots.

(b) What major factors should be considered when evaluating the suitability of particular word processing packages?

(c) Describe the features of a word processing package, including the use of a spell-checker, that can improve presentation.

(d) Describe the software which you would recommend to the company to enable it to prepare its own brochures and advertisements.

Chapter 7

6 ACE MACHINE TOOLS (12/94)   *45 mins*

Ace Machine Tools is a medium-sized engineering company. The sales director proposes to purchase a stand-alone computer to automate the sales department's quotation and customer order processes. You believe that there may be further advantages to be gained by linking the new software to the existing stock control and accounting software.

Answer two questions from the following.

(a) Outline the potential benefits and drawbacks to linking the systems.

(b) Identify the factors that must be considered when installing and using the new system.

(c) You have a choice of purchasing standard applications packages and adapting them for use, or commissioning a software company to write a dedicated suite of programs for your company. Compare and contrast the two approaches.

(d) It is clear that Ace Machine Tools has no company policy for evaluating the performance or development of its applications software. Sketch a system flowchart which will give a suitable approach to software maintenance and redevelopment.

Chapter 9

7 BARGAIN BASEMENT
45 mins

Bargain Basement is a company specialising in retail operations and has over one hundred shops. The shops are located in town centres throughout the country and are linked to the head office and warehouse by private data communications links. All data communications equipment used by the company adheres to protocols defined by the ISO Open Systems Interconnections (OSI) 7 layer model.

A customer at one of the shops uses a catalogue to select the item he or she wishes to purchase and gives the catalogue number to a checkout operator who enters it into the shop's computer system. The computer system checks to see if the item is in stock and, if it is, informs the shop staff that the item is required and that they must retrieve it from the stock room. The computer also checks the stock level of that item and will automatically re-order from the company headquarters when necessary. It also prepares a bill of sale for the customer and processes the transaction. A summary of all transactions and stock levels is transferred to the company mainframe computer on a daily basis for corporate management use.

Answer two questions from the following.

(a) Why is a database approach a suitable solution for this application?

(b) Explain the role of a database administrator within an organisation of this type.

(c) Sketch a flowchart to show the processes carried out by the shop's computer system when a customer purchases an item or items. Ignore any processes involved with communicating with a company mainframe computer.

(d) Briefly explain the purpose of the OSI 7 layer model and discuss the relative merits and disadvantages in using it to design a communications network.

Chapter 9

8 DATABASES

(a) Explain briefly what characteristics are fundamental to a database.

(b) What are the advantages of the database as a means of file organisation?

(c) Describe the software facilities which commonly form part of a DBMS.

(d) Discuss the implications of introducing a database system into your organisation.

(e) Within the context of the database explain the terms data integrity and data security.

Guidance note

This question tests your knowledge of databases and covers most of the important topics, albeit at a fairly basic level. In discussing software facilities, you should consider creation of the database, input of data, retrieval of data and production of reports. The implications of introducing a database system can be considered under the headings of hardware, software and personnel. You might also wish to demonstrate the benefits of such a course of action.

Chapter 11

9 ULLOCK PIKE   *45 mins*

Ullock Pike plc is a group of companies which provide office cleaning and related services, mainly to industrial sector customers, across the UK. The group has grown rapidly in recent years, largely through the acquisition of local concerns. As a result it has a wide range of systems, some of which are not computerised at all.

A major re-organisation has just taken place and the group is now divided into ten regions, each with a regional head office reporting to the centre. Because many customer operations are spread across several regions, it is now considered that the introduction of a single group computer system is a high priority. You have been invited to join a study group to consider the feasibility of such a project. You have learned, from speaking to a number of people, that a key demand, at all levels, is for the provision of management information.

Answer two questions from the following.

(a) Explain what is meant by the terms data processing system and management information system and clarify the difference between them.

(b) Describe the three levels of management which you might expect to encounter, referring to the characteristics of decision making at each level.

(c) Identify the information needs of each level of management and the potential contribution of computing at each level.

(d) Consider how important it is that management information is presented in the proper format.

Chapter 12

10 PROBLEMS

The chief executive of your organisation, which is planning a major systems analysis and design project, has read a recent article in a computer journal suggesting that many system development projects are not satisfactory upon completion. Symptoms which are highlighted in the article include:

(a) development costs which exceed the budget;

(b) completion in excess of planned timescales;

(c) systems which do not meet users' requirements;

(d) systems which are unreliable and difficult to maintain.

You are required to draft a report to the chief executive identifying the problems which may be faced by the systems development section of the organisation when carrying out its major analysis and design project.

Guidance notes

1   The emphasis should be on addressing the problems which give rise to the symptoms described.

2   One approach would be to work through the stages of systems development in turn, identifying potential problems which may arise at each stage.

Chapter 13

11 COSMETIK (6/95)   *45 mins*

Cosmetik is a new research company which is responsible for the testing of new cosmetics and their ingredients. It is funded by a large number of cosmetic manufacturers who wish to have an impartial body to approve their products. Forty scientists are employed by Cosmetik for this task. In addition, there are thirty laboratory and administrative staff.

It is proposed to develop a computer system to analyse the results of the research, maintain records of the research and the reactions of individuals to a given product or ingredient as well as providing standard word processing and spreadsheet facilities.

Answer two questions from the following.

(a) Explain how you would conduct an initial investigation in order to justify the new system.

(b) List the steps required to develop and maintain the new system following a successful feasibility study.

(c) Explain why the developers of the application software should adopt a modular design for the software.

(d) Suggest methods that could be used to evaluate the performance of the new system.

Chapter 14

12 STAFF TRAINING (IS, 6/90) *45 mins*

In response to a high staff turnover your senior DP manager has asked you to prepare a brief report outlining the actions required and potential benefits of a programme of staff training and development.

Chapter 15

13 GREEN GABLE *45 mins*

Green Gable Ltd is a private bus company operating scheduled services in a large city and its suburbs. The company has been successful in its first six months of operation, in spite of one or two timetabling errors which have been widely reported in the local press. A minicomputer is to be installed at head office to control all aspects of the operation, including fleet management, route optimisation, staff planning, maintenance scheduling, passenger analysis and accounting functions.

The company's information systems manager has no experience of systems installation and has asked you for advice on all aspects of computer security. In particular he has expressed concern 'off the record' that the company's major rival might seek to obtain confidential information from the new system.

Answer two questions from the following.

(a) State the guidelines which should normally be followed in determining what controls should be built into a system.

(b) Identify the different physical risks, both natural and man-made, to which a computer system is exposed, describing steps you would take to minimise these risks.

(c) Explain why standards are necessary to aid control in the information systems environment.

(d) Identify the main types of systems documentation which will be produced, explaining why systems documentation is often poorly maintained.

ANSWERS TO MULTIPLE
CHOICE QUESTIONS

Chapter 1

1   C   Word for Windows is wordprocessing software. The printer, the CPU (Central Processing Device) and the keyboard are all hardware.

2   B   The keyboard is an input device. The screen and the printer are output devices, while the CPU performs the processing function.

3   D   DOS stands for the Direct Operating System. A modem connects your computer to the telephone line, the mouse facilitates input into your computer, a scanner allows you to copy text or pictures into your computer. All are attached to your computer and are peripherals to your computer.

4   B   You are likely to play games on your PC. PCs penetrated the home market on the back of games and educational software. Playing games on a mainframe or supercomputer would be a waste of an expensive asset, and an electronic organiser would not necessarily have the memory capacity to allow for an interesting game.

5   D   A printer need not be connected to the PC - it would still work, displaying its output on the screen. Input devices, such as a keyboard, are necessary, as is the screen. The CPU enables the PC to process the input information.

6   A   The CPU is divided into 3 areas, the control unit which receives program instructions, the ALU (arithmetic and logic unit) which performs the calculations allowing the instructions to be carried out, and the memory which holds the instructions in memory while the computer is operating.

7   C   16 KB is $16 \times 1,024 \times 1,024$. Answer A (1,024) represents 1 Kilobyte, Answer B (8,388,608) is $8 \times 1,024 \times 1,024$ or 8 KB. Answer D (17,179,869,184) is $16 \times 1,024 \times 1,024 \times 1,024$ or 16 Gb.

Chapter 2

8   D   RAID, used by mainframes, has several disk units each with its own read/write head. A CD-ROM offers 660 Mb of storage. A typical PC hard disk offers 1.2 Gb of memory, while a floppy disk provides 1.44 Mb.

9   C   It is not recommended to use a floppy disk as a coaster for a coffee mug – the disk and the data stored on it are likely to be damaged. A floppy, however, is a useful device for storing information, for backing up important files stored on a hard disk, and for transporting files from one PC to another.

10   C   It would waste expensive storage space to back up (or keep duplicates of) multiple copies of a standard letter, although you might make a backup copy of the original standard letter. Client databases should always be backed up, as they contain important information, as should the company report and memos, letters etc pertaining to a business.

11   A   The mouse is an input device and displays data. Data can be stored on CD-ROM disks, on magnetic tapes, and on WORM (write once read many) disks.

12   **B**   A phone number is data, which would be entered in the field area on a record – in a field possibly called PhoneNo. Title, Lastname and Postcode are all suitable field names.

13   **B**   Price should be typed as a numeric field, which would allow calculations to be performed, such as adding and multiplying. Date of birth should be typed as a date field. Phone No and Catalogue Nos will not be used for calculations, so should be typed as alphanumeric fields.

14   **A**   Sort means re-arrange. Data can be accessed serially (in the order in which it happens to be), sequentially (in the order of a key field – for example, Surname) or randomly (through an index or a database query).

15   **C**   Human-sensible means directly accessible to human beings. COM requires special equipment (eg a microfilm or microfiche reader) for humans to use it. Answer A is therefore not true. Impact printers (answer B) hit inked ribbons against paper. An inkjet printer fires jets of ink onto paper using an electrostatic field. A pixel, abbreviated from picture element, has nothing to do with printers at all, being the smallest part of a picture held in digital form on computer. Daisy wheel printers have all the characters held like spokes in a wheel, which rotates until the desired character is found.

16   **C**   Tape writers (on tape decks) write to tape; tape spoolers are buffers and tape copiers copy tapes.

17   **D**   In a magnetic disk system, records can be accessed directly. In a tape system the tape has to be run from the beginning until the required record is reached. An updated tape file is always written to a different tape than the file which preceded it. Direct access storage media allow a single input transaction to update a number of files in one processing operation. Whether data becomes corrupt does not depend on the qualities of any particular storage medium, but rather the security measures used to guard it.

Chapter 3

18   **B**   The RETURN key, which moves the typing line down, is also present on the typewriting keyboard. It performs the same function on the computer keyboard. In addition, it often signals 'confirm' or 'execute' for computer instructions.

19   **C**   A mouse will not key in text, but it will increase flexibility in drawing, choosing menu items and moving around the screen.

20   **A**   A dot matrix printer has a print-head with a matrix of pins which are presented in different combinations against a print ribbon. It is therefore an impact printer (answer C) and as it prints one character at a time it is a character printer (answer D). As the print head can be pressed in any number of combinations, a dot matrix printer can print graphics (answer B). However, as there is a space between each dot, the output is often not considered good enough for correspondence. Dot matrix printers can print near letter quality (NLQ), however.

21   **D**   DOS is an unfriendly language, involving keyboard input which is error prone. GUI (graphical user interface) is user-friendly allowing dialogue using images rather than typed text. WIMP (windows icons menu pointer) is a GUI. Icons are images used to represent an abstract idea or process.

22 C WYSISYG (what you see is what you get) describes the fact that what you see on the screen is an accurate representation of what will be printed. OCR (optical character recognition), OMR (mark sensing and optical mark reading) and MICR (magnetic ink character recognition) are all computer readable methods of conveying data.

23 A A line printer prints out one line at a time. A thermal printer is a line printer. Thermally sensitive paper is heated by a hot printhead. Impact printers (answer C) require metal to hit ribbon. An electrosensitive printer (answer D) uses special aluminium-coated paper onto which characters are burned by sparks of electricity.

24 C Laser printers print on to individual sheets of paper, much like photocopiers, and do not use continuous stationery.

Chapter 4

25 A To access data stored by another system (answer D) you would use what is called a *gateway*.

26 C Protocol is not so much concerned with the transfer of data between different systems, as ensuring the integrity of data transfer itself. Answer C is the definition of protocol provided by the British Computer Society.

27 B Answer D describes a computer bureau. Answer A describes what is commonly termed a network. Multi-user systems link the CPU to several terminals.

28 B The work of an emulator (answer A) is described in the comments on the next question. Many microcomputers use a different character code to many mainframes, so these have to be converted. An ethernet cable (answer C) links several computers in a network together. A simulator enables the imitation of modelling of the behaviour of an existing or proposed system by another system; see the comments on question 29 below.

29 A Answer B describes simulation. Answers C and D both occur, but they are not emulation. Emulation is used when, for example, a microcomputer has to imitate the terminal of a mainframe in certain types of network.

30 A A LAN is linked by direct cables not by the telecommunications network. A WAN is linked by the telecommunications network.

31 D A multi-user system (answer C) refers to a system where a processor serves several users.

Chapter 5

32 A Some software (eg the operating system) can be hardwired into a computer's ROM. Answer B is incorrect, as computer circuits can only be either ON or OFF. Answer C refers to programming tools. Applications software refers to software for which a user has a particular purpose, and utility software is provided to perform routine processing requirements.

33   A   Utility software is applications software (eg a standard sort program, a standard print program, and other standard routines that are used regularly in different computer systems). Firmware is a generic term for software that is hardwired into ROM. An interpreter program is a program that translates computer languages into machine code.

34   B   The operating system is a program or set of programs controlling the operation of the computer. Its tasks include 'booting up' the computer when it is switched on, and responding to commands from users to carry out such tasks as deleting files or formatting floppy disks. Translating programs is not one of its jobs.

35   B   Answer B refers to the bootstrap program which is part of the operating system. Answer C is wrong: both UNIX and MS-DOS for example are used on machines made by different manufacturers. Answer A is wrong, as some microcomputers can use more than one operating system (though not at the same time!) The user must select the operating system that he/she wishes to use when the computer is switched on.

36   A   Software is written in a programming language, but the programming language itself is not software.

37   D   High-level languages have to be converted into machine code, and on the surface appear completely different from machine code or assembly language. The logic of the program (ie what it sets out to achieve) is described in a high-level language, but how it is displayed in binary form (which indicates how the computer will implement it) will be quite different. *Low-level languages* are more efficient than high-level languages in that they are tailored to individual machines whereas high-level languages are not. Low-level languages can therefore make better use of a computer's particular processing capabilities. They should be *quicker* in execution than programs written in a high-level language for the same data processing application (and so answers A and C are incorrect). However, as high-level languages are more brief, and the logic of the program more clearly displayed than in a low-level language, high-level languages are easier to test and correct (answer B).

38   D   Syntax are rules for forming statements correctly, but they do not refer to the logical content of the statements. A compiler program checks that the program instructions in the high level language are correctly constructed and so correct for syntax, but it does not check that statements are logically accurate in what they say. A compiler only checks for errors of syntax and reports them: it cannot *correct* them.

Chapter 6

39   D   Desktop publishing is a widely used but slightly vague phrase. If you are creating artwork for a document, you need to be able to cut and paste text with more freedom than is offered by most word processing systems. Desktop publishing software would incorporate a graphics facility. A daisywheel printer, however, would not be sufficient for your needs, and so you would need a laser printer.

40 **B** It is the combination of text with graphics, both of which can be easily manipulated to design or construct each page of text, that is the distinctive feature of desktop publishing (answer B). A phototypesetter is a specialised machine used for high quality typesetting. Modern phototypesetters can accept as input the output from a WP system.

41 **C** Access is a database program produced by Microsoft.

42 **C** There is no point in devising a spreadsheet if you are not prepared to let it work for you, so answers A and B, although they give correct answers, are not appropriate. If you are updating the model every month, for example by adding July and deleting April, you will not wish to do the addition manually (answer A) or to have to adjust the total columns (answer B). Answer D is wrong: cell references given are incomplete in that they refer only to columns and not to rows. The brackets describe the logic of the formula. Answer C is correct for Excel, as it describes the sum of the data in the range of cells from C4 to E4, which is what you wish to show in your 'Total 3 months' column – the updating calculation for cell 34 will be performed automatically.

43 **C** Answer B adds across the monthly net profit figures. Answer A subtracts the costs listed from fee income in the year-to-date column. Answer D is effectively the same calculation as answer A. Answer C is wrong: Excel requires that the opening cell reference in a formula, in this case B4, must have an indication (an '=' sign) to show that it is a formula. Without such a sign, B4 would be treated as an item of text.

44 **A** Both formulae in answer A are correct. Both formulae in answer B are incorrect. Formula (1) in answer B, =C4–D4/D4 can be translated as £21,500 – £22,000/£22,000 which equals £21,500 – 1. Operations in brackets are performed first, so that, in answer A the result of £21,500 – £22,000 is divided by £22,000. As for formula 2, answer B will generate an *error* message as no priority has been given to one of the calculations: either cell C19 divided by cell C4 is first performed, or cell C4 divided by 30 days.

45 **C** Note that if you have already saved the file before, you will be asked through screen messages b the program whether you wish to cancel the command, or replace the previous version of the file with the file you are saving.

Chapter 7

46 **C** Questionnaires are not suitable for large amounts of data, as the complexity of the data required may preclude the asking of appropriate questions. For small numbers of people, a more reliable method of fact-finding would be interviews, which ought to be manageable when the number of interviews is small.

47 **B** Equipment is normally categorised as a 'fixed asset'. Hardware maintenance and staff training are likely to be regular costs. The cost of recruiting staff is a 'one-off' non-capital cost.

48   D   An essential document will be one for making orders for stock items from the factory (materials requisition notes). Suppliers' invoices and confirmations will be a part of the purchasing system and are not central to a stock control system. A list of reorder quantities is not essential: the reorder quantity for each stock item will be held on file in the computer system.

49   C   The customer file will be accessed to record the sale, the stock file to requisition the goods that the customer wishes to buy, the orders file to record the order (and generate an invoice) and the sales commission file, assuming that the salesman will earn a commission on the sale, will be updated too.

50   A   The open item method identifies specified invoices.

51   D   Answers A and C are the same and refer to a situation where some of the data is run in *parallel* on the old and new systems but not all of it.

52   B   When data is run on both old and new systems this is an example of parallel running.

Chapter 8

53   C   The term feedback is widely used in everyday speech (as in answer B). This question was testing your understanding of it in systems terminology. Additionally, answers A and D were descriptions of open loop systems where control is exercised irrespective of the system's output.

54   A   Note that an open loop system cannot feature feedback. Feedback is control information generated by the system itself. In an open loop system, control action is not automatic, and is exercised from outside the system.

55   B   Feedback expressions are used in every day speech. Positive feedback, in system terminology, has the specific meaning given in answer B. For example, if you are driving along an empty motorway breaking the speed limit, and your passenger encourages you to go even faster, you are being given positive feedback.

56   A   Answers B and D are types of management information system. A decision support system (answer B) assists decision making by allowing the manager to specify the information he or she needs, from the variegated data to which the system has access. An expert system contains a database of specialist knowledge. For example, medical expert systems can be used to assist doctors make diagnoses. A database management system (answer C) is a specific type of system related to the structure and organisation of a database.

57   A   Information can be classified as being either planning information, control information, or operating information. Answer B is planning information, as it will be used to inform the organisation's long term business strategy. Answers C and D are operating information, used to conduct day to day operations. Control information (answer A) is so called as it is required for the monitoring of organisational activities against plans and targets, so that corrective action can be taken.

58　　A　　In this example, the information was not *clear* (answer D). The message was not timely because it arrived just two days before you were due to leave and doesn't really give you enough time to book a ticket. The information which included the travel agent's advice was not accurate. The information was relevant (answer A) and that is the only good thing that can be said about it.

59　　B　　Exception reporting is the analysis of those items where performance differs significantly from standard or budget.

Chapter 9

60　　B　　The term database is rather vague, but it is a general principle that databases seek to minimise, if not eradicate, the duplication of data, and so answer B is not a description of a database.

61　　A　　Data in the database can be presented in a number of different ways depending on the application. Answer D describes the *opposite* of what a database should provide.

62　　C　　A key field needs to be a unique identifier.

63　　B　　The database management system determines how a file is stored physically. A single item of data can belong to two or more logical records, but be held physically in just one place on the file (answer B).

64　　D　　With a ring structure (answer C) pointers exist both ways so that an item of data can refer to other data further 'up' the structure as well as further down. A ring structure is like a chain structure.

65　　C　　A network structure links many data items together, and as such is not a rigid hierarchy (answer A), or a one-to-many arrangement (answer B) in that an item of data of one type can be linked to several of a different types. A relational database works in quite a different way, by separating the data structure from the data items, so that a record is composed of a number of fields, and can be accessed through any of its fields. In hierarchical or network structures an enquiry has to be directed through other data. This is not the case with relational databases.

66　　B　　A database administrator is a person with responsibility for the database.

Chapter 10

67　　C　　E-mail is virtually instantaneous.

68　　B　　Ceefax is a teletext system.

69　　C　　In document image processing a document is scanned into a computer. PABX is a telephone system and EDI stands for electronic data interchange.

70　　B　　Although much data can be conveyed electronically, there will always be the need for personal communications.

71	D	Timesharing involves a number of different users sharing the central processing unit, which allocates its time rapidly between different jobs, so that it appears that each job is performed at the same time. It is controlled by special software (a timesharing supervisor).
72	D	Polling occurs where it is not feasible for a terminal, in a system with many terminals, to transmit data at any particular time. Several terminals may use the same piece of transmission equipment. Moreover, the central computer may not be able to deal with so many instructions at one time.
73	C	Modems connect computers (1 and 5) to the phone line (3).

Chapter 11

74	D	Detailed analysis takes place at a later stage.
75	D	Discounted cash flow using either NPV or IRR is a technique which takes into account the time value of money.
76	C	As above, this level of detail would be examined at a later stage.
77	D	As above.
78	A	Custom-built software would fit the user's exact requirements.
79	B	Better decision making is a benefit, but is difficult to quantify.
80	C	A methodology used might be SSADM.

Chapter 12

81	A	
82	A	
83	B	
84	B	Answer A refers to the document number, which is to do with the individual document, rather than the document type. The individual document you have chosen is less important than the type of document it is.
85	D	A document description form will be used to design what a form should contain, but not how the data on the form will be laid out on the page.
86	C	Item 6 is concerned with the *content* of a message, not the way that it will be *formatted* (set out) on the VDU screen.
87	D	This question tested your knowledge of the basic ways of human interaction with the computer via a VDU screen. A command system allows the operator to type instructions in directly. The operator does not have to pull instructions from a menu, or follow a rigid format.

Chapter 13

88	B	The word reflects the 'standing' nature of the data.
89	A	
90	D	
91	D	
92	A	
93	C	
94	B	

Chapter 14

95	C	The effectiveness of such a training method would be difficult to monitor. CBT stands for computer based training.
96	D	
97	A	
98	B	Staff may fear that they will be reduced to operators tied to the machine.
99	B	
100	C	Line managers have considerable autonomy with responsibility for managing their own staff.
101	D	An analysis of training needs would be the first stage in an HRM-based training strategy.

Chapter 15

102	B	The generation cycle technique of master file reconstruction is also known as the *grandfather-father-son technique*. A copy of the master file (the 'father') which preceded the current version (the 'son') is kept. If the current version becomes corrupted, then it can be re-created by inputting the transactions data to the old master file again. In addition the 'grandfather' tape is kept, with the transaction files that will allow the 'father' to be recreated if necessary.
103	C	You could in theory use the grandfather-father-son technique for any *batch* processing applications including those held on disk files, but it is likely to be very expensive. In a real time system, where files are being updated all the time, it is not a viable option. You might dump files to tape, say, at the end of every day. There should also be a means of keeping a record of daily transactions.

104   C   Encryption involves the replacement of the correct text by cipher. The transformation from a cipher text to the original is called decryption. An authentication code is a coded check, derived from an algorithm, which can reveal whether a message has been tampered with in some way.

105   C   A check can be made to ensure that the product code in a record is compatible with the warehouse code.

106   A   Check digit checks should pick up any transposition errors or other transcription errors in a stock code.

107   C   At specified intervals during the running of an application program, a checkpoint program 'lumps' the entire contents of main storage to backing store. Should processing be interrupted for whatever reason, it can be recommenced from the point where the checkpoint program was last executed. The result of processing to that point will have been saved.

108   D

Chapter 16

109   C

110   C   If payroll details are used for any purpose other than payment of wages or pensions and keeping simple books of account, then no exemption is available under the Act.

111   D

112   C   Data needs to be misleading as to fact rather than opinion for a data subject to sue.

113   B

114   C

115   A

ANSWERS TO
EXAM STYLE QUESTIONS

Chapter 1

1 FEASIBILITY STUDY

The person chairing the feasibility study group should, prior to the commencement of the study, be satisfied that the terms of reference have been properly established by the board of directors or the steering committee (if there is one). Particular attention should also be paid to the membership of the feasibility study team. At least one person must have a detailed knowledge of computers and systems design (in a small concern it is usually necessary to bring in a systems analyst from outside). In this instance the computer manager should be involved. At least one person should have a detailed knowledge of the organisation and in particular of the workings and staff of the departments affected. As financial controller, the person chairing this group would be suitable, but, in addition, another user department representative should form part of the study team. All members must be objectively critical and have some training or experience in data processing techniques and systems design.

The current feasibility study is required to consider expanding or replacing the existing computer system. It will, therefore, concentrate on the use and limitations of the existing system before putting forward the alternative possibilities. The aim of any feasibility study is to assess the data processing requirements of the organisation, to investigate and recommend possible solutions and to provide management with information on which a decision can be based. This information should include the advantages and disadvantages of each suggestion from the technical, economic, organisational and social points of view. A plan should be made for the development, implementation and control of the recommended solution.

In this particular study, the factors which must be considered include:

(a) economic advantages over the present system;

(b) greater speed in information processing;

(c) improvement in reliability of equipment;

(d) capability of further expansion and undertaking of tasks previously not contemplated;

(e) time period for the study.

In the first phase of the work, the team has to determine, for example, input data details and methods, establish growth areas etc. This may be achieved by the use of questionnaires, interviews and study of existing procedure manuals, and the results of the investigation must be properly recorded (eg by narrative, flowcharts, decision tables etc).

Up to this stage the feasibility study has comprised an examination of the existing system and of management's requirements, in accordance with the terms of reference set by the steering group. This should lead to a strict definition of current inputs, outputs, files and procedures, and an identification of existing inefficiencies, eg bottlenecks, redundant procedures. Before commencing the second phase of the feasibility study the strengths and weaknesses of the existing system may be evaluated and reported to the steering committee. If it is apparent that a replacement computer is unnecessary and a strengthening of existing procedures is all that is required, the terms of reference may have to be amended.

The next stage is to work out the requirements of the new system, taking into account legal, auditing and accounting requirements. A new cost/benefit analysis study of the proposed system (compared to the old one) should be produced as well as an analysis of the alternatives available. All the areas required to be reported on would have to be properly investigated. These would include:

(a) general introduction including summary of proposals and terms of reference;

(b) description of the existing system (and its faults);

(c)   system requirements;

(d)   details of the proposed system;

(e)   costs and benefits including comparison with existing systems;

(f)   development and implementation plans; time scale and effort required; and

(g)   a clear recommendation as to the preferred option.

Chapter 2

2   WHIN RIGG

Tutorial note

It is important that you take note of any requests by the examiner for answers to be in a particular format, in this case a table.

(a)   Computer storage is divided into main storage and backing storage. The central processing unit (CPU) of a computer has a limited amount of internal (main) storage, more often referred to as memory. Most computer applications require more data and processing capacity than can be provided by the memory. External (backing) storage holds the data, in machine form, which is not required by the CPU. This division also helps to maximise the efficiency of the system and to ensure adequate security of data.

The main storage of a computer (also called memory or immediate access storage) holds programs, some input/output data and has a work area to process data. Data is held in main storage in two forms; read only memory (ROM) is normally used for start-up programs and other fixed data, and random access memory (RAM) (more important from the point of view of the user) has a read/write capability and is essential for effective main memory. The primary feature of main storage is fast processing speed. The larger the main storage, the more expensive the configuration, so the limited size of main storage results in the need for external storage, held on hard disk or perhaps peripheral devices outside the CPU.

Backing storage devices hold large quantities of data in machine form until required by the CPU for some form of processing. The data is accessed and transferred to the main storage for processing and then transferred back to the backing store when the operation is complete. Hard disks, although sometimes located in the same 'box' as the CPU, are a form of backing storage.

Another application for backing storage is in the maintenance of duplicate records in case of data loss or corruption on the main system; this is an important feature of most computer systems. The ability to recreate data following system failure or other disasterS should always be given a high priority in any computer system.

Main storage is physically made up of electronic integrated circuits or silicon chips, which are cheap to produce, small in size and can hold large amounts of data. Backing storage devices are either in disk or tape form and use magnetic or optical technology

The division between backing store and main store can be eliminated by the use of virtual storage, which allows programmers to use backing storage as though it were main memory. This effectively eliminates the size limitation of internal memory but is only available for larger systems, and requires a sophisticated operating system.

It appears that Whin Rigg needs additional backing storage. Once hard disks are substantially full, data and files stored on them become fragmented and access times become slower. Defragmentation is possible, by which related clusters of data are grouped together, but unless data can be deleted the company needs either larger disks or additional storage media.

(b)

Storage type	Primary	Secondary	Secondary	Secondary
Medium	Internal circuitry	Magnetic disk	Magnetic tape	Optical disk
Function	Stores data within the CPU while the computer is operating	Provides capacity not available in main memory	Mainly used for backup and archiving	Reference information mainly read-only at present
Attributes	Silicon chip	Circular disks Concentric tracks	Plastic tape Parallel tracks	Circular disk Concentric tracks
Capacity	Limited, ranging from 512 kb – 64 Mb on micros up to 20 Mb+ on mainframes	40 Mb – 1 Gb (hard disk) 360 kb–1.44 Mb (floppy)	20 Mb	1,000 Mb (1 gigabyte)
Speed of operation	Immediate (less than one millionth of a second)	Fast	Slow	Fast
Cost	Included in cost of computer	Medium	Low	High
Access	Random access	Direct or sequential	Sequential or serial	Direct or sequential
Read method	Electronic	Disk rotated past fixed head	Tape played through fixed head	Disk rotated past fixed laser
Risks	Volatile. Very reliable	Magnetic fields	Physical damage	Developing technology, so risk of obsolescence

(c)   File conversion is the process by which master file and reference file records in Whin Rigg's old system are converted on to a file suitable for the new system, as the new system cannot become operational until master files are set up. It is important to ensure that master file data to be converted is *complete* and *accurate*, and that the data can be loaded on to the new system. Every record relevant to a file should be transferred to the new system, and so the file conversion must be planned with sufficient detail to ensure the accuracy and completeness of the process.

Stages

The steps governing file conversion can be summarised as follows.

(i)   Ensuring the original record files are complete and up to date.

(ii)   Recording the old data file on specially designed input documents.

(iii) Transcription of input documents and verification of what has been transcribed.

(iv)   Validation of data, performed by the computer.

(v)   Correction of any errors.

(vi)   Reconciliation of old master files to new, by means of control details, listing of all records for one-to-one checking and so forth.

Where the existing files are already held on a magnetic medium, it may be possible to write a conversion program to transfer the records into a form suitable for use in the new system and so avoid the transcription stage, which is itself an obvious source of potential errors.

Controls

The types of controls over file conversion will include the following.

(i) Full planning, with documentation relating to staff employed, records to be converted and a timetable for conversion and review procedure.

(ii) File design checks to see that file designs specified in the systems specification have in fact been followed.

(iii) Checks to ensure all data transferred accurately.

(iv) Manual check of new master files to old (each record).

(v) Reconciliation of accounting records, for example, total of balances.

(vi) Segregation of duties between conversion staff.

(vii) Procedures to ensure errors are investigated.

(viii) Procedures to ensure users know how to use the new system (training, courses, documentation).

(ix) Particular attention should be paid to the coding system. Code numbers must be unique and should bear a clear relationship, or be identical to, those used on the previous system.

(x) No transactions should be posted during the changeover. Files can be created over a weekend or during a bank (public) holiday.

(d) Techniques of collecting relevant data about the current and proposed systems include the following.

(i) *Interviews*

A percentage of existing personnel involved with the system are asked for their understanding of how the system works, why events happen as they do, what forms are used and what improvements could or should be made to the system. With interviews bias is a major factor, as is the interaction between the interviewer and interviewee. If the personal bias of either the interviewer or the interviewee is strong, then the questions or the answers could be slanted to distort the actual picture. If there is any degree of interaction between the two people, in the form of either attraction or antipathy, then this might also reflect itself in the interview results. Lastly, the act of writing down or taping someone's responses can be inhibiting.

(ii) *Questionnaires*

All existing users of the system are asked for their views and the facts regarding the various attributes of the system. The accuracy of the response from those who reply is often high. However questionnaires can tend to be completed at a higher level or quality or with more thought or care by people with a specific reason for completing the form than by those who are neutral. Questionnaires are an inexpensive way of gathering data, but the lack of interaction is a disadvantage.

(iii) *Observation*

This is performed by watching what physically happens to a document or file, etc. The results can be more accurate than with other methods, but as with interviews, the fact of observing can change behaviour, and the cost of maintaining someone in a fixed position to perform such an observation can be high.

(iv) *Document investigation*

This involves physically tracing the passage of a document from one end of the organisation to the other. This method has limited use since it is very time consuming, especially when dealing with documents which have multiple paths that they can follow through an organisation depending on the specific contents of the document.

Chapter 3

3 CLAIFE HEIGHTS

(a) The introduction of office automation will yield several benefits.

(i) Routine data can be handled more quickly, economically and with greater accuracy.

(ii) Data will be more easily accessible, particularly on corporate databases or telecommunications systems.

(iii) Office productivity will typically increase; this is partially due to the automation of systems and partially due to improved paperwork and data handling procedures. Productivity in automated systems is often gained simply by imposing a discipline upon previously uncoordinated activities.

(iv) The use of office automation systems often results in improved customer service since enquiries may be dealt with far more quickly than manual systems allowed.

(v) Office automation can also raise employee morale. Since these systems are more complex and challenging they may provide job-enrichment to some clerical employees.

In addition to these benefits a number of additional ones are available due to improved managerial effectiveness.

(i) Databases and decision support systems can allow users more readily to obtain and use the data they require.

(ii) Spreadsheets and sophisticated modelling packages may be used to analyse data so that more complete or better decisions are made.

(iii) Many recurring reports and analyses may be quickly and easily performed so that management time is more efficiently used.

(iv) Management reports or presentations can be made more effective through access to graphics or desk-top publishing packages and high quality reproduction or typesetting systems.

Office automation can then offer significant benefits to both clerical and managerial staff in the organisation's operations.

(b) A management information system (MIS) is a system which converts data collected from internal and external sources into information for use in an organisation. It communicates that information in an appropriate form to the management of the organisation to enable them to make decisions in planning and controlling the operations of the business. A good MIS provides good information to management at all levels appropriate to their needs.

A typical MIS draws on the output from data processing and operational systems. It uses this to generate information which is regular and formal in nature, for example analyses of budget against actual results and margins by product or region. It may be less efficient at presenting information which is informal or unstructured.

The information required by senior management, particularly for strategic purposes, is, however, often informal, qualitative and *ad hoc* in nature. This means that an MIS must be capable of doing more than providing summary information from the results of transactions processing if it is to meet the needs of senior management. It must therefore be adaptable, flexible and responsive.

An MIS for senior management may therefore need to comprise certain manual elements, particularly in relation to external information needs. There are public databases which subscribers access as required, but these can become expensive if used regularly. Processes may be adopted for subscription to a press-cuttings service, review of trade journals and receipt of official bulletins and releases from relevant government departments. An *adaptable*

MIS will be able to incorporate this kind of information flow and communicate relevant elements of it to management.

Flexibility is also a key characteristic. Because senior management need to set objectives, they are very much concerned with the future. Systems design cannot incorporate every possible future permutation, which means that management will often make demands of a system for information which it does not currently produce. For example, local authority boundaries may change or there might be changes to local government taxation structures. This may entail a redrawing of the organisation's regions or changes to processing operations and consequently a requirement for a restructuring of the reporting process. A flexible MIS will be able to accommodate this. Programmers will be required to make adjustments to existing software, which may be bespoke or off-the-shelf.

An MIS for senior management must be *responsive*. Executives may require information during the course of a meeting, a telephone call or a negotiation. They must be able to retrieve this information without having to spend time defining report formats and colours etc. There must be some facility to manipulate data (eg comparisons with prior year, with current year budget or with latest forecast). These criteria will be satisfied by an efficient database. Report formats showing information in a form useful for senior management can be pre-set so that they do not have to be re-specified each time the database is accessed.

(c) Feedback is the process of incorporating into a system changes which are shown to be necessary by the previous results of, or outputs from, the system. The changes usually follow from any differences measured between the desired results and those actually received.

The life cycle of a system encompasses all the stages from conception to that point where the system ceases. During this cycle there are two levels of feedback which are possible. The first is at the design or structural level of the system while the second is at the detailed operational or control level.

(i) *Feedback at the design or structural level of the system.* This occurs when differences measured in the output indicate that there are errors in the design or implementation of the system. Details of the errors are passed to the personnel responsible for the design of the system, and this should result in a re-design or re-working of the affected parts of the system. This re-design should take place quickly as *ad hoc* modifications if the errors are serious. However, it will be left to be incorporated in the next full version of the system if they are less serious or if the economics of the changes indicate that the benefits from implementing the change are outweighed by the costs of doing so.

(ii) *Feedback at the detailed operational or control level.* This occurs when differences measured in the output indicate that there is poor performance or problems with the operation or control of the system. Details of the errors are passed to the personnel responsible for the operation of the system, and this should result in changes to, or a re-design of, the method of operating the system or of the controls used in the system. The nature of the level at which the feedback is taking place in this instance means that the changes should be implemented quickly.

A danger with feedback is that of the effect of timing problems. If there is a delay in getting information about poor results to the controller of the system, then it can happen that the system controller will compensate for the poor result but receive further reports of poor output (and assume that these indicate more changes are needed) before the effects of the change generate outputs. The controller will then make more changes which are not necessary, and have to adjust again when the results of those changes reach the monitoring point in the system.

A management control system should be in a semi-permanent state of control feedback. As changes are perceived to be necessary they should be implemented. The amended system will then produce different results, and any changes which are then necessary will again be fed back into the design or operation. This ongoing process of feedback is vital to the capacity of the system to cope with long term changes in requirements and to the ability of the system to adjust to errors or problems in its design and to changing needs.

(d) Three of the important aspects of an MIS are the physical hardware, the software and the personnel who manage the system. Each of these is affected by the type of system on which the MIS runs. Some of the advantages and disadvantages of using different networking solutions are as follows.

Local area network (LAN)

A local area network consists of a number of PCs and printers, usually with a dedicated computer performing as a 'file server' attached to the network. Each PC has access to the facilities of the network, which may include fast printers, communications and the hard disk in the file server. A local area network generally operates on one site only.

(i) *Advantages*

   (1) Lack of dependency on hardware. Individual components of the system can fail without, in general, affecting the ability of the system as a whole to operate.

   (2) Wide availability of equipment. Standard hardware is used, so it tends to be widely and freely available.

   (3) Lower cost of individual pieces of equipment. Because of the wide availability of the hardware involved particular parts of the system can be purchased or replaced at competitive rates.

   (4) Avoids potentially high communications costs. As the processing is contained within a relatively small area there are no telecomms line costs.

   (5) The use of multiple PCs leads to a high individual processing capability.

   (6) LAN network managers do not require as high a level of expertise as other network managers.

   (7) It is reasonably simple to incorporate graphical user interfaces (GUIs) such as Windows into the system. These GUIs tend to increase productivity through their ease of use, lower training requirements and clear presentation of data.

   (8) Lower software costs. Because of the number of systems sold, the costs of software can be significantly lower.

(ii) *Disadvantages*

   (1) The MIS software available on LANs does not usually offer very sophisticated security, and so breaches can be easier than with mini/mainframe solutions.

   (2) Running LANs can leave less memory available in each PC for user programs. This can cause difficulty in running some software such as spreadsheets.

   (3) Viruses pose a major threat.

   (4) The probability of individuals working with outdated data (eg when extracting it for use in spreadsheets, Executive Information Systems etc) is reasonably high.

   (5) The time needed to re-generate management reports, if these are not an integral part of the software (perhaps using other programs such as spreadsheets), can be relatively high.

(6) It may be difficult to allocate responsibility for security.

(7) Short distance of operation.

Wide area network (WAN)

A wide area network consists of computer systems at a number of locations (which themselves might contain LANs) geographically distant from each other, which are connected by dedicated phone connections, dial-up phone facilities or packet switch systems. Each location can have hardware ranging from the simplest level (a terminal) to a full multi-user system in its own right.

(i)   *Advantages*

    (1) If data has to be moved between sites, a WAN avoids the necessity for physical transportation of media by hard copy.

    (2) WANs can avoid duplication of data storage, with attendant difficulty of keeping all sets of data current.

    (3) Special processing requirements can be handled by purchasing the resources at just one site.

(ii)   *Disadvantages*

    (1) The potential for data theft via unauthorised access or wire tapping is high.

    (2) Communications charges will be high.

    (3) It is difficult to maintain different sites' software and data at the same level.

    (4) In batch processing, control becomes a major factor.

    (5) Network management personnel can be expensive.

    (6) Viruses can pose a threat.

    (7) If a site handling special processing fails, the whole network might be impacted.

    (8) Graphics require large amounts of data. If images are to be moved across the network the impact on performance and costs would be high.

Mini/mainframe multi-user solutions

A mini computer or mainframe usually consists of a larger and more powerful computer with a number of relatively less powerful terminals attached to it. Programs run in the central computer, and all data is held on the central system.

(i)   *Advantages*

    (1) The single set of hardware reduces some of the complexity of writing programs for updating and keeping data current.

    (2) The MIS function is generally under the management of a single person or department and is therefore better controlled from batch and audit points of view.

    (3) Viruses are generally not a potential hazard.

(ii)   *Disadvantages*

    (1) High costs of hardware. Larger centralised systems tend to be more expensive to buy and to run.

    (2) An organisation may be tied to specific proprietary hardware and software. Systems are often available on a limited range of equipment and are specific to particular computers or operating systems.

    (3) Non-portability of data and software. With proprietary systems, it is usually difficult and expensive to move either the data or the software to different systems.

(4) Need for specialist staff. Mini and mainframe computers tend to require more expensive specialist staff.

(5) Higher costs of software modifications. The cost of modifying software is usually related to the size and cost of the computer on which the software runs.

(6) Support for GUIs is currently far lower than on LANs and WANs. If GUIs are supported they often demand such resources from the central computer that they become impracticable to use.

There is no single answer to every organisation's needs. All three types of system (LAN, WAN and centralised) will provide the essentials of an MIS. All three will provide the processing and reporting which would be needed. Although there is a move towards 'downsizing' (replacing larger systems with networked PCs) all three types of system still have their place in different situations. The impact of choosing one solution over another will in general lie in the personnel/hardware/control areas rather than in what the systems can do.

Chapter 5

4   GRAPHICS

Computer aided design

Computer aided design (CAD) is the use of a computer, often a dedicated workstation, to produce drawings for, and to calculate the characteristics of, components and systems in a wide range of activities from planning motorways to designing the layout of circuit boards. CAD is used especially in architecture and in various types of engineering including electronic, mechanical and aeronautical. The inputs to a CAD consist of the technical expertise of the user and vast amounts of data stored in libraries which contain standards for components, circuits, regulations etc, for example standard pipe lengths, gauges and connectors. CAD requires an extremely high resolution monitor and produces output in the form of printouts of specifications and other information, for example stencils/artwork for printed circuit boards.

Graphical presentation package

Another use of computers is the production of information in the form of pictures, diagrams or graphs. Computer graphics is the representation of information by a computer in graphical form, the display being either as charts or diagrams in hard copy or as animation on a VDU.

Graphics software packages will incorporate the facility for displaying charts or diagrams on a VDU screen, and pictures can also be animated. Home computer games are a good example of the use of animated graphics. A graphics software package will be of limited value if the images it produces can only be displayed on a VDU screen, so there needs to be a way of producing the image either on paper or on photographic film.

Programs *for presentation graphics* are programs which allow the user to build up a series of graphical displays or images which can be used for presentation. With additional hardware, this type of software can be used to produce 35mm slides for an on-screen slideshow or storyboard (which can be synchronised with a sound track) or material for videotape. Alternatively, the software can be used to produce overhead projector (OHP) slides.

For a computer to be able to produce graphics, it must have the appropriate CPU hardware. With PC systems, a graphics card can be inserted into the PC (there are monochrome graphics cards and colour graphics cards). This hardware (as a minimum, a 386SX with 4 Mb of RAM and a large hard disk) will then be used with suitable software to produce graphics. With IBM PC systems, for example, a Hercules Graphics Card (produced by Hercules Computer Technology) can be inserted into the IBM PC and used with graphics-based word processor software, such as Microsoft's Word for Windows.

Use of a presentation package to improve delivery

It might be thought that presentation graphics is superfluous and that it is possible to use, say, spreadsheets to draw graphs and VT to add words. However, presentation packages, which have grown steadily in popularity over the last few years and now have over 6% of the PC software market, enable the user to design a coherent sequence of frames to present a message, reinforced with graphics and, at the higher end, sound and animation. An integrated system allows a whole presentation to be created, organised and presented, including speaker notes and audience handouts.

Most modern packages, for example SPC Harvard Graphics, Lotus Freelance, Microsoft PowerPoint and Wordperfect Drawperfect, have three operational modes for creation word chart, graph and drawing. They also allow slide ordering and a range of additional features.

Chapter 6

5   THORNWAITE CRAIG

(a)   File organisation and access methods for a mailing list to be used each month for direct mail shots.

File organisation

File organisation may be serial, sequential or random

A file has an unordered, or serial, organisation if the records are in no particular order or sequence on the file. (Transaction files may have an unordered organisation.) This is *not* the same as *random* organisation.

A file's organisation is *sequential* if the records on the file are in a logical sequence according to their key field, for example, in alphabetical order, or in numerical order. Sequential files must be maintained in sequence. New records must be placed in their correct position in the file, and records which follow pushed back to make room for the new records.

Random file organisation is a bit more difficult to understand. With random organisation, records are put on file in one of two ways. Either records are filed in some way that corresponds to a key value, which is calculated from data on the record when it is filed, or they are fixed by means of an index. When a record is put on file, its key field is listed sequentially in an index, which shows the address location on file where the record is to be placed. An index on a computer file is similar in principle to an index at the back of a book. This is called *indexed-sequential organisation*.

File access

File access means locating individual records on the file. The way in which a file can be accessed will depend on how the file is organised, but access might be one of the following: serial, sequential or direct.

The *only* way of retrieving records from an unordered file is to start at the first record on the file, then go on to the next record, and the next, and so on through to the end of the file. This is known as *serial* access, which is the access of data by reading all records physically preceding the required record until the required record is found.

Sequential access is the access of data in accordance with the order of a particular key. With sequential access, the records on the file must be organised sequentially. Sequential access is the access of records on a sequentially organised file, *without* using an index.

Direct access may be defined as access to backing storage (normally disk) or memory locations, the access time for which is apparently constant regardless of the previous location addressed. It may be indexed sequential or random.

The factors involved in the file type selection include the following.

(i)   How often the file will be updated.

(ii)   Whether most changes to the file would be based on a change to existing records on the file (as in the case where an address on the file needed to be updated) or additions to the file which could be added to the appropriate point in the file.

(iii) Whether the file should be printed in post-code order to take advantage of any mailing rebates.

If the number of changes to records in the file was small, there might be a case for maintaining the file in sequential order. This would result in some time savings when the file was being used for the monthly productions. However, if the mailshots were selection driven this would point very firmly towards using an indexed-sequential access method. This would give the following.

(iv)   Fast access to specific records (for updating) using keys as the search pointer.

(v)   Fast access to records with attributes which had been included in indexes. So, for instance, if the post code has been indexed, the file could be printed in post code order very quickly.

(vi)   A similar speed of access to a sequential file for processing records via attributes which had not been indexed. So, for instance, if only records within the file which contained a specific code needed to be printed, and the code was not indexed, it would be quicker to construct another index containing the code and then use that index to access the records needed.

(b)   Factors to consider include the following.

(i)   The *needs* of users. Users must know what they want the software to do, so that they can assess whether a package meets their requirements.

(ii)   *Budget.* What is the cost of the package?

(iii) *User friendliness.* Does it use a WIMP system or offer WYSIWYG?

(iv)   *Ease of use.* Does the package come with training manuals and/or tutorial disks? Is it a popular enough package for training courses to be available?

(v)   *Flexibility.* Is it likely that the scope of the particular application will change or be extended.

(vi)   *Hardware.* Will the package operate with existing hardware? Do the organisation's PCs have the storage to run it?

(vii) *Status.* Is the package tried and tested? The version under consideration is important – many popular packages are released with new features on an almost annual basis.

(viii) *Updates.* What arrangements are there for purchase/supply of updates when these become available? Is it worth having these?

(ix)   *Add-ons.* What add-ons are available (eg graphics features)?

(x)   *Maintenance.* What service is offered?

(c)   Word processors have two main functions. The first is to allow the user to enter the text and get it correctly laid out (inserting text, moving and copying sections, setting margins, paragraph and page breaks, etc) and otherwise accurate. In this regard the use of a spell-checker routine can be useful. A spell-checker matches each word in the document against the program's dictionary and indicates words which are not in the dictionary. Correctly spelled words which are not in the dictionary can normally be added to the dictionary, increasing its ability to cope with a particular organisation's documents. Typical tailored additions would include proper names (customers, clients, place-names) and abbreviations (company names, departments, job titles, Acts of Parliament). Adding these to the spell-checker's thesaurus would prevent their being highlighted every time it is run.

The second function of most current word processors is to allow users to enhance the look of the document they have produced by applying various style changes to the text. These include changing the font of the text, changing its size, setting the text to be bold, italic or underlined, and using facilities such as boxes to emphasise particular points. These features are not as sophisticated as those provided by a desktop publishing package but their use in preference to DTP does make any further text amendments or additions simpler.

Once text has been entered and set out, the document can be saved onto disk, printed, recalled from disk and modified.

Word processors also often include facilities to merge standard documents (such as a mailshot) with a list of other data (such as names and addresses) to produce a number of tailored documents.

(d)   Desktop publishing (DTP) programs take the files produced in two other areas of the computer, word processing files and graphics images and allow the user to create a composite publication with a professional finished appearance through facilities such as placing text, placing graphics, rotating text and graphics, cropping images, changing fonts, alignment, text attributes and wrapping text around graphical images. Generally DTP systems are used with good quality printers, and sometimes are used to generate files to send direct to printing companies for printing on their higher quality printers. Due to the rapid advance in word processing programs many of the distinctions between word processors and DTP systems are becoming blurred.

The capabilities of DTP mean that organisations wishing to produce a wide range of documents no longer require outside typesetters, make-up studios and printers. Annual reports, sales catalogues, marketing brochures, reviews of the business, newsletters, press releases and other documents for which a high quality finish is required can be produced in-house without any necessity for specialist facilities or staff. The only equipment required is a PC and a laser printer. DTP packages are becoming increasingly user friendly, so that any operator can learn how to use a package without difficulty. The lead time necessitated for sending documents to external printers is eliminated and documents can be produced to extremely tight deadlines.

An organisation may easily invest far more in DTP software and associated hardware than it needs to. It may be that the package is to be used for internal newsletters, salesmens' price lists, internal notices etc. In this case it is unlikely that the organisation will require a sophisticated package and it certainly will not need either a colour monitor or a colour printer. However, these may appear extremely attractive!

A risk of user-friendly packages with a wide range of applications is that they can become addictive. Discipline is required to ensure that what was acquired as a means to an end, (ie the production of high quality published material) does not become an end in itself (ie an office toy). Documents which could be prepared perfectly adequately on WP will suddenly 'have' to be produced with a range of fonts and perhaps with symbols such as starbursts, balloons, maps and other pre-drawn graphics which DTP packages may offer.

A mastery of the features of DTP is only one aspect of successful desk top publishing. The user must also pay attention to style and layout of documents.

A consistent style between related documents will improve their effect, and layout is important too. Pages which are not well balanced will lose impact, and too much use of fancy features will detract from the basic message that the user intends to convey.

Chapter 7

6   ACE MACHINE TOOLS

> **Tutorial note**
> In part (b) you should focus your answer on 'installing' and 'using' rather than describing the whole development life cycle.

(a) Benefits of linking the two systems may be as follows.

(i)   *Avoiding duplication*: some reduction in the work effort will result from having access to prices, quantities etc directly from the same system.

(ii)   *Speed of response*: it may improve the response time in the issue of quotations.

(iii) *Error reduction*: it will reduce the chance of human error incurred whilst transferring information between separate systems.

(iv)   *Reorder levels*: it may help to establish more accurate re-order levels for stock

(v)   *Ad hoc queries and reports*: may be generated for accounting and management purposes

(vi)   *Integrated approach*: it will promote a more integrated approach to sales and order processing which may be more 'customer focused'.

(vii) *Customer service*: in addition to improved response times (above), staff will be able to give customers a better picture of existing stock levels and consequently of likely lead times for orders.

Drawbacks may be:

(i)   *Time*: it will certainly take more time to introduce an integrated sales/order processing system.

(ii)   *Expense*: the cost in terms of feasibility, development/design costs and hardware and software including network will be higher than if a stand-alone PC were to be introduced.

(iii) *Technical challenge*: reliance by the company on the system will increase the pressure to maintain it.

(iv)   *Non-standard orders*: automated ordering of non-standard products may prove difficult to deal with.

(v)   *Ownership*: staff in their separate functions may feel threatened by the removal of boundaries.

(b) The factors that must be considered when installing and using the new system are set out below.

(i)   Installation should be carefully planned.

(ii)   Steps will include:

(1) site preparation (physical location of micro-computers, disks and documentation);

(2) installing the hardware and software including cables for the network (if chosen);

(3) a training programme for staff;

(4) system and acceptance testing;

        (5) data transfer – creating new files or file conversion as appropriate;

        (6) changeover – choice of method;

        (7) review and maintenance.

(iii) Test procedures should be rigorous.

(iv) Disruption to existing work schedules must be minimised eg by choosing slack working periods for activities such as installation and changeover.

(v) Training: users and management need to be fully trained in the use of the new system.

(vi) Full technical back-up and user support (especially from the system's suppliers) must be in place.

(vii) Security of the system and data must be ensured.

(viii) Ergonomic factors and health and safety legislation must be considered.

(ix) Requirements of the Data Protection Act 1984 must be complied with.

(x) Ongoing evaluation of the effectiveness of the system is required. A post-implementation review should be carried out once the system has been run live for two or three operating cycles (weeks, months, etc), so that bugs can be eliminated. The system should thereafter be reviewed regularly, perhaps at 18–24 month intervals.

If you convince Ace of the benefits of installing an integrated system, this thorough attention to detail will help reduce any potential resistance to the change.

(c) The comparison and contrast may be seen by reference to the table below.

Applications package		Custom built software
(i)	Less costly to produce	Potentially very expensive to produce
(ii)	Rapid installation with little or no debugging	Longer development time
(iii)	Some compromises likely in terms of business requirements	May be written to encompass all present and anticipated future business needs
(iv)	Likely to be compatible with other software	Knowledgeable programmers needed to write compatible systems.
(v)	Probably supported by supplier as technology advances	Difficult to support as technology advances
(vi)	Supplied with documentation and possibly on-screen tutorials for training	Documentation and training needs to be developed: most costly
(vii)	Developed as user-friendly	User-friendly features to be addressed
(viii)	Modifications may be difficult, time consuming and expensive to introduce	Written to meet optimum needs, modifications less likely
(ix)	May be easy to integrate with other standard applications in the future	May be harder to integrate with future applications
(x)	Relatively easy to maintain and upgrade	Expensive to maintain and upgrade
(xi)	Basic security features	More sophisticated procedures for security may be written

In summary Ace would certainly save money by buying and possibly modifying packages but may need to sacrifice some quality elements in meeting their needs. However since their business needs would appear to be for quite straightforward commercial functions, they should consider purchasing well supported and tested application packages.

Chapter 9

7 BARGAIN BASEMENT

(a) The database is a suitable solution for this application for the following reasons.

(i) The data can be shared, thus when items are out of stock at one site it can easily be seen where the goods may be found at other shops.

(ii) Integrity of the data will be preserved. The data will be reliable, as users will only be able to make valid alterations. For example, details of price changes will only be entered by authorised personnel at head office. The database approach means that the same prices will apply and be in force at all branches immediately. There is no risk of some stores inputting incorrect prices or of delays/omissions in input.

(iii) Improved access for the users, who will be able to get all the information they need to help each customer. They will be able to supply order times if goods are not in stock or recommend neighbouring stores where it might be possible for goods to be reserved pending a visit by the customer or for goods to be transferred to the store required.

(iv) It will provide up-to-date information on the performance of individual shops and of regions.

(v) Managers can have reports to support their planning and decision making eg statistics, sales, stock levels.

(vi) Security will be easier to control, eg standardisation of procedures, clear policy and documentation.

(vii) Software maintenance may be less costly.

(viii) It can evolve to meet future needs. New applications will be easier to implement.

(ix) Stock re-order modules should allow re-ordering, not only from regional/central warehouses to stores, but also from external suppliers to the company's warehouses.

The critical advantage for Bargain Basement will be in stock control allowing them to establish accurate stock levels to reflect demand, without tying up excessive working capital in stocks.

(b) The role of the database administrator would be as follows.

(i) Managing the data as a vital company-wide resource for the organisation.

(ii) Maintaining the database by adding the required new data in consultation with users, systems analysts and programmers; ensuring consistency.

(iii) Monitoring the performance of the database, particularly in relation to management and user needs.

(iv) Controlling the access to the database, keeping valuable records secure.

(v) Establishing and reviewing validation procedures and checks.

(vi) Minimising or eliminating data redundancy (duplication of data items).

(vii) Arranging suitable training for all users.

(viii) Establishing and maintaining a data dictionary defining the data items and their relationships.

(ix) Providing up-to-date manuals for users.

(x) Liaison with suppliers, eg for technical support.

Bargain Basement may benefit from appointing a database administrator who also has a good overview of the business functions. This would promote good understanding and communication. The administrator could also be pro-active in recommending further developments to meet changing business needs.

(c)

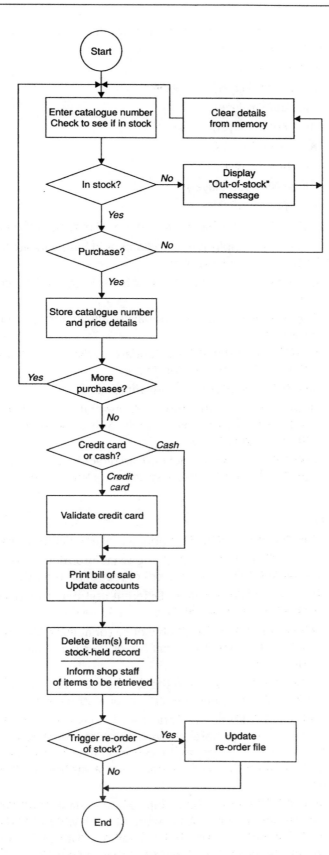

(d) The purpose of the OSI seven layer reference model is to provide a complete specification of all the protocols required to transfer data from one machine to another. Thus by using the model as a guide a user can use standard protocols to, say, send e-mail from a LAN-based Ethernet to a terminal connected to a completely different system, eg a token ring LAN. It was developed by the International Standards Organisation (ISO) to promote open systems interconnection (OSI).

The seven layers are:

(i)   the physical layer;

(ii)   the data link layer;

(iii)   the network layer;

(iv)   the transport layer;

(v)   the session layer;

(vi)   the presentation layer;

(vii)   the application layer.

For Bargain Basement the use of the model may have the following merits.

(i)   Because the applications, software and hardware are 'open' the company is not locked in to one supplier.

(ii)   Competition among suppliers is likely to lead to cost savings for the company.

(iii)   The modular nature of the layers allows for upgrading as technology advances

(iv)   As OSI is an international standard backed by USA and UK, it is likely to remain supported for a long time.

However, there are possible disadvantages.

(i)   Upper layers of the model (presentation, application) are not well specified relative to lower levels. Some equipment is only compatible with, say, layers 1 to 3.

(ii)   There are competitive network architectures, eg, SNA which mean that it may be a long time before systems are truly open.

8   DATABASES

(a)   The characteristics which are fundamental to a database are as follows.

(i)   It is constructed by considering what information could be provided and comparing this with the *needs* of user departments.

(ii)   It is a *shared bank of data*. Different user departments must all be able to access the same information at the same time.

(iii)   Data is input and stored only once (or at least with minimal duplication) but may be used by a *number of user departments* in any number of applications.

(iv)   Data relationships within the database are organised in *defined structures* – eg hierarchical, network or relational structures.

(b)   A database is a collection of data files which is integrated and organised so as to provide a single comprehensive file system. The purpose of a database is to provide convenient access to the common data for a wide variety of users and user needs. Advantages of a database as a means of file organisation are as follows.

(i)   It avoids the unnecessary duplication of data. Suppose user A and user B wish to use the same data, although each wishes the data to be presented in a different way. Without a database, both users would have to keep a set of the data (and indeed each may even have to collect it). But with a database, the data is conveniently held in one place, ready to be output in whatever form the user wants.

(ii)   As there is no need to duplicate data, it follows that the data held can be used for more than one purpose – as in the user A and user B example above.

(iii) The organisation of data into a database, rather than into separate files, encourages the integration of data and makes it more widely available.

(iv) As the data is only held once, it is relatively straightforward to ensure that it is up-to-date. The need to make sure that sets of data held by different persons or departments at different locations are kept up to date is eliminated. This gives the additional advantage that separate departments will use the same data and therefore they should not reach different conclusions or come to different decisions simply because they were based on different data.

(v) Data can be used in a very flexible fashion, because it is independent of the user programs which access the data. New programs can easily be introduced to make use of existing data in a different way, without the need to disturb the data itself.

(c) A database management system commonly contains four main facilities.

(i) *Creation of database structure*

This facility enables the user to specify what file or files will be held in the database, what records and fields they will contain, and how many characters will be in each field.

(ii) *Entering and amending and updating data*

Having created the database structure, a user will need to be able to input data (to create files), and then amend or update that data. A database system usually provides more than one facility to enable these operations to be carried out. For example:

(1) *Append* – this allows new records to be inserted on to the file;

(2) *Edit* – this allows records to be accessed and amended;

(3) *Browse* – this allows several records to be viewed at the same time and any part of them amended;

(4) Delete – this is for deleting individual records for a file, or for wiping out a whole file.

(iii) *Retrieving and manipulating data*

Having input the data – ie created the files in the database – the user will want to be able to recall it subsequently, in various forms for various purposes. Again, most database systems offer a number of facilities to enable retrieval and manipulation of data. For example:

(1) Data can be retrieved by specifying the required parameters – eg, from a database of employee records, records of all employees in the sales department who have been employed for over 10 years and are paid less than £12,000 pa could be extracted.

(2) If certain search and retrieve parameters are used regularly, they can be stored on a search parameters file for future use.

(3) Retrieved data can be sorted on any specified field (eg, for employees, sorting might be according to grade, department, age, experience, salary level etc).

(4) Some calculations on retrieved data can be carried out – such as calculating totals and average values.

(iv) *Producing reports*

Most database packages include a report generator facility which allows the user to design report structures so that information can be presented on screen and printed out in a format which suits the user's requirements and preferences.

Report formats can be stored on disk, if similar reports are produced periodically, and called up when required.

(d) *The implications of introducing a database system* include both the provision of resources to implement it and the benefits arising from it. Resources may be categorised as hardware, software and personnel.

(i) *Hardware requirements.* A database system requires large capacity and direct access storage devices as well as a large capacity and cheap central processing unit. Owing to technological advances and economies of scale, these items are constantly decreasing in cost.

(ii) *Software requirements.* A 'database management system' is needed to control the storage and retrieval of data in an efficient manner. The effectiveness of the database depends on the convenience of the means of access to the information it contains. To construct an efficient system, a logical relationship between data items must be decided upon and the applicable file structure implemented.

The three main categories of file structure are 'hierarchical structures' which store data items 'from the top downwards', 'network structures' in which a data item may be related to any number of other data items, and 'relational structures' in which the relationship of one data item to another is indicated by having the same data field value in each.

(iii) *Personnel requirements.* A database administrator should be appointed to supervise the structure, physical storage and security of the data. The database administrator will maintain user manuals, ensure that individual privacy is not violated and generally serve the best interests of all users. In addition, it will be necessary to provide training in the new system for the staff of user departments.

The benefits of introducing a database include:

(i) savings in input times and costs, as a single input will update all the files affected;

(ii) increased availability of information, as user departments will be able to access data easily and generate information in the formats appropriate to their own purposes;

(iii) flexibility in processing methods. Both on-line and batch processing may be used, according to the needs of different users.

(e) *Data integrity* is a critical issue in database management systems particularly because the data is held in a single, integrated database. Any corruption or degradation of the data will then have the potential for causing major problems. There are several mechanisms used to ensure data integrity: databases typically employ a wide and powerful range of security devices to prevent unauthorised use. Additionally data is frequently 'backed-up' so that faulty databases may be readily reconstructed from previous ones. Another significant problem seen with databases is the possibility that many users may access the data simultaneously. If this happens it is possible that a user can undo or overwrite another's work. To prevent this problem, database management systems often 'lock' data so that only one user at a time may alter it. Maintenance of data integrity is essential if a database is to operate successfully.

Data security is the ability of a database system to preserve and protect the data which it holds. There are two aspects to this function:

(i) the preservation of the data in spite of various kinds of hardware, software, operational and human errors or faults which might occur; and

(ii) the protection of sensitive data from unauthorised attempts to use it.

The first of these functions is typically provided through using back-up facilities which provide excess capacity or some provision for reconstructing data from earlier database holdings. In excluding unauthorised users database systems most commonly use some form of password protection so that only the authorised personnel who have the appropriate passwords are allowed access to the data. It is also common to limit physical access to the system in order to increase security, particularly for large mainframe systems.

Chapter 11

9   ULLOCK PIKE

(a)   A data processing system is a system designed to take raw transaction data and to produce output of a routine or operational nature. For example, in Ullock Pike plc, a sales order processing system, takes the basic details of the sales order, processes it, posts it to the sales ledger and sales account, and issues an invoice. Another example is a payroll system, where operating data (eg, time sheets) is fed into the system and operational output (payslips, BACS transfer tapes) are produced.

A management information system on the other hand is one designed to assist managers plan and control the business. It is an information system making use of all the available resources to provide managers at all levels in all functions with the information from all relevant sources to enable them to make timely and effective decisions for planning, directing and controlling the activities for which they are responsible. In Ullock Pike, management might receive details of turnover, profitability and market share by region and/or by activity for example, office cleaning, window cleaning, hire of overalls, sale of consumables, hire of plant etc.

A management information system is not really concerned with the detail of transaction data, but more with aggregates, ratios, trends, variances from budget and so forth. It is used to support decision making, and planning for the future of the business as well as the critical review of current operations. For example, an MIS would show which areas of the country were the most successful for selling goods.

(b)   It is common to distinguish three different levels of management, analysed by reference to their decision-making activities.

(i)   Senior management, who are responsible for strategic planning.

(ii)   Middle management, who exercise management control.

(iii)   Operational management, responsible for operational control.

Characteristics of decision making at senior management level

Senior management, it is felt, take strategic decisions. These focus on the long-term needs of an organisation, its internal structure, and its market profile. For example, senior management in the organisation are likely to be responsible for, say, taking a decision to take over another company, opening new regional offices, or pulling out of certain product markets. Financially, senior management are responsible for the major financing decisions (eg, size of dividend payment, whether to raise loan or equity capital).

The decisions are likely to be arrived at after a certain amount of deliberation. They affect the organisation and activities of the company, and also its profile in the outside environment. However, these decisions are unlikely to be routine decisions.

Characteristics of decision making at middle management level

Middle management are held to take decisions of a tactical nature. Senior management are also likely to take those kinds of decisions. These decisions are normally management control decisions. Management control operates within the framework of strategic plans and is the process by which it is ensured that resources are used effectively and efficiently in pursuit of organisational objectives.

Characteristics of decision making at operational level

Operational control ensures that specific tasks are carried out effectively and efficiently. Operational information is used by front-line managers watching over specific processes. Decisions made are of a programmed nature: specific situations can be predicted in advance, and the actions taken to respond to them can usually be described in a procedures manual.

(c) *Information needs*

The information needs of management at strategic level are various. Some information might be informal. As senior management is concerned with long-term influences on the organisation, relevant information may come from outside (eg trade journals and bulletins, customer sources and newspapers). Other information may be provided internally. These may include market surveys, monthly management accounting information, key business ratios, and so forth.

The type of information needed at middle management level can be referred to as tactical information. It includes, amongst other things, productivity measurements, budgetary control or variance reports, cash flow forecasts, short-term purchasing requirements and so forth. It is likely to have an accounting emphasis. It is produced regularly.

Operational information describes exact conditions of processes occurring. For example, types of operational information include the number of cleaners that need to be allocated to cleaning an office of a particular size, and the exact level of stock at a particular time, for example window washing fluid or carpet cleaner.

Potential of computing

Computing can be used to allow senior managers, or their specialist assistants, to manipulate information they have. A decision support system will be useful. A spreadsheet package may enable a financial model to be prepared which will help indicate the financial consequences of a particular decision. More recently, executive information systems have been developed. These enable senior management to interrogate an organisation's data files at any level, and programs to manipulate the data once it has been called up/retrieved.

Much tactical level information will be generated internally, as feedback. Given that the reports needed are standard, computers are very useful in the production of this information. Such information can be analysed further, using decision support packages such as spreadsheets. Computers can be used both in the production and the analysis of this information.

Many computer systems provide operational information. A sales ledger system is an operational system. In a sales ledger application, it would be possible for chasing letters to be sent automatically to slow payers after a certain time as the decision to send letters is a programmed one. Additionally, many production processes are controlled by computer, and the computer can be used to provide information about the operation of the system.

(d) Information and communication are the means by which the activities of an organisation are unified. Information is communicated within an organisation so that appropriate action can be taken. An organisation obtains information by means of processing and analysing selected data. Once data has been collected and processed, the resulting information must be communicated to users. It may be disseminated in a number of forms, including:

(i) scheduled reports, routinely prepared on a regular basis;

(ii) exception reports, highlighting variances against plans or expected figures;

(iii)   reports produced on demand, in response to a specific request; and

(iv)   planning reports.

All of these reports should share a number of features. Information must have a purpose, otherwise it is useless and valueless. It might have an immediate purpose, in which case it should be presented in a suitable format for use, or it might be stored for future use, in which case a different format might be more appropriate until such time as it is required. If information is to fulfil its purpose, there should be clear indication of who needs it. A report will only fulfil its intended purpose for that user if it has the additional characteristics of relevance, completeness, accuracy, clarity and timeliness.

A key factor which will affect the extent to which all these requirements are met is the format in which the information is presented. The two most widespread types of output suitable for all the types of report described above are the VDU and the printer. The most obvious difference between these is the *permanence* of the information presented. Information presented on screen is only accessible until the display is overwritten/replaced or the user exits from the particular screen mode. (A screen print can be taken if required; this becomes more laborious if many items are to be printed.) A printout produced on a printer can be referred to more than once, and different items can be reviewed by turning pages; this avoids the need to flick between screens by using menus and entering key fields to facilitate searching.

The *type* of report, as identified above, will govern to a large extent the 'proper format'. *Scheduled* reports may be produced on printouts if they are required for immediate reference (for example, aged debtor analysis or allocation of staff/workgroups to premises for the coming week) or on microform (COM) if they are produced for archiving purposes (for example, month-end purchase ledger listing). *Exception* reports should be printed out – actions taken/authorisations can then be evidenced in writing by reviewers. Information produced on *demand* may be printed out (eg, analysis of sales by region for a meeting) or may simply be retrieved on screen (eg, status of a customer account prior to a telephone call). *Planning* reports, for example, location of outside window washing lifts/hoists for the next month, may be drafted on screen and printed out when they have been finalised.

Within each *method* of output the format in which information is presented can vary. VDU output screens are likely to have been defined for many applications at the systems design stage, others can be designed as required. Output from application packages and bespoke packages will usually fall into the former category; output from general purpose packages is more flexible as there are no present limitations.

Printout format will be specified to meet the user's requirements; a credit control manager may require an aged debt analysis by customer, whereas the chief accountant may require the same information summarised to show simply domestic and overseas aged debt totals. The manager's report will be irrelevant, voluminous, wasteful and unclear; what is more, because it will have taken longer to print out than the summary the chief accountant will have had to wait longer for it. It may still be useful, but it will also be inefficient and probably cause frustration. To be useful, information should be presented in the proper format.

Chapter 12

10 PROBLEMS

To: Chief Executive

From: Systems analyst

Date: 30 March 1995

Subject: Systems development

Introduction

This report identifies the problems which may be faced by the company's systems development section when carrying out the forthcoming major analysis and design project. The project will have two distinct stages. The systems analysis element will involve a study of current operations and problems followed by the preparation of a specification of requirements. The systems design stage will involve design of data, processes and physical elements. As the project is a major one it will be led by the systems development section, but users have an important part to play at all stages.

Study of current operations and problems

During the first phase of systems analysis the project team will acquire detailed information about the existing system. This may lead to difficulties as the existing system environment is continually changing, as are the requirements of the users. The analysts and users will have to understand each others' requirements: the analysts to comprehend the users' operational view of the system, and the users to appreciate the way in which analysts operate and handle information. This process will require a high degree of co-operation between the two groups.

Because the project is complex, the analysts will need to adopt a structured approach to the acquisition of information, and they must consider how they will control the process of fact-finding and recording of data. This is an area which can lead to cost overruns if it is not adequately controlled.

The analysts will need to ensure throughout this process that they corroborate information and explanations received from users. They will be likely to use a selection of techniques including interviews and questionnaires. In either of those, users may interpret questions in unexpected ways or may be unintentionally misleading, particularly if they are subject to particular sensitivities about the future of their job or their job definition.

Specification of requirements

This phase of the analysis also requires close co-operation between analysts and users. The users will specify what they want the new system to do and give details of required data input and information output. The analyst has to prepare the specification with due regard to those requirements. The users have to be persuaded to 'buy in' to the specification, and so the analysts have to prevent problems by striking a balance between producing a specification which is too vague and therefore not a satisfactory foundation for design work and preparing a specification which is too formal for the users to understand, in which case they may be unwilling to commit to what is being developed. If they do not commit to the development they may restate the requirements and this will lead to time and cost overruns.

Systems design

One of the key issues at the design stage is the necessity for a clear demarcation between design elements. What is critical, following the specification of requirements, is the design of data and of processes. It is important that this process, that of defining the functional specifications, is kept distinct from the process of defining non-functional specifications. Non-functional specifications set out not what the system is to do but how it is to do it, for example, extent of use of existing hardware and any constraints such as response times, data volumes and cost. If the new system is to meet user requirements it is important that data design and process design are considered before physical design. If this is not done, then systems will not meet users' requirements and may also be unreliable, as a result of sacrifices made at the design stage.

Recommendations

The planned system analysis and design project is a complex one and it is recommended that the company adopts a framework within which this project should be controlled. It is recommended that a formal system analysis and design methodology is used throughout the project; this will help break it down into stages so that effort is directed at each task as appropriate.

Chapter 13

11 COSMETIK

(a) The following are the steps for an initial investigation of Cosmetik's system needs.

    (i) Identify the goals and objectives of Cosmetik as a business.

    (ii) Gather information on the future plans from reports, interviews and commentary in order to predict future needs.

    (iii) Form a development team to discuss the business objectives and future systems needs. The team should include people with authority, IT knowledge and users.

    (iv) Investigate, with the help of the team, the technical needs, the management/decision making needs, any financial constraints, operational implications. In particular it may be necessary to consider the socio-political climate in relation to testing and developing cosmetics.

    (v) Devise possible solutions based on time, technical, financial and operational considerations.

    (vi) Select and recommend proposal to the Cosmetik board to include a full project plan and costings.

If approved the proposal will go forward to a detailed feasibility study.

(b) Following a successful feasibility study, the steps required to develop and maintain the new system are as follows.

    (i) Produce a clear and agreed systems specification detailing all the requirements. Set clear systems standards of performance. This document sets out the objectives of the system, gives instructions for design and programming, sets out operating procedures, users' roles and responsibilities, security, audit and maintenance procedures.

    (ii) Design hardware configuration required: to include such matters as memory size (RAM), storage devices, input and output peripherals. Ensure compatibility of components.

    (iii) Design software: this may mean software selection where packages are to be used or programmers will be asked to write programmes for specific needs. Certain packages for analysis and administration (eg, spreadsheets) are likely to be suitable for Cosmetik.

    (iv) Decide on communication links: may use a LAN (local area network) to link each partner and practitioner to the system.

    (v) Selection and training of staff: the identification and possibly recruitment of suitable staff to operate the new system, and training to begin as soon as possible.

(vi) Review and identify physical threats to system and security of personal records: plan suitable protection measures.

(vii) Devise an implementation schedule; preferably to coincide with a quiet period (or a weekend).

(viii) Write and check final code to integrate programs. Acquire OS/communications software.

(ix) Test the system, if possible by pilot run. Correct 'bugs' in the programs, check accuracy of documentation/manuals.

(x) Run system making regular careful checks on all aspects. Keep feedback open for rapid reporting on any system technical or staff problems.

(xi) Maintain the system to meet ongoing needs: monitor performance against agreed standards.

(c) The developers of the applications software should adopt a modular design for the software because the applications can be broken down into a series of modules which can be further broken down into simple tasks which are easy to define. This in turn should make each task simple to code and test.

It also allows for the rapid production of prototypes for a given task or module. Related tasks can then be linked to form modules. The modules are easier to debug and to test.

Each module can be brought on-line on an individual basis as required. It also facilitates the upgrading of modules. Upgrading or amending an individual module can be done without having to re-program right across the suite of modules which constitute the system. Similarly, it allows for the addition of new modules without major alternations to the existing software.

Modular development would entail drawing up a structure diagram, usually top down, to illustrate the steps and components parts of the system.

Cosmetik would benefit from the relative simplicity of this approach as they are new to the challenge, and from the ease of operation, whereby errors should be minimised and cost savings made.

(d) In order to evaluate the performance of the system, first it is necessary to define the criteria and systems objectives against which performance is to be measured. This would first be carried out by the systems development staff with the fullest possible consultation.

Once the system is fully operational, it is suggested that an evaluation committee be formed comprising the systems manager, a representative of senior management, a senior scientist, head of all major functional areas/departments, users and general staff representatives. They will review the suitability of the performance criteria and may change it from time to time. The criteria set is likely to include such matters as: timeliness of information, response time, reliability, frequency of errors, relevance to needs (scientific, operational and business), data security, suitability of presentation, staff performance and training. Overall, they will be interested to know the extent to which the system helps to support the goals of Cosmetik. They will also be vigilant about ensuring the system gives good value for money. In this connection, the views of the wider community may be particularly valuable. The committee will report recommendations to the systems manager and the company board.

System audit will also influence the evaluation of performance in that it ensures that the system performs to the requirements specification and evaluation criteria set, in particular in relation to security and minimising the possibility of fraud. The auditor may also make recommendations for improvement.

Any deviation between the expected, required performance and the actual performance should be reported immediately to the systems manager and senior management. Immediate action should be taken to ascertain the reason(s) and take appropriate action to rectify.

Chapter 14

12 STAFF TRAINING

To: DP Manager
From: KH Chang
Date   7 June 1996
Subject: Proposals for staff training and development

This report is written in the context of a significant increase in the number of DP staff leaving the company, or seeking other jobs within the company, in the last few months. If adopted these proposals will help to settle staff concerns and also improve the services provided by the department for improved training and staff morale.

Objectives

Our primary objectives must be to settle staff uncertainties and reduce the number of leavers, especially in key positions. There are several factors which have led to the increase in staff turnover. The major culture changes in the department and throughout the company following the appointment of new executive management has led to uncertainty over the future; there appears to be considerable fear over possible reorganisation and redundancies. The recent introduction of networked systems and finance software has resulted in changes to working practices which have not been well accepted by those DP staff involved.

Staff morale must be improved by generating motivation and interest in jobs as well as price in working for the department. A better understanding of the value of our IT function and of individual's jobs is therefore required.

Both the objectives and the actions taken should be applied to managers as well as clerical and technical grade staff. Improved staff morale will be initiated in the first instance by the function managers.

Immediate actions

(a) Review the organisation structure of the department to ensure that lines of command are clear and that key staff can see career prospects in the department rather than outside.

(b) Hold meetings with function managers to put detail to the problems highlighted above. These should result in specific proposals which may range from re-training to individual appraisals.

(c) Prepare a programme of staff training and development throughout the department. This is discussed in more detail below, but the main objective is to improve the skill level of staff, improve their understanding of the department's activities and status in the company and finally to emphasise the need for high quality work.

Training and development programme

The programme should fall into two categories. Firstly, general staff development, which will include dealing with customers, understanding the latest technology developments and understanding the department's function in the company. Secondly, specific training requirements should be identified and the necessary courses set up. The following paragraphs provide more detail on these proposals and highlight the potential benefits of the programme.

General staff development. A series of informal discussion chaired by the DP managers and the function managers should be held for each group of staff. The topics discussed should include:

(a) IT department future – new systems, impact on jobs;

(b) company IT strategy;

(c) function activities – need for team work;

(d) training needs – emphasise commitment to staff.

These meetings will show management's commitment to IT and to the staff and will allow staff to discuss their concerns in an informal atmosphere. If staff gain a better understanding of their position in the organisation and are encouraged to be achievement-oriented then the meetings will have been worthwhile.

Specific training needs. In the course of preparing this report it has become apparent that there are several area where specific training on application software and some hardware is needed.

(a) The most urgent need is on the new finance systems. The initial training on the system was broadly unsuccessful because the courses were more theory than practical and were held away from the working environment. As a result our staff do not have adequate knowledge of the systems and their potential problems to be able to support the end-users.

It is recommended that further training takes place in small groups using the live systems data and simulating real problems in a training environment. The courses should also seek to improve confidence in dealing with end-users. To this end an emphasis on social development (especially a patient and confident telephone manner) should be given in part of the course structure.

Retraining on the financial systems must be a priority which will provide the benefits of a much improved service to our customers and of improving the skill and morale level of our staff. Staff who consider themselves expert in their subject will be much more confident in their abilities and are more likely to develop in the future.

(b) Training is also required on the new spreadsheet and database application packages which have been adopted on a corporate basis. External courses with the software suppliers should be set up. Expertise in this area will allow the department to be pro-active in the development of *ad hoc* systems throughout the company. Staff will become more integrated with the rest of the company and will develop an understanding of end user requirements.

The measures mentioned under immediate actions and staff training and development are designed to improve staff morale and thereby reduce staff turnover. In addition, considerable benefits will accrue in the department's service to the company. It is recommended that, following the arrangement of the various internal and external courses, a detailed action plan is produced including course and meeting dates as well as a procedure for reviewing the success of the programme.

Chapter 15

13 GREEN GABLE

(a) A typical computer installation represents a considerable capital investment and makes use of the skills of highly-qualified and experienced personnel. These valuable resources will not be utilised effectively if proper control is not exercised over the flow of data through the system. The systems analyst should build controls into the system, based on the following guidelines.

(i) *All data* due for processing should in fact be processed. For example, all journeys made by each vehicle must be recorded so that maintenance schedules are up-to-date and adhered to.

(ii) Circumstances which may give rise to the possibility of error should be avoided. Whenever possible error situations should be *designed* out of the system.

(iii) Errors which do occur should be detected, located and corrected *as soon as possible*. The sooner the error is located the easier it is to correct and the longer it remains undetected, the more complicated the subsequent amendment procedures.

(iv) Controls must be simple and, whenever possible, should not interrupt the flow of data through the system. The ideal control fits smoothly into the system and becomes an *integral part* of it.

(v) Controls must not be excessively *costly* to apply. A reasonable level of control must be set, as any attempt to ensure 100% accuracy would be uneconomical.

(vi) The controls should be part of a general *strategy*, over the whole area of data processing activity, to prevent and detect fraud. A systems analyst should consult with the company's auditors when the system is being designed, not after all the work has been done.

An example of the application of these guidelines is given in the UK Auditing Practices Board's Auditing Guideline on *Guidance for internal auditors*, which addresses, among other issues, evaluation of an organisation's internal control system. It states that 'controls ensure that processes act to meet the system's objectives' and goes on to set out the main objectives of an internal control system.

(i) To ensure adherence to management polices and directives in order to achieve the organisation's objectives.

(ii) To safeguard assets.

(iii) To secure the relevance, reliability and integrity of information, so ensuring as far as possible the completeness and accuracy of records.

(iv) To ensure compliance with statutory requirements.

(b) Physical security comprises two sorts of controls: protection against natural and man-made disasters, such as fire, flood and sabotage; and protection against intruders gaining physical access to the system. (These threats can be grouped alternatively as accidental and deliberate.) The physical environment has a major effect on information system security, and so planning it properly is an important precondition of an adequate security plan.

Natural disasters

Fire is the most serious hazard to computer systems. Destruction of data can be even more costly than the destruction of hardware. A proper fire safety plan is an essential feature of security procedures, in order to prevent fire, detect fire and put out the fire. Fire safety includes:

(i) site preparation (eg, appropriate building materials, fire doors);

(ii) detection (eg, smoke detectors);

(iii) extinguishing (eg, sprinklers); and

(iv) training for staff in observing fire safety procedures (eg, no smoking rules/locations).

Other natural disasters include flooding and abnormal weather conditions. It is difficult to envisage the form and effect of these, but certain steps can be taken. It may be unwise to site a computer in a basement, even if this is considered to be a more suitable location for machines than people, as this is likely to be the first area affected by flooding. Lightning may adversely affect power supplies.

A proper environment must be provided for mainframes. Mainframe computers in particular are susceptible to damage from poor atmospheric or environmental conditions. A typical installation would provide air-conditioning, a dust-free environment (provided by use of special clothing and double sets of sealed doors), antistatic protection and 'clean' power supplies. Power supplies must be protected from both loss of power and irregularities in supply, both of which can corrupt data and processing activities.

Man-made risks

The other main area of physical security is access control, to prevent intruders getting anywhere near the computer equipment or storage media. Methods of controlling human access include:

(i)   personnel (security guards);

(ii)   mechanical devices (eg, keys, whose issue is recorded); and

(iii)   electronic identification devices (eg, card-swipe systems).

Theft is also a problem, particularly where so much computer equipment is easily portable. A microcomputer need not be larger than a briefcase and even a laser printer can be carried by one person. To some extent this can be guarded against by means similar to those described above, but with much equipment located in ordinary offices and no longer kept in a single secure location other measures must be taken. Regular 'stock controls' or physical inspections may be necessary, and a strictly imposed form of bookings used when staff take PCs off-site, either to customers or home.

One possible approach to disaster recovery is to use the services of a specialist disaster recovery company. These companies are becoming more widespread as computer users are made more aware of the potential dangers of a major disaster. These companies offer office premises with desks, telephones and storage space which are equipped with hardware, including terminals, of the same type as that used by their customers. In the event of a disaster, the customer can 'invoke' standby procedures and load backups of software to carry on essential business.

Disaster standby companies generally offer services to users of one hardware manufacturer's equipment only, and clearly require a number of subscribers if they are to offer a cost effective service. The upper limit on subscribers is governed by the probability that two customers require facilities at once; this is determined by insurers.

Alternatively, computer bureaux can agree to make their own systems available in the event of an emergency. Such an arrangement has to be specified in advance, as there might be other demands on a bureau's resources.

However, the key is to draw up a formal disaster recovery plan and to ensure maximum staff awareness of the appropriate procedures. (*Note.* Passwords and similar measures are concerned with logical access, not physical access, and so are outside the scope of this question.)

(c)   Information systems standards are standards for the development, procedures and documentation of computer systems. Standards are necessary to minimise the likelihood of errors and misunderstandings in the development and operation of computer systems. Standards are of particular relevance and benefit in the following areas.

Documentation of a system

Documentation is needed for systems and program specifications, and also for operator instructions. The existence of standards for specifications provides a standard format for documenting the system and helps to ensure that nothing is omitted from the specification. Operator instructions give users and operators a point of reference for looking up and learning the system's operating requirements.

Management control

Standards should provide guidelines for managers to plan and control systems development and operations. These guidelines will cover scheduling of steering committee meetings, project costing methods, performance standards and job specifications, allocating responsibility and 'ownership' of the system. This is particularly important here, where the IS manager has no development experience.

Communication of information about the system

The existence of standard documentation facilitates communication between different groups of personnel involved with the system, for example, analysts and programmers, or developers and users.

Continuity after staff changes

People leave their job from time to time and may be temporarily absent by reason of holidays or illness. Standards of operation will make it easier for stand-ins or replacements to pick up the job.

Aid to training

Standards help people learn how to use a system. Standards of documentation across an organisation help staff transferring between departments/work groups, as they will have some familiarity with formats/practices. With privatisation, it is possible that the company may seek to run services in other areas as well.

Aid to systems analysis and design work

Standards will help the systems analyst in the following ways.

(i)   No aspect of design is overlooked.

(ii) As an aid to thinking. Standards can help to steer a systems analyst's mind in the best direction when designing a system, eg, they can suggest controls to be built into the system.

(iii) The standard documentation also provides evidence that systems development controls have been carried out and the system incorporates sufficient procedural and processing controls.

(d)   The main documents which ought to be prepared and standardised in an organisation are the following.

    (i)   The systems specification.

    (ii) Program specifications and other program documentation.

    (iii) User manuals and user documentation.

    (iv) Operating software manuals.

Systems documentation may be poorly maintained for a number of reasons. Documentation can be perceived as unimportant and therefore as someone else's responsibility. Practice and theory can diverge at an alarming rate, and strict controls must be in place if documentation is to keep pace with the environment it is supposed to describe.

    (i)   *Systems specification*

        This document is sometimes seen just as a means of communicating with management to obtain their approval for a system. However, it has a number of other uses in the systems development cycle, including giving programmers details for program preparation, detailing procedures for operations staff, allocating responsibility to users and providing information to auditors. Any of these readers may be involved in suggesting changes to the system, either during development or after it. Because the systems specification is associated with the early stages of development, it is highly probable that subsequent changes will not be reflected in the document.

    (ii) *Program documentation*

        During the life of a program it is likely that users or user groups may request changes to the program. These may be made without corresponding changes being made to the documentation.

(iii)   *User manuals and user documentation*

Users may learn how to use systems by experience or by on-the-job training and word of mouth. Pressures of the job can lead to a reluctance or lack of time to read user manuals. This can lead to a divergence between documentation and practice.

(iv)   *Operating software manuals.*

If manuals are distributed at all, they may well not be replaced when software is upgraded or new versions acquired.

INDEX

W